VIA PODIENSIS, PATH OF POWER

Other Books by Marie-Laure Valandro

**Camino Walk**
Where Inner & Outer Paths Meet

**Letters from Florence**
Observations on the Inner Art of Travel

**Deliverance of the Spellbound God**
An Experiential Journey into Eastern
and Western Meditation Practices

**Touched**
A Painter's Insights into the Work
of Liane Collot d'Herbois

**Wisconsin Hills Farm Stories**
Adventures of a Biodynamic Farmer

**Nutrition for Enlightened Parenting**

# Via Podiensis, Path of Power

## A Walk from le Puy, France, to San Juan de la Peña, Spain

Marie-Laure Valandro

2015
Lindisfarne Books
An imprint of SteinerBooks/Anthroposophic Press, Inc.
610 Main Street, Great Barrington, MA 01230
www.steinerbooks.org

Copyright © 2015 by Marie-Laure Valandro.
All rights reserved. No part of this book may be reproduced, stored in a retrieval system, or transmitted in any form or by any means, electronic, mechanical, photocopying, recording, or otherwise, without the written permission of SteinerBooks. Translations throughout this book have been revised by the editor.

Book and cover design: William Jens Jensen
All photographs by the author

LIBRARY OF CONGRESS CONTROL NUMBER 2015930148

ISBN: 978-1-58420-183-0 (paperback)
ISBN: 978-1-58420-172-4 (eBook)

## To the Reader

*This book makes no pretense whatever of being "learned." The author has brooded over these things for many years, painfully aware of the overshadowing mass of research and scholarship, compared with which her efforts are no more than little glow-worm lamps in the night....*

*Such a book, too, can have no "style." It must, all the time, be struggling with the necessity to create a conversation between the accepted facts of history and the visions of the Hills of Dream, and it has to be a friendly conversation and not an argument.*

—Eleanor C. Merry, *The Flaming Door*

Learn to keep silent, and power will come to you
Give up power, and the ability to will will come to you.
Give up willing, and feeling will come to you.
Give up feeling, and knowledge will come to you.
—Rudolf Steiner, *Esoteric Lessons 1904–1909*

The silence of the tongue and of the imagination dissolves the barrier between ourselves and the peace of things that exist only for God and not for themselves. But the silence of all inordinate desire dissolves the barrier between ourselves and God. Then we come to live in Him alone.
—Thomas Merton, *No Man Is an Island*

Perhaps there are some among you who feel oppressed by the fact that you cannot convert what you have learned here into practical work but are continually simply absorbing spiritual teachings, and now you have to ask yourselves: Am I not a gourmet of spiritual delicacies? Wise masters of the East give us an answer: By absorbing spiritual teachings, you do something that has eternal value. The spiritual development of humanity could not progress through the activity of the "yesterday's spirits"—whether they are people who lived in former times or gods who preceded us in earthly evolution—if there were no souls into which they could pour their teachings. It's not unlike the seed of a plant—so long as it is still in the blossom or fruit, it has no value. Only when it is placed into the earth can it sprout. More important than artists themselves for the Earth's evolution are those who take into their souls such works of art such as the *Sistine Madonna* and the *Faust* drama.
—Rudolf Steiner, *"Freemasonry" and Ritual Work*

People strive for esoteric knowledge and may attain it through human faculties, but esoteric knowledge has greater significance for the world than it does within only the human soul. In the world around us we can distinguish among substances and materials, through which various phenomena and manifestations are expressed. All creatures and phenomena of the Earth and all the worlds are rooted in that primal principle that can hardly be expressed in human language. In the physical world, individual instances of this primal principle are expressed in the substances of earth, water, fire, ether, and so on.

One of the subtlest substances accessible to human striving is called *akasha*. Beings and phenomena manifested in akashic substance are the subtlest of all those accessible to us. What people acquire for themselves as esoteric knowledge not only lives in their souls but is also impressed in akashic substance. When we bring an idea from esoteric science to life in our soul, it is inscribed immediately in akashic substance. It is significant that such impressions, which are significant for the general development of the world, can be inscribed in the akasha only by human beings....

When a soul still on Earth forms clear, strong spiritual thoughts and ideas for itself, and another soul living between death and a new birth looks down on that soul it left behind, the soul between death and a new birth can pursue the soul life of the one on Earth in the present because that soul life is inscribing itself into the akashic substance.

Here we touch a point that shows how anthroposophic teaching will remove the chasm between the so-called living and the so-called dead....

If, as a result of true understanding, only a small part of humanity works as suggested to strengthen moral courage, all materialistic theories will gradually disappear from the world. As we have seen, esoteric knowledge is needed for the whole process of evolution, because it must be written in akashic substance.

—RUDOLF STEINER, *Approaching the Mystery of Golgotha*

## Chant des pèlerins de Compostelle

*Tous les matins, nous prenons le chemin*
*Tous les matins, nous allons plus loin*
*Jour après jour, la route nous appelle*
*C'est la voix de Compostelle*

Ultreïa, ultreïa, et suseia, Deus, adjuva nos !

*Chemin de terre et chemin de foi*
*Voie millénaire des jacquets*
*La voie lactée de Charlemagne*
*C'est le chemin de tous les pèlerins.*

Ultreïa, ultreïa, et suseia, Deus, adjuva nos !

*Et tout là-bas au bout du continent*
*Messire Jacques nous attend,*
*Depuis toujours son sourire appelle*
*Le soleil qui descend au Finisterre.*

Ultreïa, ultreïa, et suseia, Deus, adjuva nos !*

—Jean-Claude Benazet (tr. M-L. Valandro)

---

\* The ancient words *"Ultreïa, Ultreïa, et suseia, Deus, adjuva nos !"* may be roughly translated to mean "Ever farther and higher, God help us!"

# Song of the pilgrims of Compostelle

Every morning we take to the road,
Every morning we go farther.
Day after day the path is calling us,
It is the voice of Compostela.

Ultreïa, ultreïa, et suseia, Deus, adjuva nos !

Dirt road and path of the fire,
Millennium-old path of Europe,
The Milky Way of Charlemagne,
It is the path of all the pilgrims.

Ultreïa, ultreïa, et suseia, Deus, adjuva nos !

All the way down at the continents' end,
St. James is waiting for us.
For all time, he is smiling upon
The dying sun of Finisterre.

Ultreïa, ultreïa, et suseia, Deus, adjuva nos !

(tr. M-L. Valandro)

*The author on the first day of her journey*

# Via Podiensis, Path of Power

It is a long trip across the Atlantic for this second pilgrimage, which this time will take me across France from the central eastern region of Le Puy (not far from Lyon), trekking straight in a southwesterly direction to the Pyrenees, and then on to Spain, the city of Jaca, and the famous monastery of San Juan de la Peña, where I will end the walk. I will cross the Pyrenees at a different pass since I have already walked the other route further to the south in Saint-Jean-de-Pied-de-Port. It will be around the same distance, approximately 850 kilometers, or 650 miles. This walk will be mostly in France, and a few days in Spain—the opposite of the Camino walk where I spent most of the time walking in Spain.* The pilgrimage should actually be done in the reverse order; begin in Le Puy, France, and end up in Santiago, as it was done in the Middle Ages. This route was taken by pilgrims coming from Germany and Switzerland, and they still take this route to cross France. It is a region very rich in history, culture, literature, farming, agriculture, architecture, geography, spiritual events, and geology. Le Puy itself used to be a pilgrimage site in the Middle Ages.

I left France when I was fifteen years old, and returned when I was twenty-four, after finishing my university studies and teaching for a

---

\* See Valandro, *Camino Walk: Where Inner and Outer Paths Meet*.

couple of years in the Boston school system. I left from New York City on a bright autumn day and partied for four days on the luxury ship *France* to spend a year in Paris, studying at the Sorbonne and teaching English to make ends meet. Mostly not.

After that one year, I made sporadic trips to France, but never stayed very long, because my life took me elsewhere. Now it is a kind of return to my roots from which I had been suddenly uprooted against my own will to follow my parents to our new country, the United States, where I still choose to live, at least for part of the year.

I am to walk and live with the French and many others for six weeks. Of course, I have reasons for walking this ancient route—to live history, to watch history coming to life, and to penetrate the invisible threads that brought me here and would lead me on to other adventures. Most of all, however, I love walking for days on end; I love the solitary walk along soft dirt paths and meeting total strangers. My other love is to share the most beautiful words of wisdom written by others, which you will see sprinkled throughout the text. They are meant to shine out like diamonds and awaken in your soul, healing it from the dreadful abstraction and dried-up, dead concepts of materialism. Then this tale will have done its task. Now back to the meeting of total strangers:

> People can never attain a truly good, upright, and strong personal inner life without having the warmest interest in others. All inner life that we seek remains false and seductive if it does not go hand-in-hand with a kindly interest in the character and qualities of other people. We should automatically assume that we find our inner selves as human beings when we take an interest in the characteristics of others. Entering with love the individualities of other people, which is sometimes united with a deep experience of life's tragedy, can bring us self-knowledge. The knowledge of self we seek through delving into ourselves will never be true. We deepen our own inner nature by meeting other people with full interest. Nevertheless, this statement as expressed here implies

something that cannot be carried directly into actuality because it must interact with another statement.

The other statement is this: We never gain a true knowledge of the outer world unless we resolve to examine the universal humanity in ourselves and come to know it. Therefore, all modern natural science will be purely mechanical science and knowledge—not true but false and inverted unless it is based on the knowledge of the human being. In the science described by me as "esoteric science" in my book *An Outline of Esoteric Science*, knowledge of the outer world is sought along with the knowledge of the human being. We find the inner through the outer, the outer through the inner.[*]

I first started walking on paths when I was very little, when we went to visit my grandparents' farm in the hills of Burgundy, a few miles from Dijon, where we lived until I was six. My parents would take us there for the weekend and we would enjoy the farm life I loved. The farm was tucked away in the hills, far from the road. It had only a very bad dirt road through fields that my grandfather worked the best he could. The whole family had hardly any money. We ate a very frugal diet—milk soup, bread, cheese, potatoes, fresh churned butter, and no meat—but to me it was heaven—young lambs to play with, milking the cows, going into the fields with my grandfather. He would sit me on his big fat horse; I would plant potatoes and peas with him, and then I would play in the dirt eating his bread and chocolate snacks. I played with my aunts and uncles, who were barely older than I was. My mother had twelve brothers and sisters, and her youngest brother was one-and-a-half years older than I. They all played musical instruments—accordions, trumpets, drums, flutes—and after supper they would all jam, except my mother; she liked to dance. Besides all of this, what I enjoyed the most was the walk to the village from the farm. The farm was on top of those

---

[*] Steiner, *Inner Impulses of Evolution*, pp. 58–59 (translations throughout this book have been revised by the editor).

hidden Burgundy hills, with beautiful pine trees in the surrounding fields. We had to walk to the village down the hill, through a beautiful, still forest—probably two or three miles.

That was my first introduction to walking—walking to the village of Lantenay to buy fresh bread and camembert (my favorite), and of course walking back up the hill in the evening. It was a fairytale to me to be on these walks. It was as if I could talk to the silence: the moss, the worn-dirt path that seemed to radiate happiness by our very walking on it. The sunlight streamed into the thick forest, my aunts and my sisters laughed, and we would arrive in the village near the old washing building, where the village women still washed their clothes on flat stones, beating them and using rough-looking soaps. The river flowed through the little town, and we slowly emerged from the woods into the village; that was always mysterious. Then we would go back into the darkness of the woods and emerge from the woods again into the meadows filled with flowers such as poppies, *bleuets,* and daisies. Slowly, the large stone farmhouse would come into view in the distance surrounded by the barns. These first impressions never left me, and I could not wait to go back along the walking paths. Over the years, I think these strong memories have sent me on many paths—Peru, months in the Himalayas, Iran, Argentina, Chile, Ecuador, the Canadian Rockies, the Pyrenees, and more. I think I was looking for the paths of my youth.

Thanks to my walk on the Camino in Spain the previous year, I am renewing my interest in my own country. So there I am.

⸻

In addition to my love of walking, people, books, and the lands, I have always had a strong interest in the period of history from the seventh to fourteenth centuries and—for reasons that I cannot explain—on this trip, I wanted to concentrate on Charlemagne, crowned emperor in AD 800, to see what that would bring. I had many other interests as well: the Roman de la Rose, the troubadours, the knights and ladies, the Benedictines and the Cistercians in their abbeys and their involvement in the shaping of the land, the Templars, Parsifal, the Cathars, the spiritual implication and influence of the Moslem conquest, the rise of great churches, and the cosmopolitan aspect of life in the Middle Ages. When I was studying French and Spanish literature, I wanted to get a doctorate by writing a thesis on the grand *L'amour* portrayed in French literature. Nevertheless, I stopped at a Master's degree and taught high school, adults, and children; it seemed more practical. Perhaps I am now doing what I wanted to do thirty-five years ago, but in a different way. Am I walking into the unknown or reminding myself of what I already knew?

Crossing France in that region, I would visit these ancient sites and perhaps get a taste of the past and see how it might shape the future. Of course, my companions along the way—many with the same intentions—help in this reenactment of the past. We were living together in past lives and perhaps we did tread these paths together before at some point—perhaps on a horse, in an abbey or castle, fighting somewhere, dying of the plague, or burned at the stake. Where does this impulse to revisit places come from? Perhaps it is to return, to retrace one's steps and even have a chance at looking at the future, because we make the future in the present. We were all on a path, whether we knew it or not. We had been called to travel together for a few weeks to share each other's lives, and to meet perhaps long forgotten friends or make new ones for the future.

I remember a different sort of dream a while back that came from nowhere, about traveling in a wooden cart pulled by a bullock. I was sitting on top of bags, along some small, winding dirt path during the Middle Ages; someone else was driving, and I was just a passenger. Just a picture, but I knew it was a truth of another lifetime.

Along with my history–literary–French upbringing baggage of the past, the people I meet will keep me totally in the present as I take step after step on this ancient, eternal path of acquiring wisdom, looking for answers from Sophia, but the modern way—*Anthroposophia*, the wisdom of being human. The earlier walking paths have transformed themselves into inner paths. How wise life is.

> Spiritual paths above all were necessary from the thirteenth, fourteenth, and especially the fifteenth century onward, if one wanted to receive true Rosicrucian instruction. For the temples of the Rosicrucians were hidden from the outer physical experience. Many true Rosicrucians frequented those temples, it is true, but no physical human eye could find them. Nonetheless, there were disciples who came to these old Rosicrucians; true Rosicrucians could indeed be found in scattered places. They were like hermits of wisdom and consecrated, human action. Anyone who was able to perceive the language of the Gods in the gentle radiance of their eyes would find them so. I am not speaking in mere pictures. I am relating a reality, one that was of utmost importance for that time. To find a Rosicrucian master, the student must first gain the faculty to perceive the language of Heaven in the gentle light of the physical eye. Then it was possible to find here and there in Central Europe during the fourteenth and fifteenth centuries these remarkable men, living in the most simple and unpretentious way—men who were God-inspired, connected in their inner life with the spiritual temples that did indeed exist, though access to them was no less difficult than access to the Holy Grail, as described in the well-known legend....
>
> It was with an infinite peace and rest that pupils departed from their masters in those days. Their countenance expressed the great comfort they had received, and from that look of peace gradually developed a mild and gentle gaze of which the language of Heaven can speak. Therefore, we find in those earlier times and on into the first third of the fifteenth century a profound instruction of the soul being given in these humble and secluded haunts. It is indeed unknown compared to the events related by conventional history. It went on nonetheless, and was an instruction that took deep hold of the entire human being, an instruction that made it possible for the human soul to link its own nature on to the sphere of the Cosmic–Spiritual.

> This whole spiritual atmosphere has disappeared over the later centuries. It is no longer present in our civilization. A superficial, God-estranged civilization has spread over the countries that once saw such a civilization.... From the spiritual revelations that have been accessible to humankind since the last third of the nineteenth century is born a longing to speak to people once more in a spiritual way.*

I walk to find such deep wells of wisdom.

༺༻

From Chicago, I flew to Barcelona and spent time with my daughter who lives there. I was a tourist in a very charming, busy city full of Europeans who come for rest and relaxation, thanks to the cheap Ryan Air flight. They come for the weekend—Germans, French, Irish, English, Dutch, Italians, and others. Many kids from around the world come there for longer periods—New Zealanders, Autralians, South and North Americans, including Canadians and Québecquois, Israelis, Africans, Japanese, and Chinese, all to work and have a good time. Many are multilingual, with at least three to four languages, like my daughter's new roommate. She came from Montreal and speaks French, English, Spanish, and Greek because of her Greek father. These new young adults are all open to new ways. The youth are our future—let's hope that they will find new ways to live. It appears they are trying to find something else, and Barcelona is one of the stops on their adventurous find-yourself life.

My daughter had a week off, so we planned a little walk. From the airport, the cab driver told me I should visit the Montserrat Monastery, a short train ride from Barcelona. On one of my discovery walks in Barcelona, I encountered the tourist bureau, which had a little flyer about walking to Santiago de Compostela from Montserrat. The path had been recently inaugurated, so we decided to walk

---

\* Steiner, *World History and the Mysteries*, pp. 131–135.

on it for a week or so. We soon packed up, and my daughter reluctantly put on her hiker's outfit and backpack. She said to me, "Mom, now I look like one of those *alternativas* [hippies]." It was not the look she wanted. We headed for the train.

Montserrat was beautiful and full of tourists. We arrived on the day of *les Rameaux,* Palm Sunday weekend. We were given our credentials as pilgrims and a place to stay free at the monastery. We left our packs in our room and hiked up into the mountains surrounding the amazing complex that houses a famous choral school for boys, and then turned around a bit early owing to ominous clouds in the southern sky. In the evening, we treated ourselves to a great dinner at the luxurious hotel. Then I wandered into the cathedral, which had a beautiful statue of the Black Madonna. Many people came to this place as a pilgrimage destination just to see the Black Madonna. People touched her very reverently, as did I. Something very powerful came from that statue full of gold, the direct glance, the standing child, and the huge globe in her hands. It kind of jolted one's consciousness—nothing magical—just straightforward presence. Eyes looking straight ahead. What comes at you is something that stirs you deep inside, and then she says "WAKE UP." The previous fall I had spent a lot of time looking at, and experiencing, the healing power of the Madonna paintings and statues, but none had this feeling of *je ne sais quoi.* It came from another realm; I can't explain it.

> All the ancient Black Virgins I have seen have a numinous and hierarchic calm, as with the Virgin of Notre-Dame d'Espoir in Dijon. She is a manifestation of a level of being and experience infinitely beyond human failings and sufferings and it is, perhaps, precisely because she possesses this freedom from misery that she is able to comfort and to bless through her presence. The atmosphere she generates is the evidence that there is, in truth, a level of peace that is attainable and is full of succor for human griefs and hopes.[*]

---

[*] Francke, 2007.

This next, somewhat long passage requires concentration and is good training for the mind. To understand what lies hidden, we *cannot* be lazy or passive, but must participate with our thinking. Try to live into these words and make them come alive; then the spirit of the Black Madonna will be present.

> What, in terms of Spiritual Science, has happened to the old clairvoyant faculty of the human soul? This rape of Persephone has, in fact, been going on from the earliest times right up to our own day; the old clairvoyant culture has vanished. Nevertheless, nothing in the world ever really disappears; things are really only transformed. Where, then, has Persephone gone? What is the Regent of the old clairvoyant forces [i.e., Persephone] doing today in human nature?...
>
> The human soul encompasses far more than what it knows intellectually. A more comprehensive soul life, subconscious soul life, is at work in us (it is better to call it subconscious rather than unconscious)—a soul life that, in most modern people, does not emerge into consciousness at all. In this subconscious life, Persephone is at work today in human beings without our being able to give a reasoned account of it; this is where the suppressed clairvoyant forces have gone. Whereas in primeval times they worked so that the soul could see into spiritual worlds, today they work in the depths of human souls. They assist in the development and formation of the "I" principle, making it ever-more firm.... Thus, the Persephone forces have been drawn down into the human subconscious; they have been embraced and have, so to speak, been raped by the depths of the human soul... forces that in outer nature are represented by Pluto. According to Greek mythology, Pluto is the ruler of the underworld, the interior of the earth. However, the Greeks were also aware that the same forces at work in the depths of the earth are also at work in the depths of the human soul. Just as Persephone was carried off by Pluto, likewise the soul was robbed of its ancient clairvoyant capacity through Pluto's intervention.
>
> Now Persephone is Demeter's daughter. Thus we infer that, in Demeter, we have an even older ruler, both of the forces of external nature and of the forces of the human soul.... Demeter

is a figure of Greek mythology we associate with the kind of clairvoyant vision that belongs to the very oldest endowment of wisdom of Atlantean humanity; it is in Atlantis that Demeter is really to be found. When Atlanteans gazed into the spiritual world, they saw Demeter; she actually came to meet them. What did they say when this whirling of constant movement and changing forms, the archetypal mother of the human soul and the fruitful forces of nature, appeared to them from the spiritual world? They might say to themselves (though not in full consciousness, but in the unconscious), "I have done nothing myself; I have not gone through an inner development, as later ages will do, to see in the spiritual world. The same forces of nature that have given me my eyes, brain, and organism that are active in me, these very forces also give me the power of clairvoyance. Just as I breathe, likewise I have clairvoyant vision.... Through the forces under the control of Demeter, the fecundating goddess of the whole world, the clairvoyant capacity represented by Persephone is born in the human organization." Thus Atlanteans felt that they, too, had their place among the wonders of nature. They felt this clairvoyant capacity born in them as the birth of Persephone; they felt that they owed that birth to Demeter, who spreads abroad in the wide cosmos the very forces that, in human beings, develop into the faculty of clairvoyance....

Today's human body, with its system of muscle and bone, is substantially denser and more compact than were the bodies of those who were still able to give birth to Persephone within themselves, since they still had the faculty of clairvoyance. Moreover, because our organism has become denser, it can also hold fast the clairvoyant forces in the subearthly realm of the soul. The imprisonment of the clairvoyant forces within human nature comes about as a result of the densification of the human body....

Demeter saw her child Persephone lost in human nature, saw her raped, so to speak, by the now denser human body, so that those clairvoyant forces could henceforth be used only for coarser bodily nutrition. At that point, she "gave" up imparting the moral law directly. What did she do? She instituted a mystery, thus providing a substitute, a new form of law, for the old law that worked through the forces of nature. Thus the gods withdrew from the forces of nature into the mysteries, and gave moral precepts to human beings who no longer possessed a morality drawn from the activity of nature within them.... However, as the human body became denser and denser and transformed, what happened to the original Demeter forces? They had to take a backseat in the organization of the human body; they had to become less active; humankind had to be alienated from the direct influence of Demeter and subject to other forces....

In ancient times, human beings had *clairvoyant,* or *imaginal,* knowledge; today, we have *intellectual,* or *rational,* knowledge. This is the change that has come about in the astral (feeling) body.... [Demeter] was driven from the astral body with its lost clairvoyant capacities, and Eros took her place.... The old clairvoyant form of knowledge had to be buried in the Plutonic region of the human soul, and for a period, from the time of Socrates right up to our own day, people had to remain more or less ignorant of all these things. However, under the surface the old knowledge, the knowledge aroused by those impressive pictorial images of the Greeks remained. It was buried under the load of intellectual culture. Now it is emerging again from the dark depths of the spirit....

All these figures [Hecate, Demeter, and Persephone] will appear again to clairvoyant vision, which will in the future press with increasing urgency upon humankind from the spiritual world.... The power of the Christ provides all the impulses to enable human nature to rise again and see all that has been buried in the depths of the soul—for instance, the figures of the Greeks gods. That will be the greatest event for the future history of the human soul. It is the event for which Spiritual Science must prepare, so that the soul may become capable of acquiring the etheric vision. In the next three thousand years, it will lay hold of more and more souls. The next three thousand years will be devoted to kindling the forces in the human soul that will make it aware of the etheric wonders of surrounding nature.\*

---

\*   Steiner, *Wonders of the World,* pp. 35–43.

This passage touches upon the strength which comes from the Black Madonna—why people flock to see her and priests do not understand. The complexities of where the forces come from, shown by the above quotations, cannot deter us from trying to understand them. Experiencing what emanates from the Black Madonna is a beginning in the search for the truth hidden within her.

It is no wonder that Wagner, upon visiting the Morenata in Montserrat, was inspired to compose his *Parsifal*.

⁂

We could not stay very long looking at the Black Madonna, because many people were waiting to see it. Nonetheless, I went back a few more times later that evening to view the statue.

The next day we got up early and started our walk. We could not find the path for a while, but then there it was. Just fifteen minutes into the walk, the path disappeared; it had been wiped out by a huge mudslide over the path. I proceeded very slowly with my daughter behind me not wanting to go on. "It might be dangerous," she was saying, but we made it. There were no signs saying not to go through, but this was an inauspicious beginning.

We walked on and reached a small road before starting out on a path going down the mountain. We arrived at a convent, and I rang the bell to ask directions. The nun who answered told us we were going the wrong way. We had been walking in the rain for quite a while and were both soaked and had another ten miles to walk. We needed to return back up the mountain, retrace out steps, and find the path.

After retracing our steps, I saw a local man coming down the mountain after a hike. He was going to his car, and I asked him for a ride to the nearest town. I was giving up. It was not a well-indicated path, and getting lost up here was no fun. We could be lost for days in those mountains, mudslides and all. The man was very nice and told us this path is not well marked at all; it was not made by people who walk. He told us it is dangerous to walk in those mountains. He then took us to the train station, from which we headed back to Barcelona.

Our trip had lasted just two days. I was a bit upset because I wanted my daughter and me to walk together before my big trip through France, but it was not to be. She said, "Mom, don't worry. I have things to do." At least I had seen one famous Black Madonna, and Le Puy also had a Black Madonna. On the positive side, I would have an extra week for my own walk.

The next day, very early in the morning, I left by train to cross into France and arrived in Le Puy (via Lyon) late in the evening. It is not easy for pilgrims with their backpacks after a long day on the train. One had to wander around town in search of a hostel, up and down the hilly streets. I stayed in a pilgrims' hostel on a hill. It was near the cathedral, and I stayed in a large, very empty dorm with only one French woman from the south; most people start their walk about two weeks later in the spring. The first week in April is considered early, because some places might still be snowed in, or it might snow at higher elevations, making the journey dangerous and one's backpack feel heavier. In addition, one needs more stuff to keep warm.

I made myself supper after going for groceries to a small *épicerie* owned by a North African family. I found dates, nuts, avocados, French bread, and juice. The owners reminded me of the years I spent growing up from ages six to twelve in Morocco and Algeria during their war for independence. I used to shop for my mom, and I was always welcomed by the local Moroccan and Algerian grocers.

While I was eating supper at the hostel, a group of young teenaged boys on a trip with their local priest came in noisily. Some of them looked tough; hiking was just what they needed. I had to kick them out of the bathroom so that I could take a shower. They had invaded the women's showers. Meanwhile, I missed the ceremony at the cathedral, where the local priest was blessings the pilgrims on their way. I would have to go without the church blessings, but I had received my blessings in Montserrat from the Black Madonna and her straightforward, powerful glance.

The next morning, I decided to go sightseeing in the small, picturesque city and its numerous hills of volcanic origin, many with chapels perched on them. One such chapel is dedicated to St. Michael, with a big statue to the Virgin protecting and dominating the whole city. I planned to start my pilgrimage around one o'clock in the afternoon and walk only half the day, since I would be hiking up and down the city the whole morning.

The cathedral is one of those very dark, masculine, and virile places, which is quite a paradox since this place is supposed to be a center of Marian devotion and worship of the Black Madonna. Perhaps the Black Madonna belongs to this dark, moldy place. The whole large complex had an atmosphere of old stuff—quite dead. The priests are few and the whole Catholic Church seems to be dying in some way, and this place is a reflection of that; it looked quite rundown with insufficient funds to renovate it. I saw a lot of old men and old priests. I felt that women are not very welcome here; it is a man's world. I have visited numerous cathedrals, and this one is not my favorite, Black Madonna or not.

This city was a major pilgrimage center starting in the ninth century, as well as a place to begin the Compostela pilgrimage. In later centuries, many heretics such as the Cathars were condemned to walk to Le Puy or from this place to Spain or Rome. The bishops had a lot of power at that time to abolish "heresies." It was a major rallying point for kings, knights, and armies from the north to join the crusades or for bishops from other cities to meet for "councils" to discuss decrees issued from Rome, dealing with church renewal and purges of churches, monasteries, heresies, and so on. A lot of power was at stake—the power of kings, popes, bishops, armies, men over women, and of course from under the ground: volcanic power.

The enormous statue of the Virgin, made from countless melted canons, sits on top of one of the many hills that dominate the fantastic scenery. Its function? The birth of the feminine within men—quite a task, as those priests will need lifetimes to accomplish such a birth.

Thank goodness they have the Black Madonna and her power hidden and buried in the moldy recesses of the old, dusty cathedral. I am no expert on the Black Madonna, even though I grew up within a couple of miles of one who made her home in Dijon at Notre-Dame de Bon-Espoir (Our Lady of Good Hope).

> The vast tradition of the Black Madonna and her son the corn hero, of which Our Lady of Częstochowa (in Poland) is a prime example, represents a world vision in which nature is not captured, named, and forced into servitude, but rather is understood in a compassionate way whereby the intellect presents its facts but then listens for the answer which the spiritual world provides. This listening perception of nature is symbolized in the ritual burial of the Black Madonna in the darkest recesses of the church. Traditionally, she resides in the dim alcoves, shrines, or caverns throughout the late summer, fall, and early spring months. At the winter solstice, the darkest time of the year, she is lifted out of her burial place and carried through the town in a procession. Like Persephone and Dionysos, the Black Madonna endures burial to listen to the silence of the dark earth. The ritual is an exact analogue that teaches the creative consciousness to listen in silence to the true voices of nature. In today's world such listening allows the scientifically inclined intellect to fructify its search for truth with Intuitive power. The ability to link clear thinking with Inspiration and intuitive perception makes the Black Madonna and Jaccus-Christos symbol a powerful meditational image for artists, poets, teachers, and scientists who are striving to allow the spiritual world to enter their work.
>
> Traditionally the Black Madonna is the patron of women about to undergo the dark trial of childbirth. Images of her and her gravity-defying babe were hung in birthing rooms to give strength and comfort in the chaos and insecurity of this deep, mysterious threshold between the two worlds. Thinkers wishing to transcend the brain-bound intellect and explore the realms of Intuition are in a similar situation to that of a birthing mother. Inspirations issuing from the realm of total dark are often experienced as painfully

confusing riddles or problems that are situated at odd angles to the psychic birth canal of meditation. It is here that the Black Madonna can serve as midwife between the True Self and the soul. She can provide fresh forces to continue the concentration needed for success.

Without the intercession of the Black Madonna, scientific thinking most often produces a stillborn thought—merely innovative computational sum of ideas without the spark of originality or the forces that promote growth and healing for other human beings. Although ideas such as these initially appear clever, innovative, and progressive, in the long run they devitalize the thinker and the culture into which they are born, bringing sickness and confusion into the cultural life. Linear cause and effect "inspirations" by men of "genius" coagulate the experience of earth and its life into an abstract computational landscape. This chills the heart, for it offers only bleak images of impersonal, abstracted forces of nature engaged in relentless combat, with human life caught impotently in their grip. Such alienation from nature is the price that human beings pay for the freedom we have won through developing logical, empirical thinking. The capacity to think in concepts frees human beings from the need to comply unconsciously with the directives of the Godhead. Thus freed, we experience the exhilaration of independent psychic existence and the simultaneous yearning for the union with, succor from, and counsel of a source of wisdom higher than ourselves.

Acting as mediator between the soaring conceptual life of higher reason and the spontaneous creative outpouring of the Godhead who animates and sustains nature, the Black Madonna has guided and facilitated the prayers and meditations of countless devotees. She represents a path whereby the modern human soul caught in the labyrinth of abstract thinking can find its way to a compassionate experience of nature. She enables the transcendent creative forces in the soul to resonate with the transcendent creative forces in the natural world.\*

---

\* Klocek, *Seeking Spirit Vision*, pp. 57–58.

In contrast to this large, dark, moldy complex, I visited the very light, lovely, tiny Chapelle Saint-Michel on Mt. Aiguille, at the top of a rocky hill, built by Bishop Gothescalk in 962. It sits on the former sacred site on a dolmen of Celtic worship and the former Roman site dedicated to Mercury, the God of Healing. I could have sat in that chapel all day; it had a very comforting atmosphere in which one could meditate quietly and deeply.

The name Mont Aiguille of Saint Michael means "needle" in French, reminding one of Michael's sword of light that breaks through the great Inner Darkness. He sits on a rock mountain that is very sharp and angular. Inside, one has this very light atmosphere, especially after walking up the long set of winding stairs. The chapel is tiny—unassumingly small in contrast to the large Notre-Dame Cathedral and its cloisters complex.

> The name of the Spirit of the Time, *Michael*, is a question: *Who is as God?* And only in English or German… "is" expressed. He is the only Divinity that carries a question for a name…. And today this name seems to be very near to the human being, in its form of a question as well as its meaning.
>
> Compared to a statement, a question means: permeability, searching, to be on the way—in the name of Michael, and all of this in the name of God. It is an eternal quest, directed at the highest aim. One can avoid a human question, but not one that is a *being*, such a mighty being. He who meets this question is forced by the might of an archangel and archai: "Reflect on yourself. Know thyself." Therefore this being's name, this name-being is itself the weapon of its "bearer"—again an inadequate human expression—against the two adversary forces, his archenemies. Arms—a lance or a sword—he wears only in the human image, even though an imaginative one. But those images show how unearthly he uses these weapons: his glance is never directed at the adversary or the weapon; this nevertheless finds and hits with surety, because his questioning-searching look, where he is present in concentration as it were, is his true weapon; he himself is this question which one cannot evade….

In his name—which is a question—the Spirit of the Times depicts the actual necessary human step. It was never as urgent nor as possible as today. For the period of innocence, when primal wisdom was given without questioning, was followed by the period of doubt, when questioning is the only means to find a way out....

Besides the saying "God is dead" is the experience that the Godhead is now silent; without a contribution—questioning—on the part of humankind, the Godhead is no longer given. Human beings must now begin: "Ask, Seek, and Knock." Then *Micha-el*, the Spirit of the Times, the divinity which is waiting for *his* step, *his* beginning, can offer help.... This explains why the spirit of the Times is now standing above language and fold. It says....

Michael is strictly refusing everything that is separating, for instance in the human languages. As long as one is only clothing one's discoveries in the language, not raising them into thoughts, as long as this is the case one cannot come near to Michael.... In fact we have today the strongest spiritual battle in this direction; for a great part of humankind thoughts are non-existent, because people are thinking in words. But thinking in words is not the way of Michael. Michael, one can approach only if one reaches through the words to true inner experience of the spirit, not depending on words. This, in fact, is the secret of modern initiation; to overcome the words in order to experience the spirit. This does not impinge on the experience of the beauty of language, one begins to *experience* language, it begins to stream out as an element of sensation, begins to stream within oneself.[*]

The city of Le Puy-en-Velay (1,969 to 2,913 feet) sits atop volcanic terrain. It's many hills were very active at one time. The last volcano erupted in these old central mountains of France about 8,000 years ago. This area is not easily accessible, with no direct train from big cities and no airports or main roads. It is perfect for walking paths. If one looks at the place where the Black Madonna worship is celebrated,

---

[*] Ibid., pp. 36–38.

one finds them abundantly scattered in these old volcanic mountains of Massif Central. Living in these places, where the earth forces are very active, it is no wonder that worship of a powerful Goddess continues. The strong forces coming from the unconscious needed a strong vessel, which the Black Madonna symbolizes. What is outside is also within. Dennis Klocek tells us:

> To put oneself into contact with the Black Madonna it is necessary first to develop strong powers of concentration through the practice of logical thinking based on an intellectual grasp of the life of concepts. Firmly grounded in the conceptual life, the soul can begin to rise into the realm of suprasensory cognition. In this realm thoughts have forms, and ideas are palpable realities. The discipline of the sciences serves for the modern human being as the prerequisite grounding in logical thinking so necessary for entrance into higher realms of cognition.
>
> The Black Madonna understands desire and the dark soul yearnings connected with life on earth. She gives birth to Jaccus—the Logos, the Christ—a suffering God who is able to transcend the abyss, to compassionately observe the dark side of human life, and to sacrifice the freedom of personally willed activity for the higher experience of surrender to suprasensory cognition. The Black Madonna and her black child enable the soul to observe its own darkness in the calm, clear knowledge that transcendent forces are also available to the soul. Through Jaccus the will can be purified and rectified in its currents. The purified will can then resonate with higher, finer sources of intelligence. This allows the soul's organs of cognition to induce creative thoughts much beyond the soul's native capacities. By meditating on the Black Madonna and her child the purified currents of the will and the stabilized currents of the intellect can be brought back together into a fusion in the heart—for it is from the heart that the Black Madonna and her child find their forces of transcendent compassion. In the human heart the religious impulses of the will and the scientific impulses of the thought life are nurtured into the capacity to surrender what is known in order to be free enough to create beauty, harmony, and healing. The Black Madonna offers to modern human beings the

hope of resolving the predicament of abstraction in the arts and sciences. She offers a sacred path for those who are left uninspired by layers of ecumenical varnish on the surfaces of world religion.*

Many pilgrims throughout the ages have journeyed to this old center of worship from all the corners of Europe. It was a destination; for me it is a beginning—a new beginning—as all pilgrimages are new beginnings and ventures into the unknown, the unknown area of physical places and our inner world. To dwell deeply into the meaning of the Black Madonna is a rich experience at the beginning of a pilgrimage.

> Here we may remember a phrase coined by Maurice Barres, which says much in few words... "those places where the spirit bloweth." In Le Puy, as on the hill of Sion-Vaudemont and in some other privileged places... why should such places be called "privileged"? Perhaps because it would seem that, in them, prayer rises more freely from the heart, that a suprasensory contact between the human and the spiritual worlds is more easily made.
>
> The name *Black Virgin* is given to the chthonic deity who was worshipped in those places. The image was mostly a rough carving made out of a very old piece of wood that had been buried in the ground for a long time. The wood had to be unearthed and this was connected with the ideas of resurrection and immortality. This image with a human face, thus wrenched from the densest and darkest form of matter, the earth, was taken out of its prison and brought to the light again. Through the power of prayer and the grace arising from worship the corpse became the spring of a new life, born of the hard inert wood....
>
> Again we may ask: Why were those places chosen? The study of etheric forces has provided Rudolf Steiner with the answer. In some regions of the globe, the crust of the earth has subsided in a marked degree, while the emergence of powerful chains of mountains has disturbed the concentric layers of etheric forces which, from the core of the planet, rise up to the highest reaches of our atmosphere. Thus gigantic fissures have enabled humankind

---

\* Ibid., pp. 57–58.

to come into close contact with etheric influences differing from those of our natural surroundings. Such are the deep valleys that form the bed of the river Jordan, the Dead Sea, the lakes of the Upper Engadine, and the clefts where are found the caves of Chartres, Lourdes, and Delphi. Our physical frame has lost its elasticity and become rigid but, in the distant past, human beings were highly sensitive to those differences in etheric activity. Thus when they found themselves in an area where expansive forces predominate, they felt the impact of the opposing forces with intensity, especially those of the life ether whose influence is constrictive. This impact was experienced more vividly in areas where fissures and subsidence had taken place, where the etheric, freed from its normal connection with solid matter, exercised a direct and more potent influence on humankind.

In a different way, on the basalt peak of Le Puy-en-Velay, on the hill described by Maurice Barres as "the Inspired Hill," on Mount St. Michel, on the rock of Delos, or on the highlands of Tibet, people feel the force of warmth and light ethers more fully.*

Over the past thousand years, pilgrims have taken to these roads for various reasons—for punishments, for healing, for praying for others. The attraction was sometimes reinforced by the authorities, the church, the king, and others, but sometimes it went the other way such as in the seventeenth and eighteenth centuries during the age of enlightenment, where such pilgrimages were criticized as a waste of time—better to stay home and provide for your family than run around looking at dubious relics and cure all—and some of the pilgrims were put in prison for such freedom as to run loose and free across Europe without the proper papers. The church officials and the kings did not want their serfs and slaves to live as free men and women, and the misogynists among the clergy were quick to use the word *coquaillarde* (*coquille* for shells) for women who (supposedly) went on pilgrimages as an excuse for cheating on their husbands. They also called the pilgrims derelicts and leeches.

---

\*   Morizot, *The School of Chartres*, pp. 5–6.

The romantic nineteenth century came as a breath of fresh air, and pilgrims started to take the path again. Then we entered the twentieth and twenty-first centuries with a hunger for inner renewal amid a new kind of chaos.

Now armed with the consciousness of lava power of the interior, the realm of the powerful Will in the Black Madonna, and the realm of Thinking in the Sword of Light of Chapelle Saint-Michel on Mont Aiguille, I was surely ready for my journey across France to the Pyrenees. Le Puy is definitely a site to reckon with; it has been for thousands of years. The morning had proven very fruitful, and it was time to get on the road. I walked back to the hostel, had some lunch, put on my heavy pack, and headed down out of the city through the southwestern exit, then up to a very quiet, pleasant, and deserted path among farmland. Not so busy, this road. No other pilgrims in sight.

With the blessings of the Black Madonna and St. Michel with his sword and scales, I was on my way to meet my fellow pilgrims and start the long walk. Saint James had vanished in the background of my awareness, but the spirit of Charlemagne was looming on the horizon.

What more could one want besides such Imaginations to fill one's mind as one is walking across such beautiful landscape? Nothing. And all the pilgrims who begin here experience the same awe-inspiring Images. At the cathedral's daily blessings for pilgrims, everyone is given a miniature statue of the Black Madonna to take along. I missed it, but I had the Imaginations in my mind, which was a great gift.

> Where can we come at the forces of change that seek to bring in something utterly new, though as yet but dimly felt by human beings? First and foremost we must mark the ability to *think in pictures,* which is beginning to have a most significant effect on the life of the modern soul. The picture is much closer to human suprasensory experience than pictureless—in the literal sense unimaginative—abstract thinking. It is the first step towards loosening the bonds that hold us to the physical external world. When we develop a sense for the pictorial and arouse our fantasy

*Chapelle St. Michel d'Aiguilhe, Le Puy-en-Velay*

into forming pictures, we are using the same force as works in the experience of actual spiritual reality in picture form, an experience attained with the first stage of suprasensory knowledge, the stage of imaginative consciousness.*

On the path again, my back is starting to ache from my pack, but the scenery helps me to forget the pain. Slowly I get back into the

---

\*    Roschl-Lehrs, *The Second Man in Us*, pp.13–14.

pilgrim's world, and forget plane rides, train rides, bus rides, cities, and people; all escapes my mind, and I welcome the familiar emptiness. Thoughts start to decrease, and I am on the path. I walk in the present and it grasps my attention—the rocky or grassy path, stones, April flowers, farms, clouds, smells, and silence. That is why I walk for days on end, for this bath into silence. The chatter box is quieting down, as the hours pass by. Farmland, forests, meadows, ravines, rivers—all is welcome, new, unknown, and therefore exciting. This excitement is no illusion; it is true, quiet excitement. I am seeing the world at 5 kilometers per hour, more or less. There is time to listen to the birds, see the clouds forming, feel the soft wind on my face, and feel my feet on the ground. More and more people are taking up these long distance walks across Europe for weeks at a time, and I am becoming one of them. Every year I have a rendezvous with Mother Earth.

> Walking takes away the heaviness of our thoughts. Moreover, such is also the goal of prayer as defined by the Eastern Church. Nowadays solitary walking could also be a form of praying.
>
> Walking could silence our mind while unifying it with the intuitive thinking of our right brain; this is exactly what A. Sophrony says about prayer: "Pure prayer attracts the intellect into the heart realm; prayer unifies the whole human, including the body." Because, "while the intellect is praying, it does not think; it does not reason, but lives. The intellect in a state of prayer does not function with abstract concepts, but participates directly with BEING." In the same way we can say that while walking, the intellect "is not thinking" but "IS WHAT IT IS." It is direct perception of life which does not allow itself to be imprisoned within the narrow confine of abstract concepts.
>
> Walking can truly be a form of prayer which "unites the intellect with the heart." This union is considered the usual state of the religious life.... The intellect that is united with praying through attention lives within the heart.
>
> I cannot help myself but ponder about the expression "the eye of the heart" (the title of a book by F. Schuon) which defines intuitive or spiritual vision as the silence of the intellect, and this

"revolution of the mind" which recognizes that wisdom, or spiritual experience, could very well be the union of the two hemispheres of the brain—the left, the seat of reason, and the right, the seat of intuition.*

⁕

I walked through a little village, then through a very sculpted terrain by the side of a ravine on a rocky, mossy plateau, and reached another village through a lovely rock path bordered by pine trees and a stone wall. I could see some other pilgrims far away in the distance behind me. There are lots of farms—still worked with horses—with cows in the fields. The farmers are working on spreading manure on their small tended fields because it is springtime, and they are cleaning the barns, so there is a manure aroma as we walk on these paths.

Now it is raining, and I am going through this little village that everyone loves to leave, as I found out later in the guest book at the bed and breakfast; everyone complains of having been mistreated by the local villagers, who do not seem very pleasant. Here we are in very rural France with lots of people who have never been anywhere. The place smells of ancient times—the Middle Ages—and it has not changed for centuries. They are very much ensconced in their habits and behavior. Those passing through are strangers and not to be trusted. It is not a very "Christian" environment. Fortunately, that village is not the norm, but the exception. The locals really need the Camino walkers to take their blinders off, to teach them how to be more cosmopolitan and worldly, so it is *la belle campagne*. Perhaps the place needs more Dutch, English, German natives to buy local houses.

I stopped in the local bar, and the bartender was not very keen on serving me, so I walked out. I had stopped in a little restaurant, but the woman told me off and said that they had nothing to eat, that they were closed. It was not very late. I said I would take anything they had;

---

\* Jourdan and Vigne, *Marcher, méditer*, pp. 13–14 (tr. M-L. Valandro).

she said no and locked the door. Nice beginning. When I planned this trip across France, I was getting very excited about the "good food" I would be eating. No such luck. The *boulangerie* was not any better. The *boulangere* was getting very upset because a guy was not leaving his hiking sticks outside; he was messing up the floor with the sticks, scratching it or something. Let's get out of here; we'll leave hungry. We have our legs, and within an hour we will be in another village that will surely be better; it can't get worse.

I arrived in the hamlet of Tallode and saw a sign for a "farm and breakfast" and decided to end the short hiking day there for a nice sleep. A few young, jovial farmers in blue work overalls called their mother, and she came out of the warm, restored farmhouse. "*Vous pouvez rester au premier étage, vous avez une chambre, et vous serez seule. Il y a un monsieur anglais, a coté pouvez vous lui expliquer a propos du petit déjeuner, je ne parle pas tres bien l'anglais?*"

"*Mais, bien sur,*" I responded.

I had a neighbor—the woman had given each of us a room. The *monsieur anglais* was resting, and when I went downstairs for a hot shower, he had made me a cup of tea. He was an older English man who lived in Australia, a former captain in the navy, now a barge captain. He had suffered colon cancer, which had been operated on that past January, and he was on sick leave and walking the Camino. He was also suffering from diabetes. He said that walking would make him better, and I thought he was thoroughly correct. He told me about his first marriage, which had not gone well. His new marriage, to a woman fifteen years younger than he, was much better, and his son was in London. We had a great conversation lasting well into the evening about the Masons (because he is a Mason) and numerous other topics. He told me about his Jewish Masonic leader back in Australia, whom he viewed as an exceptional human being. He was well versed in such matters, and we had lots in common. As usual, brothers and sisters meet on the way to speak about what really matters. Isn't that why we are on the road?

As for modern Freemasonry, its origins are lost in the mists of time. Practically every imaginable source has been proposed, from the Druids of megalithic Britain to Pharoanic Egypt and beyond. John Yarker even traced the origins back to the fall of Atlantis, thus making Freemasonry the bearer of the primordial wisdom of the Rishis or Sages who seeded post-Atlantean culture....

On all evidence, however, several distinct spiritual influences seem to feed into the arrival of Freemasonry on the historical stage in the late seventeenth century. At the very least, one can discern the presence of the following: the echo of the ancient mysteries, Egyptian Hermetism, and the so-called Gnosticism; ancient and medieval guild or craft initiations; monastic culture; the learning of the cathedral schools; the traditions of the Knights of Templars and the Cathars (Manicheans); Jewish Kabbalah; alchemy; certain streams of Islamic (especially Ismaeli) and Celtic esotericism; Renaissance hermetism; and Rosicrucianism.*

We could have talked all night, because my roommate had traveled all over; he had read piles of books, and so had I. Meanwhile, the woman of the house had gone to the hairdresser, all the way to Le Puy, which of course was only twenty-five minutes by car, and she had forgotten about our food. So I just ate my dates, figs, walnuts, and hazelnuts while he waited for a meal.

Around 8:30 that evening, she served a dish of leftovers—not very appetizing. Here, again, where is all that good French food? She was also charging him a very hefty price; I told him not to pay the whole price because he ate hardly anything—it was just not very good. Nevertheless, we did not care, and we forgave her; she was a friendly woman and our conversation was more nourishing than the food.

>"From where do you come?"
>"From the chasms where the gold lives," said the Snake.
>"What is grander than gold?" enquired the King.

---

\* Steiner, *"Freemasonry"and Ritual Work* (from the introduction by Christopher Bamford), xvii.

"Light," replied the Snake.
"What is more quickening than light?" said he.
"Conversation," answered he.*

Then we each went to our separate quarters. We each had a whole room to ourselves, full of empty beds—a luxury on the Camino—and we had a good sleep after all the talking.

⁂

I left Tallode (2,700 feet) around 8:30 the next morning, following a French breakfast no better than the dinner—bread with butter and jam and tea with my new friend Peter, the English-Australian sea captain and Mason.

We started our walk under ominous weather and dark clouds, so we helped each other with rain gear, ponchos, and so on. It was a beautiful walk through a plateau with endless little stone houses, farms, and barns. More farmers were spreading manure in their small stony fields. We arrived after two or three hours in a lovely village and stopped at the little Chapel of St. Roch (eleventh or twelfth century) for some quiet meditation before entering the village of Montbonnet. It was full of old stone houses, many of which had been renovated. We saw a brand new restaurant, and even though it was a bit early for lunch we stopped and asked for some food. It was time to have a real breakfast or lunch, as I had not eaten properly for a couple of days.

The inn had been very artistically done recently by the owner and his sons. They made us the best French omelet and were very friendly and happy to engage in lively conversation. We stayed for at least an hour longer, talking and drinking cup after cup of tea, and then forced ourselves to get up. We walked out of the village and went ahead on a path and into a mountainous, forested region. We were happy to have all our clothing as it began to snow; hat and gloves were welcome.

---

\*   Goethe, *The Fairytale of the Green Snake and the Beautiful Lily.*

The forest was full of pine trees and was very quiet. It became a bit muddy before we emerged from the forest onto a lovely path overlooking the whole region. The weather was getting better—still a bit foggy—and we started our descent into the next village. It was a very rocky path down the mountain, in a very old forest that had probably seen many riders and pilgrims over the centuries. It felt inhabited, quiet, and peaceful. Then we saw an old watermill, and entered a new town in this territory of ravines, mountains, and winding roads. The town was Saint-Privat-d'Allier (2,700 feet), well hidden in a region of mountains and cliffs, with a gorge where today people go kayaking in the spring. It used to be home to a Medieval castle—a proper place, easy to defend, with cliffs everywhere. From that village, we had beautiful views of the surrounding area. We saw a lot of farmhouses owned by vacationers who were probably English. Saint-Privat-d'Allier had a nice Roman church with a ravine on one side.

Peter decided to stay and sleep in the town, and I decided to continue on to the next destination after we had a coffee break and a final conversation before saying good-bye. It was only 2:30 and too early for me to stop. We had walked about ten miles since the morning, and I figured I could walk another five or so before evening without rushing too much. Peter had to turn around the next day; he was just investigating the path to see if his wife could manage it. They would do this walk next year. I had enjoyed his company and his strength. He never talked about his health or pains, but just enjoyed being on the path. He had beautiful, crystal-clear, blue eyes. I would trust being on his ship anytime.

The path went down along a river and then climbed again into the mountain in what seemed to be an old Roman road that joined a small mountain road for cars, again through a forest of tall pine trees. I noticed the spring flowers beginning to emerge through the moss, the great scent of earth, trees growing with shrubs and a myriad of other living things. This is what all the walking pilgrims love, and what brings people back year after year on these ancient paths.

It actually makes a great difference whether we pay attention to things in life, whether we take an interest in every detail or we do not pay attention to things....

When people go through life with great attentiveness to everything, they must, in the nature of things, move around a great deal.... It remains to be seen what people with an exclusively sedentary way of life will be like in their next earthly life, because sedentary existence has become customary only in this age. However, when people of earlier times were attentive to the things in their environment, they always had *to go* to them; they had to move their limbs and bring them into activity. The whole body was active, not just the senses, which belong to the organization of the head. Everything in which the whole body participates when we are attentive and observant passes into the structure of the head of one's next earthly life and has a definite effect.... The result is that in such people there is a special development of everything that depends on the earth forces. The result is big, strong bones, very broad shoulder blades, for instance, with the ribs well developed. Everything bears the stamp of good development....

Those whose karma it is to have strong bones in the next earthly life—with well developed muscles as the result of attentiveness to life—will go through life with courage. Through such attentiveness, we acquire the natural force belonging to a courageous life.... Now let us think of cowards or faint-hearted people. They are the ones who took no interest in anything during their previous life.[*]

These modern pilgrims taking to the road by the thousands is training *for the future.* The world will see many very courageous souls. Peter is definitely one of them.

❦

I arrived in the little village of Rochegude (3,000 feet), perched near the top of the mountain, and tucked away in a mountainside, with a few artists living there. One needs to be very rugged to live here.

---

[*] Steiner, *Karmic Relationships,* vol. 2, pp.120–123.

*Near Rochegude*

Sitting on top of the rocky hill a bit further up the village was a chapel dedicated to St. James. There was also the remnant of a chateau here that used to defend one county from the other. Many knights sojourned through here. It is a hidden place, very hard to reach among these rocky mountains, with no direct access, just winding around one mountain and then another, overlooking the gorges of the Allier River in the distance.

Wishing I could have stayed longer, I left the lonesome village with the sight of a young sculptor working on wooden art pieces and a gardener weeding his flowerbeds. The path turned dangerously rocky and slippery because it had been raining. It was very, very steep so I could not walk very fast. I descended all the way down into another valley and crossed another little village, and then down, down, down to the Allier River, winding among the tall rocky mountain faces and ravines. Today, I had climbed up and down a couple of thousand feet. I climbed again to find one of the pilgrim hostels in the town of Monistrol-d'Allier (1,800 feet), finding there a refreshing *gîte* and a home-cooked meal of lentils and hand-delivered sausages, as well as a house full of pilgrims. Except for Peter, I had seen no one for two days.

At the dinner table, there was a young man from the Jura who spoke German, a French man, and three German women with their nineteen- to twenty-year-old kids and friends on spring break. Another pilgrim was a former farmer who sold his farm and now travels a lot. He told me a story about l'île de La Réunion, near Madagascar off the coast of East Africa, where he had gone hiking. On that remote island, where the tourists rarely go, he saw that the Chinese were sending their prisoners abroad to places such as this island to work building factories, roads, and large complexes. They would earn twenty-five euros a month for heavy, backbreaking work—the new slave labor. Most of the prisoners had not committed serious crimes. I had been unaware of this; we learn a lot by traveling instead of just reading newspapers. That is why the Chinese are getting the contracts and can afford such projects at a fraction of the normal cost. The real cost is human slavery.

We all went to bed early, since the next day would be a very long day. We will climb 1,500 feet to reach the next town in three miles.

❦

I was the last one to leave the hostel after eating breakfast and repacking my backpack. I folded my sleeping bag and packed my clothes, bottles filled with half water and half juice, snacks, and a guidebook. I got my walking sticks, put on my hiking shoes, and was ready to go. I looked for signs but found none. I walked through the town to the highway, looked around, and started swearing in French and English. Where is this place? Then, of course, it got worse. I started walking back down to the village, this time along the river, then walked for ten minutes before deciding, *no*, this is not the right road. So I went back up to where I started, then saw the German gang going down to where I had just come from and decided not to follow them. I went back up, and then finally back down. Forty-five minutes later, I was again following the river, having found the path. I had missed the tiny, little sign.

By that time I was raving mad. I know myself. When I get to that stage, it just gets worse.

I looked at the river and said to myself, *Okay, now you have had a nice fit. Enough; you have enjoyed it fully. Good, let us get back to normal.* I was upset with my childishness, my weak point, my useless anger. What a lovely beginning for a very hard climb; I was exhausted even before I began.

The path seemed straight up, and I had to stop to catch my breath. Nevertheless, the scenery was great; I could see down into the carved riverbed. I almost took another path—the wrong path—but decided to stay on the regular, zigzagging small road. There was the Chapelle de la Madeleine, a grotto church built into the cliffs, where one could sit and recharge. A little farther up was the farming hamlet of Esclauzels, then on to Montaure (3,100 feet). I walked through forests and dirt paths, and passed lots of farms and old stone houses. It looked quite gloomy and the sun was not out. I couldn't see anything; the day was misty and everything was blanketed by fog.

Small roads were everywhere, and a mail carrier still delivers the mail. There were many granite homes, walls, and stony fields. Farmers sitting on their tractors were spraying white powder on their fields—probably lime. I enjoyed the villages of Roziers and Le Vernet, and a little dog welcomed me into the village of Rognac, all very lonely places. I walked alone until I reached the bigger town of Saugues (3,000 feet) after going through rocky paths and farming fields.

Saugues was a surprise; it sits on top of a large mountain meadow, with roads converging from all sides. The place used to be a busy crossroad for pilgrims coming from other northern directions and on toward Santiago. It has a famous thirteenth-century tower with a dungeon; no doubt many were imprisoned there—men, as well as women. It had the familiar sprawling-house syndrome and a strange wooden sculpture as a welcome to the small city. In the center, next to the Romanesque church of Saint-Medard, I met up with the first pilgrims I had seen since the start of my day, as the German party was having

*A farmer of the Montaure area*

lunch. I was looking for a place to have a warm lunch and a longer stop. I picked a busy little restaurant full of people and sat next to the bar, where I ordered a meal of stuffed cabbages and enjoyed the busy place. Everyone was all dressed up, and I must have made an unusual sight in my hiking clothes, with a big backpack, walking sticks, and disheveled hair. This area does not see many pilgrims.

A lovely woman came and sat next to me and we started a conversation. She was working for the town, and I told her I would be walking just a few miles more to a little town where I wanted to stay. She told me that the town had been closed down, so there was no place to stay there. It would be another six miles to the next town, which was a bit too long since I had already done enough—especially uphill. So she said she would give me a ride a couple of miles into town. I thanked her and took the ride. She said that sometimes the pilgrims are not very nice. She had picked up a pilgrim last year, a man who needed a ride, and as they were driving, he said, "How can you listen to such music? It is not very nice." She had nothing to say and couldn't believe that a man would say such a thing to her in her own car while she was generous enough to help him. She said that just because people call themselves pilgrims, it doesn't mean anything. I agreed with her and thanked her profusely for taking time out of her lunch hour to give me a ride.

But who was right? The pilgrim had gotten used to silence and could not take listening to the music in the car. On the other hand, his rude comments insulted her kindness.

> Would you like to join me in an exercise? Well, it won't cost you much; let us try to do it this very evening. Tonight, before retiring to bed, let us stop for two minutes. Two minutes is plenty. Two minutes is a long time for a person to *stop*. Let us ask what fills us up. What I propose, in a way, is to examine our own consciousness. Yes, but let us do this concretely, in a materialistic way, should I say? Because, within each of us there is an inner space that we need to go through, to cross like an actual space, while looking at what kinds of objects are in this real space and what they are.
>
> What we are going to find in there is a stirring, a swarming of images and sounds—sounds that burst out endlessly, bits and pieces of images that never resolve to any particular form. We are even going to find objects even more vague, all sorts of pushing movements that have the power of desires. It is the garage sale of our consciousness. That should not surprise us at all. However, we can ask ourselves another question. These bits and pieces of images and sounds, these fragments of desires—are they really mine? Are they mine? Or is it that others have instilled them within me? Is it my own voice that I hear—my own voice when I was speaking to someone? Is it the voice of my children, my wife, my friends, other living human beings? And these pictures—do they remind me of objects that I have used or places that I have visited or worked in? To tell the truth, that is highly improbable. The images will be those coming from the television (even though I watch it for only an hour). These pictures come from all those sign posts, all those advertisements that have been thrown in my face from morning until night in the streets of my town, on the first pages of the city newspapers, in the shop windows, and let us not forget the ads on the soap box I bought while coming home. The voices will belong to the people

close to me, never alone but always mixed with other voices that are strangely familiar but totally indifferent—the voices belonging to women and men that I will never meet, and to whom I will have nothing to say and who will never speak directly to me. What do you mean? They do not talk. They do nothing but that—on the radio, on the television, at the movies, on the phone, on paper, on cassettes.... They all talk, but nothing happens. They do not know to whom they are talking to, all these voices. They talk, but only because they know very well that nowadays speech is for sale.

That is the odious discovery; my inner space no longer belongs to me. I still find a few personal objects in there—needles in a haystack. And my inner space does not belong to others either. It belongs to no one. It is full of objects. There used to be cemeteries for old cars, and I used to complain about them because they ruin the landscape. But now I am becoming a cemetery myself, a cemetery full of words, screams, music, information, recipes, and habitual thought patterns repeated a hundred times that no one listens to.

It is true. All night long I have been distracted. The television—I did not really look at it. The radio was on, but who was listening? As for the Musac in the cafeteria at work and in the elevators, I do not even remember if it was working. As for the ads, it has been a long time since I have paid attention to them. So how could I ever be reached by all this? But beware; the trap is there, but how could I ever be entrapped? I think I am safe.

It is here that we need enormous courage. The courage to say something of which we are all aware but do not want to face. A human being I allow to speak to me without being able to answer back is no longer human. It is no longer a human being but it has power over me; it affects me. Music I choose not to listen to builds within me certain forms. It acts in a certain way even though I was unaware of listening to it. All these forms are no longer music; they gallop in my mind without order and shape me in their image....

Soon there will not even be an inch in our inner space that will not have been trampled every day.*

---

\*    Lusseyran, *Contre la Pollution du Moi*, pp. 17–21 (tr. M-L. Valandro).

It is an epidemic. This explains, once more, the popularity of long-distance walking to empty the mind—emptying one's mind of garbage. Serenity *in;* garbage *out.* I wish I could have told all of this to the woman who gave me that ride.

ato

I walked through lovely pine trees in rocky, granite meadows with no one around. I passed the town where I had wanted to stay; it had a nice feeling to it and another one of those tall towers. I continued on the path that went along a very quiet little road. When I got tired, I stopped at the farm lodge in Le Falzet and decided to stay. It was a no-frills old farmhouse with six un-renovated bedrooms full of single beds. It had old paper on the walls—old everything—but it would do. The farmer's wife was very warm and extremely busy. Her husband and son ran the farm, milk cows and all. I took a shower and did some washing, and then I went into the barn with the old farmer and had a chat. He showed me his beautiful milking cows, which his teenaged granddaughter was about to milk.

Meanwhile, his wife was preparing supper for seven of us—the German group of five, the young man from the Jura, and me. We would have soup and an omelet, roast meat, cheese made by her daughter-in-law, and wine from a local friend. The farmer's wife was seventy-two and worked faster than most twenty-year-olds I know. She had just served a lot of people for lunch, and would have worked a fifteen-hour day.

She arrived with all the food, which she had to carry from her home across the yard and up the stairs to where we were. We had a lively meal and conversed in German, French, and some English, as everyone got to know one another. We were getting excited about walking through the famous Aubrac plateau, a place more deserted than here that everyone talked about, including our host. She said many people enjoy that particular area the most, because of its seclusion and its rough, inaccessible terrain.

*Aumont-Aubrac country*

In the morning our host was up early and had breakfast ready. She served us freshly made yogurt, bread with butter and jam, coffee, and tea, and we all went on our way. It was a beautiful day, a bit misty. I walked through pasture land down to a typical old French village, whose small cobblestone streets passed old renovated farmhouses with lilacs blooming, into a lonely forest, a valley with a riverbed, and through another quiet village with numerous vacation homes. I was looking for the path, but somehow could not find it, so I had to make a detour through a place called Le Sauvage, which added five or six miles to the day. We all made that mistake. Our reward was coming. We had to climb through a beautiful forest, up a mountain, and then through more beautiful, soft meadows with snow still on the ground. Then we arrived in a fantastic place where pilgrims often stay. The German group had settled in for lunch on the high meadow overlooking the site. I continued walking down through the snowy path. It was an enchanting scene, and spring had not reached this high, still place.

*A farm in the Domaine de Sauvage (Le Sauvage) region*

It looked like a castle–farm–monastery on a soft hill facing mountains with tall pine trees, with other mountains in the distance. Walking down to Domaine du Sauvage (4,200 feet), we had to pass through a foot of snow that had not yet melted. It was a hospital built for the pilgrims and run by the St. John's Knights. It was a Templars place, they said. It had a great feeling to it—majestic because of the scenery, but deeply quiet.

From a distance, the silhouette of the architecture was magnificent. I loved the long, stone, central building, which had arches and buttresses against it. It was a simple mixture of a monastery, farm, and hospital, bringing together religious celebration, healing, and working the earth. This left a strong impression that one could actually breathe in while walking through it.

> In Wolfram von Eschenbach's *Parcival*, the Templars are described as "Guardians of the Grail."... The Grail represents the higher ethers creating the energy of the terrestrial locations over which the Templars chose to settle. The Templars carried on the mission

*Farming mosnatery, Le Sauvage*

of those who had worked from very early times to purify and raise the energy that had been subjected to the dynamic of the Fall as it manifests in the Earth. The ancient peoples of northwestern Europe built dolmens and stone circles over the energy points, thus connecting them directly with the approaching Christ, the Sun Being, who was descending to bring back the higher vibration, pure life, and chemical ethers to the Earth.

We know that cathedrals, abbeys, and churches have been built over areas of concentrated etheric activity ever since the time that Christianity took over their stewardship. The energies of those places were often transformed by pagan acts of worship long before they were rededicated to Christian saints. Their original fallen quality was gradually raised by constant religious practices, so that one could describe them as having been restored to the pure etheric state. One might also conjecture that they had never lost that state since paradise faded at the beginning of Earth's evolution. Rudolf Steiner has said, "Such places were...sought after by the Druids—places where imaginations lingered long in the atmosphere and where the influences of nature on human beings was stronger, owing to archaic layers coming to the surface."

In Druid times, the sacred grove would have been composed of several varieties of trees, each corresponding to a different planet. The grove itself would be imbued with the harmony of the spheres, which merged with the upward rising Earth energy over which the grove was positioned. Much later, the sacred geometry of the religious buildings covering those same holy places brought in the Cosmic Word in another way. The soaring arches and fan vaulting of the sublime Gothic cathedrals, built with Templar knowledge, subtly echoed a distant memory of the sacred grove....

The "mystery of humanity and the cosmos from which we have been created" is the mystery that the Templars materialized by incorporating cosmic and human dimensions into the buildings they created: "As above, so below."*

⁂

The young man from Alsace stopped for lunch, and I continued on. The road out of this unusual site was heavily forested. I walked on the main road for another two miles to a lovely chapel and Fontaine Saint-Roch, where I took off my shoes and had a great lunch of goat and local cheeses, bread, water, olives, chocolate, hazelnuts, and dry figs in the sunshine. I had climbed up to about 4,000 feet. This place used to be a hospital for pilgrims, as was Domaine du Sauvage. It was especially important when crossing this small mountain path, which must have been perilous in the Middle Ages, owing to its geographical setting and roaming bandits. This place still had a certain magic, Two hospitals had been built here for pilgrims within a couple of miles, so the energies in this area must be beneficial.

After my long lunch break I traveled on just as the German group arrived for a rest and to get a drink at the crystal-clear fountain. This time the mossy path went down through old pines and meadows. Sweet-smelling pine needles scented the air and carpeted the path. It

---

\*    Francke, *The Tree of Life and the Holy Grail*, pp. 63–64.

was a bit warmer. I met up with Alexander from Alsace, and we walked into town at a leisurely pace, telling jokes and stories. My back was hurting a bit. We had a nice conversation with a local farmer who was complaining about how hard it is to make a living; he was cutting wood and brush for twenty-five euros per hour. A tall, skinny guy, the farmer was a hard worker who tried to make ends meet on his farm in this difficult territory.

We continued on, and Alex injured his legs by walking too fast. We descended into St. Alban, a psychiatric center. There I met a Spaniard from Seville who is a psychotherapist living in Geneva. Then I met two couples from Québec who drank four bottles of wine and were totally drunk and full of fun as only the Québecquois can be; they were walking the path on a two-week vacation. The German group was also staying there, and then a French man with two kids, aged seven and ten, arrived after walking almost twenty miles. After these few days on the road, I am finally meeting quite a few pilgrims and walking tourists.

I walked into the local church, which was very cold and humid, and then went shopping and bought some country pâté, whole-meal bread, apples, oranges, and pear juice. We would have a noisy evening with everyone packed in that small room.

Walking around in that psychiatric-center town I noticed several people who had shaved heads and large scars from brain surgery. They seemed to be thoroughly pacified and very docile in their demeanor, which did not fit their outer appearances. The hospital compound was a few miles down the road. In the shop where I bought my lunch was a man in his early thirties. He was sweet and saying that he loved butterflies and flowers. Meanwhile, he was completely drunk and buying some wine. His soul seemed to have gotten lost, probably with the help of new "wonder drugs" that French pharmaceutical companies have become experts at developing. We were sitting on the terrace outside, and he wanted to join us for a drink, but someone drove him away like an unwanted dog. I felt misery surrounding this place. The "Washing of the Feet" image came to mind, reminding me that all the knowledge

I accumulate and am allowed to know is not for myself but to help others who have been thrown down as I have risen to heights of knowledge. This is a most difficult meditation and brings one down to sober reality. I and the other pilgrims are having a good time while walking, eating, drinking, talking, and seeing the countryside—at a cost. The cost is the suffering of that man and countless others who are experiencing Hell on Earth.

When I got to bed, a pilgrim was upset because he said I had taken his bed. I told him that he should have put his backpack on the bed. I gladly gave him the lower bunk, because I saw that he was extremely overweight and could not climb to the top bed. He was a lawyer from the southern United States and was trying to walk the path, but he had many difficulties. His feet and legs could not really carry him, but he was trying as much as he could.

> Take for instance, a man who thinks and ponders a great deal in one incarnation. In his next incarnation, he will be a thin, delicately made man. One who ponders little in one earthly life but lives a life more concerned with grasping the outer world tends to accumulate a great deal of fat in the next life. This, too, has significance for the future. Spiritual "slimming cures" cannot be well managed in one earthly life; such a person must resort to physical cures, if indeed they will help. However, for the next earthly life it is certainly possible to undergo a slimming cure if one ponders and thinks a great deal, especially if one thinks about something that requires effort.... It needn't be meditated but simply pondered about a great deal, with the willingness to make many inner decisions.*

All the lights went out and I had trouble sleeping after seeing so many lost souls—too many for a little town—and having difficulties acknowledging the price of knowledge and freedom. Besides, the lawyer pilgrim sleeping under my bunk bed was snoring very noisily all night. Well, I

---

\* Steiner, *Karmic Relationships*, vol. 2, p. 125.

will stop the whining. I do not want to be called a *pinone*, Italian for a whiner. On the pilgrims' path, one never knows what is coming. Not knowing is the beauty of it, but it is not always beautiful.

I am constantly reminded that in previous times this path was not a pleasant excursion. Many pilgrims were driven out of their homes for being heretics or thieves or for not cooperating with Church officials, monks, or royalty. As punishment, they had to undertake pilgrimages to Le Puy, Santiago, Rome, or even all the way to Jerusalem. Some had no shoes and had a cross sewn onto their clothes to identify them as heretics. Many pilgrims were sick and sought cures for their illnesses. The ones who were not sick to begin with became sick along the way, and many died. The geography is very demanding, with very rough terrain, mountain passes, rugged stony paths, deep valleys, rivers, and deserted plateaus—which we were about to traverse. Those poor pilgrims also had to contend with and fight off thieves, or *routiers,* or hired soldiers from all over Europe, especially Germany or northern Europe in general. They were hired by local dukes and *seigneurs* to fight skirmishes for pay. They were certainly not *chevaliers,* but rough, thieving, and plundering soldiers. Often, instead of being paid, they would be encouraged to take whatever they wanted from the local villages they passed through. Life on the road was often a death sentence for the pilgrims. Now we walk here in relative safety, comfort, and freedom, thanks to the fighting of our ancestors.

Tomorrow I will walk a longer day, about twenty-one miles, and reach the famous Aumont-Aubrac.

⸙

I arrived in Les Gentianes (4,100 feet), a farm hostel, at 5:30 in the afternoon. I was exhausted after the twenty-one-mile walk; I thought I would not make it. My back was sore from my too-heavy pack again. I had to get rid of stuff, but what?

In St-Alban-sur-Limagnole, I started the morning after an almost sleepless night of listening to the lawyer pilgrim snoring all night, plus a night-light shining in my eyes. I got up early. Alex from Alsace could no longer tolerate the snoring and bolted from his bunk and out of the dorm around 4:30. I started to pack while trying not to make noise, and then everyone got up for the same reason—no sleep. The lawyer pilgrim was still snoring despite all the morning noise and commotion of plastic bags, paper bags, and backpacks being repacked—the familiar sounds of beginning the morning.

I walked to the *boulangerie* and bought two delicious chocolate croissants, which I ate with tea. Then I left the *gîte* after listening closely to directions from the hostel keeper. He said, "No, don't take that road; they make you climb the mountain. There, in the opposite direction, just follow the road, and you will save yourself at least two kilometers."

Although we are on a pilgrimage, we do not have to walk extra miles and climb all the mountains within sight of the town. I guess some feel that we need to suffer and that the path is not long enough. "You are a pilgrim after all, so let us make you more miserable than you already are." And many did indeed begin the day with an early mountain climb.

Later, I discovered that this pilgrims' path from Le Puy follows a path called GR 65 (*grande randonnée*), which is the designation for a long-distance vacationers' footpath, which more or less follows the pilgrims' way. However, the designation "GR" means it follows small nature paths and avoids town roads. They are great, long-distance paths for tourism all over Europe. For pilgrims, it means we have to do a lot of extra Sunday walks on our long way to Spain or the Pyrennees. Nevertheless, after a while what most pilgrims do is find their own road and avoid the very long detours; they are lovely for tourists but unnecessary for the pilgrims. These added miles mean less time to visit a church or monastery, keep a diary, wash one's clothes, or recuperate.

I gladly took the hostel keeper's shortcut. I went through a thickly wooded path. This time there were many more pilgrims but the same scenery—villages in the distance with grey stone roofs. In fact, everything seemed grey because of the local stones. I joined up with Alex, who was in pain, and met two other French men. We crossed the river into a little village and continued through more mountain forests with soft spring grass. Passing through another village, we kept a good rhythm. We climbed through more forest and saw beautiful, golden longhorn Aubrac cows in the meadows. I ate lunch on the soft green ground under the cover of a tall pine forest, and Alex caught up with the two French men. We arrived in Aumont-Aubrac at a lovely farmhouse and decided to go on for another ten miles; it was too early to quit. Alex continued on, too. While I had a coffee, another French man used his cell phone to make a reservation for me at the next place. I generally never make reservations. I saw the American lawyer pilgrim walking about the town. He had taken a cab, as his legs had given up on him, but he had not given up.

I left Aumon-Aubrac and started climbing through a deserted forest. I was not sure it was the right place. I arrived in a couple of villages and, in the middle of a deserted field, stopped and spoke with a local woman who was walking very briskly to confession with her priest—at least five miles each way. I wondered what sins she had to tell the poor priest. A few minutes later, by the side of the road, I had a little conversation with an old farmer, bent by hard labor, who was getting ready to take his longhorn, honey-colored cows back to his home in the next village. Around the corner, I reached the lovely little town of La Chaze-de-Peyre and Chapel Lasbros, where I stopped again to rest my aching back.

Later, climbing through forest paths, I reached the high Plateau of the Aubrac. It had very restful, expansive scenery with no trees, just soft plateaus all the way to the horizon. Clouds were gently shedding their rain with a wonderful play of diffused light. I saw lonely, abandoned stone huts in the distance, and tiny, lacy, curvy roads with few people on them. Sometimes one could see a pilgrim in the far distance—a dot moving alone in the vast countryside.

I had a few miles to go before reaching the next hamlet and considered stopping there, because it was getting late and I was tired. Along the way, I had met a group of eight Irish men and women on vacation as pilgrims. Due to my usual numerous stops along the path, I lost track of them in the distance. You are supposed to drink as much as you can to help with muscle pain, but then you have to pee frequently, too.

I finally arrived at the *quatre chemins,* or four corners stop, and gladly took off my backpack for some well-earned rest. The Irish group was there in a daze; perhaps they'd drank too much. Then I understood why; it was a kind of bar-farm stop, so I went in to order a café or something. The woman at the bar had red lipstick that had been applied quite clumsily, and her arm was in a sling; she said she had fallen. Well, from the look of the bar, she must be drunk 24/7 under the influence of cheap French wine. The place was incredibly dirty, so I ordered lemonade. The farmer, her husband, was very skinny with disheveled, thin hair, rain boots, and blue work clothes. He appeared to be a drunkard, as well, and he had a kind of preoccupied look.

When I arrived, I saw a startling sight near the dazed Irish party. A bull was running full speed after several young Aubrac cows to perform his spring ritual. He was running in and out of the tables after the bewildered cows, which were not being very cooperative. Of course the tables were outside for the pilgrims to sit on while sipping beers or coffee, not for a *corrida,* or bullfight. It felt like I was home in the Midwest. I thought to myself, *Hey, this is not very safe.* I couldn't believe my eyes. I tried to get my camera, but I was too late. The *corrida* had moved inside the stone barn next to the bar. The farmer, fork in the air, was trying to manage the breeding session. He returned, looking more disheveled than ever, probably to have a well-earned drink. The look on his face said, *Well guys, what is all the fuss about? No need to worry; I have it all under control.*

The Irish group was very cool and collected as though nothing had happened, or like they see this every day where they come from. I was laughing like hell, thinking that my son and husband would have absolutely loved this little incident and would have laughed about it for days. It was a real scene for films. I drank my grenadine/lemonade and then took off after the Irish group; I had had enough of hiking alone in this very desolate, as well as backward, mountainous region.

As I was leaving Alex came in with another Frenchman. He had intended on staying here; well, forget it, knowing him. He will have to walk with pain for other three or four miles, because the only place to stay was a very old and dirty caravan, probably full of lice and old bedding. The deserted moor-like scenery was truly breathtaking, especially the dark clouds in the distance, the spring-green meadows, and the soft walking path between old stone walls. Nonetheless, it was a long three or four miles for all of us before we saw a building in the distance. The French man went on ahead of Alex, who had been walking too slowly because of his leg pains. He and I chatted until we arrived.

A larger group was staying at this very nice farm-hostel; more than twenty people were in the various rooms, and supper was served at a very long table. I sat with the Spaniard Alphonso, who lives in Switzerland; the Québecquois Marie, who studies in Paris; a woman from southern France; three Swiss Italians; the Irish group; and Alex, who arrived later. We had a typically lengthy French dinner, until the woman made us go into the sitting room. She had been working non-stop since early that morning.

Our dinner conversation was about the *botello* parties in Spain, which had been upsetting all the moms and dads. Their kids would drive somewhere in their car with their friends, park by the side of the road or street, open their enormous bottles of alcohol, and proceed to get drunk and raise hell until all hours of the night. The kids say it is cheaper than going to bars; all they need is a car, their *botellas,* and lots of friends and music. The Spaniard was very upset, but Marie said they are young and should have fun. Then everyone talked about their own humorous experiences—the usual tales of being fed beans and being smoked out of the dorm.

We laughed a lot, and then I retired, leaving them to talk into the night; I needed my sleep. After washing my socks and clothes and putting them on the warm radiator to dry (it was still cold up here), I went to bed to sleep before another day in the even-more deserted Aubrac Plateau. There we were at almost 4,000 feet in altitude.

In the morning, we met again for a long breakfast and more conversation. Then everyone left, except Marie, who was talking with the young man from Alsace. I experienced more great scenery with no one around, reminding me of Scotland and Ireland. The pilgrims had dispersed. I loved the old stone farmhouses, which were everywhere.

I stopped in Nasbinals for a coffee and to buy bread and cheese for a sandwich, and then had a picnic in the forest. The little town was busy with tourists and Sunday drivers because it was after Easter. Locals were coming into town for fresh bread and to a little market selling artisan goods. I enjoyed meeting people in the café. They told me that they see no one from November through March, and then in April it is exciting to finally see human beings as the town wakes from a long, grey, lonely, cold winter.

The high plateau area is ancient, dating back to the last great ice age, 15,000 years ago, with its limestone, granite, schist, volcanic lava, and acidic sandstone. It is a very humid place, with lots of peat deposits. Before reaching the plateau, there was a forest of heath, juniper, birch, beech, oak, and hazel trees.

The area was also famous for its pastureland; shepherds used to bring their sheep to spend the summers up in the higher altitudes, staying in little stone huts, taking care of their sheep, and making cheese. In former times, they came long distances and used special paths for transporting their animals. Now, someone told me, they bring their animals by truck. They also continue to celebrate a big festival in late spring as a remembrance of those former times. Much of the land was owned by well-known abbeys in the Provence area; they used the land for the same purpose and built enormous farms. The monks used to grow buckwheat, but this all ended during the French

Revolution. The monks were chased out and the land holdings were divided up and sold.

After passing through the village of Mongros, I became tired and wished for a shorter road. All of a sudden, as the going got rough, I saw a picture-perfect scene coming slowly into view—a fairytale village and a church steeple. Because I was walking, I had ample time to enjoy it. It had been hiding in a fold of the valley I was traversing. Mesmerized by the quiet scenery, I forgot that I was tired and was again thankful for being here, walking, enchanted, and wanting to stretch the minutes.

Following a picnic stop, the road became increasingly rugged and deserted. There were large, wide mountains with just a few trees tucked between enormous meadows. The clouds had been coming in ever since lunch, and I was worried about being out in the open as thunder and lightning would inevitably come.

As I walked higher and higher into the bare, empty mountains, I could see the sky changing; it was that indigo color that at home means nasty business. But there was nothing I could do. I had to climb into the meadows, and it did not look like a path at all. I said to myself, *If it starts raining or snowing, I won't find my way here. It is too vast.* A few old abandoned stone huts—probably for shepherds—were up the hill here and there. I trudged along, but just when I started to doubt the path I had chosen and my sense of direction, I spotted the Irish group in the distance.

I went ahead a little faster in their direction; I'd rather be lost with others than alone. Then they disappeared, but the path became a little more obvious. It was going down...and then it started to snow and hail. I saw some kind of medieval farm or monastery on the far eastern side, which announced a bit of civilization. It must have been another one of those Templar monasteries. I had put on all my rain gear, including gloves and multiple hats to prepare for the bad weather. As the path descended, I saw a runner and a few tourists walking up, and the old village of Dômerie d'Aubrac came into view.

The village of Dômerie d'Aubrac was founded in 1120 by a Flemish knight, Adelard de Frandres, who was attacked by bandits on his way to Santiago and who almost died there in a storm on his return journey. In gratitude for his deliverance, he founded Aubrac as a place of refuge for pilgrims. Church of Notre-Dame des Pauvres is all that remains of the monastery, plus one other building.*

The old village had several restaurants and was full of tourists on Easter break. I went into the teahouse, where the Irish group had been having their teatime. I was soaked, and the town was under a blanket of heavy snow and hail, which I had just missed. I sat there and was going to order tea or something in this very busy place but decided that twenty-five dollars for a cup of coffee and some cake was outrageous, so I walked out. Too bad—it had looked promising. Nevertheless, I just could not spend that much money; we were not tourists, and they should not take advantage of us pilgrims.

I regretfully put on my backpack and started walking out of the village. The path headed down into a forest, and I walked with the Irish group for a while. They were on a two-week holiday, and every year they did two weeks on this Camino path. They said they do not hike on paths, but instead use a compass to hike anywhere and everywhere. They were great hikers.

We finally arrived in Saint-Chély-d'Aubrac, another beautiful old village. It had a communal *gîte* built by the town to house the numerous pilgrims passing through. This way they could make some money for the town. It was brand new, very clean, and tastefully done. They put me in with the Irish group. I walked around the town and joined another, new group of hikers for supper. Marie and a German hiker and I shared our food. Marie from Québec and I had a lovely discussion. She told me she had gotten completely lost for several hours up on the plateau, but then found the way. Then she started talking about

---

\*   Raju, *The Way of St. James, France*, p. 61.

a favorite topic for twenty-four-year-old women: her love life and how difficult it is.

> Friend if you had shown consideration,
> Meekness, candor, and humanity,
> I'd have loved you without hesitation;
> But you were mean and sly and villainous
> Still, I make this song to spread your praises
> Wide, for I can't bare to let your name
> Go unsung and unrenowned,
>
> No matter how much worse you treat me now.
> I won't consider you a decent man
> Nor love you fully nor with trust
> Until I see if it would help me more
> To make my heart turn mean and treacherous
> But I don't want to give you an excuse
> For saying I was ever devious with you;
> Something you could keep in store
> In case I never did you wrong.
>
> ..........................
>
> All other love's worth naught,
> And every joy is meaningless to me
> But yours which gladdens and restores me,
> In which there's not a trace of pain or of distress;
> And I think I'll be glad always and rejoice
> Always in you, friend, for I can't convert;
> Nor have I any joy, nor do I find relief,
> But what little solace comes to me in sleep.*

This poem is in a vein similar to Marie's contemporary complaints, 900 hundred years later. Affairs of the heart do not change much. Then Marie decided to make a chocolate fondue for everyone at the hostel.

---

\* By Castelloza, from the Auvergne in the region of Le Puy. She was probably the wife of a nobleman who fought in the fourth Crusade (in Bogin, *The Women Troubadours*, pp. 119–120).

Lovers were soon forgotten and replaced by chocolate and laughter; we all pitched in fruits and sat around for dessert with lively discussions and laughs. I met three new couples from France, who were walking all the way to Santiago. There was also a very devout Catholic couple, so I had to watch my jokes about nuns and priests. The other couples were more modern. They were all going all the way to Santiago. I had already walked half the path the previous year, so I would finish on the Spanish side shortly after the border. They would continue on for more than another five hundred miles, hoping to reach their destination by June 15. *Inshallah.*

Except for the Irish group, who continued their drinking party, we all retired after the long day. I just didn't have their stamina. The Irish group walked in around midnight while I was sleeping, and they were drunk. It seems they were on a drinking binge rather than a walk. There were two women and four men, all in their late fifties and early sixties. I wondered how they would get up in the morning. My own body cannot tolerate alcohol, and I was puzzled by how different we all are; obviously alcohol was necessary for them. The room took on that rancid smell of alcohol's by-product—acetaldehyde—which was pouring out of their skin. The dirty air made me very uncomfortable. I made sure the window was opened, bringing in some welcomed, pure, fresh air.

> In the cult of Dionysus an attempt was made to counter these dangers (dangers of selfish isolation and conflict for humanity had been abandoned by divine guidance, and people had to learn to find their own way and build new social structures with the help of the newly awakened intellectual capacities) by drinking wine in large quantities communally, so that people experienced a new sense of community, *different from the ties of blood and the family* [author's emphasis]. People were taught to control themselves as much as possible—despite being under the influence of large amounts of wine—so that they could dominate the inner "animal." That is why the cult of Dionysus was a cult of celebration, an orgiastic cult in which animals were sacrificed communally,

particularly the goat and the bull, as a symbol of people's inner "animal" forces, which were being sacrificed.

Rudolf Steiner described the cult as follows: "You know that the cult of Dionysus was related to wine.... In the course of human development, alcohol had a mission to fulfill. No matter how strange it may sound, its mission was to prepare the human body in such a way that it was cut off from its relationship with the Divine, so that the individual "I AM" could emerge. Alcohol works by cutting human beings off from the spiritual world in which they operated before. Alcohol has certainly served a purpose. In the future, people will be able to say in the most literal sense that it was the task of alcohol to pull humankind down into the material world, to the degree that they would become selfish, so that alcohol would lead them to demand the use of the self for their own purpose, so that it would *no longer serve the whole nation*.... Alcohol has removed human capacities to feel united with the universe in the higher worlds."*

We might understand why alcohol is forbidden in the Islamic cultures. An inebriated man or woman is no longer part of the Nation of Islam, but would start to feel "I am" as an individual, separate from the state and religious body. The situation is similar for the those born into nations with very strong blood ties, such as Native Americans and the Jewish people—there is enormous alcohol consumption in those nations, mostly hidden for obvious reasons.

I am reminded of another story. I lived in Iran during their revolution in the winter of 1979/80. I had rented a chalet with my boyfriend (now husband) in the Alborz Mountains, the Alps of Iran, north of Tehran, where I was writing a book (still in a drawer) and skiing every day. Khomeini had arrived in Tehran, and the newly formed revolutionary guards were driving around the city and countryside terrorizing the people—"keeping the peace," as they called it. One day in a little hamlet at the foot of the ski area called Dizeen, the guards arrived

---

\* Dunselman, *In Place of the Self,* pp. 158–159.

in their brand-new, green Toyotas, entered the Westernized hotel, and proceeded to smash all of the liquor bottles. I watched as they were smashing them, not bothering to clean up the broken glass that was now everywhere. If they had known there was an unmarried, French-American couple there, who knows what might have happened. They left a mess. It was a perfect picture of things to come.

The next morning, I got up early and had breakfast at the little restaurant next door. The owner had tied his dog by the door so he would not run away. He served me bread, tea, jam, and cheese, which was enough to get me going. I walked through the narrow medieval street by the old church and down to the river. After crossing the river, I noticed a woman wearing boots. I had thought she was fishing, but she was cleaning the small riverbed, removing the detritus that crowded the riverbanks. She was hard at work very early in the morning. We had a chat, and she said she had moved here a few years ago and had bought a house by the river and renovated it. She was now retired and living in that town full time with her husband, and trying to keep the area clean.

I walked on and arrived in Saint-Côme-d'Olt. It was a bit hot, so I stopped in the center of the small town for a coffee break. Formerly, Saint-Côme had a pilgrims' hospital. It is a medieval town with great charm. I saw a pilgrim with a large backpack enjoying a beer, so I invited myself to his table. He was happy to have some company. He was an older German pilgrim, and we immediately began to exchange stories.

After enjoying a very expensive coffee and beer, we put on our backpacks and went on our way together for the last leg of the day. His English was much better than my German. I love languages, but I find German difficult, so we spoke English. He said that he had gone on this pilgrimage the previous year, starting from his home in Germany, not far from Cologne, and had stopped about two days from where we were now. He had suffered a massive aneurism in his stomach. He said he was lucky to be alive; someone had been there at just the right time. Now, after a year, he was fine and wanted to finish what he had started.

*The old German pilgrim, a former miner*

He would be hiking for roughly three weeks, and then next year he would finish the pilgrimage all the way to Compostela. I thought he was very brave, especially after such an attack.

This walking is very strenuous for anyone, but for someone who has a heart problem it can be fatal. He was a very big man, at least 6 feet 4 inches, and we made a funny pair because I am only 5 feet 2½. He is a former miner and worked all his life deep in the ground. I found his stories fascinating and was all ears. We walked together, and I cannot remember much of the scenery until the next town, because I was paying more attention to his stories than to the scenery.

We crossed the river Lot and walked along the shady river for a bit, and then walked up the mountain. It was one of those very indirect routes, causing the pilgrims to walk many miles up and down into the forest, whereas we could have simply walked along the river Lot into the city of Espalion, which is on the river itself. (My guidebook actually mentioned just following the road.) Nevertheless, on we went, very grumpy.

An older French pilgrim from the Vosges was also walking with us, and she was tired. The German miner had to stop quite a bit to catch his breath, because he had just started on his trip and was not used to the rhythm yet. So we all stopped and cursed the people who failed to warn us about this very steep, out-of-the-way path and that we could have enjoyed the river walk instead. At one point, we could see the other pilgrims walking along the river roadway in the distance, and they looked like ants. We did have a beautiful view of the Lot Valley from up high. It was a hot day, and we were quite a way up, so we decided to bushwhack our way back to the road. We finally descended over a dirt path back to the road. After a few more miles of quiet, tired walking by the river Lot, or Olt, we arrived in the lovely medieval city of Espalion. On the left side of the river we saw its ancient castle in ruins, speaking to us of former times. Everyone stayed at the new and clean local *gîte* for pilgrims. We took showers, changed and washed clothes, and decided to eat supper together—la dame des Vosges, the old German miner, and me.

This entire area has a very rich history.

> Born in the very learned quarters of a Europe in the middle of transformation, heresy very naturally found a home amid the *petite noblesse*, where it crystallized questioning the new order imposed by the Gregorian reforms. When Pope Gregory VII declared the supremacy of the religious order over civil law, he upset the many secular traditions.
>
> From the time of antiquity, the minor squires and or noblemen, many of whom lived off the same meager landholdings, were very poor and survived only thanks to the many taxes. The tax revenues were fought over tooth and nail by the bishops and wealthy abbeys. When the papacy decided to free the clergy from the laypeople, it provoked the impoverishment of many minor nobles and consequently the thriving of the upper-clergy....
>
> So for the *petite noblesse* it was all about rethinking the exorbitant demands of this clerical theocracy, which although it wanted to reform society, it was not in the least preoccupied with

changing its own morality. The nobility then tried to stop as much as possible any reforms rather than install a "new" Christianity, the exception being the noble women who became *bonne femmes,* or *parfaite,* by conviction.

On the other hand, the Cathars did not pay the least attention to materialistic preoccupations. Money was merely a means of providing for the daily bread of the common church.\*

Louis VIII fought in these areas for many years, first against the English kings, then against the heretics. He gained victory over Jean sans Terre. Jean sans Terre was one of the five sons of Eleanor of Aquitaine. She is a remarkable figure in history for many reasons. For one, she married Louis VII when she was fifteen and he was seventeen in 1137, and after having had two daughters the marriage was annulled for "consanguinity"—a bit too late, don't you think? She then remarried, this time the famous Henri II Plantagenet in 1152, two months after her divorce. Henri Plantagenet was described as a strong, robust, and restless redheaded man. He was cautious but passionate, nonreligious but superstitious to the point of terror, and well read for a man of his time. Strangely for a king of England, he didn't speak any English but was the "father" of English law.\*\*

By that time, Eleanor of Aquitaine was thirty, Henry II Plantagenet was nineteen and had become king of England, and she had five sons and three daughters. Henri Plantagenet was infamous, having had Thomas à Becket put to death in 1170, when he was thirty-seven years old, and had his own wife Eleanor shut up in the Tower prison (no doubt during one of his fits) from 1173 until the king's death in 1189. Being married to such a king, we see that she was no weakling but a match for such a man of will. She was queen of France from 1137 to 1152, and then queen of England from 1154 to 1189. Her grandfather was a famous troubadour, Guillaume IX. Her

---

\* Bordes, *Cathares et Vaudois,* p. 131 (tr. M-L. Valandro).
\*\* See, for example, Dark, *St. Thomas of Canterbury.*

favorite son, Richard Coeur de Lion (1157–1199), before embarking on the crusade in the south of Italy, met the by-then amazing personality of Joachim of Fiore:

> Joachim made a dramatic impact on some of his contemporaries. The most famous encounter occurred in the winter of 1190/01 at Messina, where Richard Coeur de Lion, en route for the third crusade, asked to see the Abbot Joachim. So Joachim was fetched down from the mountains of Calabria to stand in the eager and curious circles of English Courtiers.... He offered little to strengthen the morale of the crusaders.... The discussion turned largely on his exposition of the Dragon with Seven Heads.[*]

During the Crusades, a great deal of knowledge was imported from the East by the knights and merchants and shared with their mothers, sisters, and others. All the famous sages, such as Joachim of Fiore, were visited by the well-known knights and kings for their incredible insights and knowledge. They did not have our information system, but there was nothing that they did not know; things traveled just as far then as it does now. People walked and rode on horseback, covering vast territories in very short time; they regularly crisscrossed Europe and beyond. They could cross Europe in a month or less. They visited one another in castles and monasteries for long periods of time, unlike our little weekend visits. Their trips often lasted half a year or longer. They would visit famous hermits living in the mountains of Central Europe, in the hills of Italy, or elsewhere. It is no wonder that the very large royal family of Europe had access to the best-known troubadours, writers, and theologians. If we remember that all the kings of Europe married several times each and had a great many children, then we can understand the extent of their influence in Medieval Europe. They helped shape history on a larger scale than we read about in books. There was no

---

[*] Reeves, *Joachim of Fiore and the Prophetic Future*, p. 22.

one who was not related to someone anywhere else in Europe. For example, one of Eleanor's two daughters from her first marriage to King Louis VII (1120–1180) married King Alphonse VIII of Castile and had a daughter called Blanche of Castile (1188–1252). Blanche married King Louis VIII of France and gave him eleven children, one of whom became the next king of France, the famous Saint Louis (Louis IX, 1214–1270). Looking at their ancestry, we see that Blanche of Castile and her husband Louis VIII had the same grandfather, King Louis VII.

Continuing with this larger-than-life personality of Queen Eleanor of Aquitaine, one of her daughters from her second marriage, Marie of Champagne, was a very rich personality herself.

> Chretien de Troyes was well known as a writer of popular romances long before he penned *Le Conte del Graal*. Both the matter and the manner of his earlier poem, *Lancelot*, was actually dictated by Marie of Champagne. This powerful daughter of Eleanor of Aquitaine created a "Court of Love" at Poitiers imitating the earlier tradition of Langedoc. This court was governed by a great lady, while its laws were drawn up in accord with the outpourings of the poets under the guidance of the Countess Marie herself. Chretien came under her direct influence during the four years of the Poitiers court.[*]

These remarkable women were indeed at the center of very powerful events. Their courts reached all corners of Europe. They were influential in the bringing up of their sons and daughters, even when imprisoned or dismissed by their husbands, the kings, as was the case for Eleanor. She married at the age of fifteen and was divorced at thirty. She remarried shortly after to a man eleven years younger than she and was later imprisoned at age fifty-one for sixteen years by her husband, the king, to whom she had given eight children. What a life.

---

[*] Godwin, *The Holy Grail*, p. 40.

It seems that Marie of Champagne and her mother Eleanor of Aquitaine were the great-grand-daughter and granddaughter of the first troubadour, Guillaume IV, Duke of Aquitaine. They did not write about it, *they lived it.*

I mention all of this because, when I was taught history, the *le Moyen Âge* was thought of as the Dark Ages. As we can see, this appellation is far from true. All those incredible women had an enormous influence on the shaping of the Western mind, but we generally recognize only the kings, knights, and popes, who left behind the sisters, wives, and daughters. Those women made the most of it, even though, starting at age thirteen, they often bore more than ten children.

---

We walked around the old city and ate in a small restaurant while chatting and listening to the noise. Later, we all retired for a good night's sleep, me with the two Germans so we could keep the windows wide open, while the French pilgrim was downstairs because she liked the windows closed. I got up early to shop for breakfast and lunch and found that all the pilgrims had already left. It was nice to go to the specialty shops; I bought fresh bread, an éclair for later, goat cheese, camembert, and *charcuterie* (cold cuts). I ate breakfast at the *gîte* with Marie, and we talked more about her love life and how she was afraid of becoming an old maid—at age twenty-four.

> You stayed a long time, friend,
> And then you left me,
> And it is a hard, cruel thing you've done;
> For you promised and you swore
> That as long as you lived
> I'd be your only lady:
> If now another has your love
> You've slain me and betrayed me,
> For in you lay all my hopes
> Of being loved without conceit.

> Handsome friend, as a lover true
> I loved you, for you pleased me,
> But now I see I was a fool,
> For I've barely seen you since.
> I never tried to trick you,
> Yet you returned me bad for good;
> I loved you so, without regret.
> But love has stung me with such force
> I think no good can possibly
> Be mine unless you say you love me.*

꧁꧂

It was too early in the morning to discuss matters of love, so I told her, "Just enjoy your life, and the rest will fall into place." After offering this little bit of practical advice about affairs of the heart, I headed out of the city. I walked a bit along the river, but then got lost, so that added a couple of miles to my day.

Then I met the French couple from Le Puy and Lyon—he an airplane mechanic and she a bank employee. Having cooled my anger at having wasted an hour, I enjoyed their company. I found the day too hot and decided to change my clothes, so they continued on. After that, I walked with two French men, one of whom was from Bretagne; his wife was following him in a car camper and would meet him every other day. That seemed to me a nice way to enjoy this walk with his wife. She was being a tourist and met him here and there.

Later, I met up with the German teacher, and we visited the little chapel of Bessuéjouls. It contained some beautiful stone sculptures, including an especially stylized one of Michael and the dragon carved in red stone. We stopped for a snack by the old bridge, and I listened to him talk about his divorce—his deep sorrow, his children, his misery about being unable to see his son, and how it was all his wife's fault. I must have had "confidant" written across my forehead.

---

\*   Castelloza (1200), in Meg Bogin (ed.), *The Women Troubadours*.

*A field of bright-yellow mustard flowers*

Meanwhile, the scenery was truly beautiful. High on the plateaus were lovely old farms, great views, big soft green hills, meadows with lots of longhorn cows and their calves, and mustard-yellow and green fields. Then we descended into Estaing, a beautiful old town with a great castle.

The German teacher continued on as I stopped near its famous bridge and enjoyed a coffee break with a French couple from Paris. The man from Paris was making watercolor paintings of the pilgrimage in his sketchbook and stopped everywhere for a few minutes to sketch and paint while his wife, who had just retired, looked around town. I walked with them for a bit, and then she went on as I made another pee stop.

They disappeared into the distance, and I continued alone along a forest road by the river. It was another three miles to the next village, and then I met another French couple. The path climbed very steeply toward the village of Montagu. I decided to leave my sleeping bag by a farmhouse at someone's door. The sleeping bag was becoming too

*Approaching Estaing*

heavy to carry and, besides, all the *gîtes* had blankets, so I really didn't need it. In Spain, one needed a sleeping bag, but not in France, and I would be hiking in Spain for only two to three days.

I felt a lot lighter, so I was able to hike a bit faster on the steep path. I stopped at the top of the mountain to enjoy the scenery and could see in the distance where we had started; it was a long way. I could also see the old medieval castle overlooking the river valley.

Up in the hills, after my arduous climb, I saw a herd of goats with their shepherd, who was sleeping in the grass with his dog. The goats had huge udders and looked truly content—climbing and eating to the sound of the bells around their necks. I wanted some of that goat cheese. The shepherd was impervious to my hellos; he was simply taking a snooze and letting the time go by with his happy goats. What else did he need?

As I walked on, I took a few pictures of the goats and felt the peacefulness of this place.

In former times, peasants knew the natural "empty mind" because of their daily activities, walks, and physical labor—all alone in nature. But out of this emptiness...their creative power came about only through building their homes and making objects for daily use.

Our Western civilization is based on the negation of this "empty mind," which it avoids at all cost by mechanization, fun and games, distractions, the need for objects, a frenzied lifestyle, and media. Our sense of self is muffled, and our creative power does not take part in what society makes—industrial objects that reflect a contemporary mind cut off from the eternal spring of life.

As Gary Snyder said, true power is, first of all, spiritual energy, and this spiritual energy can give us another vision of the world and change our life so that we no longer look for all those vain and useless artificial pleasures and endless desires....

This spiritual energy, which everyone can discover within, will drastically change our life and far more quickly than will our technological discoveries, perhaps up to the point that we will start to walk again in order to live, and the farming life, which has been eliminated from our ninety-percent city life, will become a way to reach that "empty mind" and creative spirit that the old mystics used to seek in their monasteries....

Daily walks are the only relationship we have with nature by which our body is allowed to find its own place. Rousseau used to say that walking enlivened his mind. Kierkegaard felt a great sense of wellbeing and complete freedom. Walking makes us attentive, concentrated. For Jacques Meunier, walkers "walk to feel lighter. They wish to awaken their senses to the road and to open their body to worldwide forces." Paths are used to express this agreement between our feet and the environment. Meunier tells us again, "Do not forget; to walk is a very basic need that unites us to the universe."[*]

I walked for another forty-five minutes in these mountains and saw some ugly modern buildings along the path. They were large,

---

[*] Jourdan et Vigne, *Marcher, Mediter*, pp. 39–40 (tr. M-L. Valandro).

newly made, rectangular structures, and I sneaked in to have a look. The buildings were filled with goats that could not leave. I was disgusted. This is probably where all that feta cheese from goats comes from. That is what we are eating, unless we eat cheese from a small goat herder like the one I had just seen. What a difference. These poor animals were in a stinking place with bad air, being milked and abused; it is called "intensive agriculture." Farmers were destroying the small meadows with their big machines to make larger farm areas, thereby causing erosion—just as in the United States. I was happy to leave; it smelled awful and looked unfriendly with "no trespassing" signs everywhere. It was a shame. Then I saw more barns—modern, rectangular, and cheaply built—in the surrounding hills. The whole area would be gone in another twenty years, poisoned by these farming methods.

Then the path went through the woods, with beautiful disintegrating rock; it looked like it had been part of a glacier, because the little rocks were imbedded in mud-like earth or clay. From ancient times, there was also beautiful rectangular marble or granite. The stones were so fascinating that I kept picking them up. I was so mesmerized by those ancient stones while walking on along the narrow path in the rain that I forgot about my fatigue. I love stones and I have a large collection of them at home, so I picked some up. Back home I could look at them and meditate on them. Meanwhile more weight was added to my pockets.

> Take a hard, natural object, like a stone, a twig, or a shell.... Set your object on a table or chair arm beside you, and look at it in detail for thirty seconds or so. Notice its surface, its texture, the marks on it, and its overall shape. You will see that there are no *words* for what you perceive of its details—subtle differences in color or contour. Yet there are *concepts:* this bit looks just this way. You have a conceptual lock on every aspect of what you are seeing.
>
> Now close your eyes for a moment to reorient yourself. Your next look will be different. You will open your eyes briefly and just

take in the stone as a whole—all of it at once, with its details, but no longer enumerating them to yourself one after the other. Open your eyes and do this whole seeing for about ten seconds.

Alternate these two very different kinds of looks two more times: details of the stone, then the stone as a whole: and again, first details, then whole. See if you can really make these two looks distinct from one another and appreciate their distinctness. In both cases, you are doing something we normally never do by lingering with a single perception and intensifying it. In both cases, you are cleansing perception from the normal prejudices and distractions that plague everyday seeing. Yet in the "details" look you are continuing the process of conceptual overlay that is the basis of normal perception, while in the "whole" look you are relaxing this overlay a bit and beginning to allow the stone itself to approach you.*

There are many such conceptual exercises in Michael Lipson's dense but crystal-clear little book.

※

While collecting stones, I walked through more forests paths, watching the lovely cows in small pastures among the woods. It was raining, but I didn't care; I had my poncho on and still had quite a few hours before evening, so there was no rush. I stopped at a small hamlet, where a farmer was feverishly working on his stone barn to make a *gîte*, and I had a chat with him. He was looking forward to finishing his place. I told him that would be great, as I would not have to walk for another two or three miles.

I had more pleasant walking in the soft rain, alone. All the pilgrims were walking at their own pace in these very out-of-the-way low mountains. Then when I finally arrived in the town of Golinhac, on top of a mountain–forest, the path emerged out of the forest onto the road where an old gardener-farmer was sitting on the wall of his old stone

---

\* Lipson, *Stairway of Surprise*, p. 102.

farmhouse. I greeted him and asked if he knew about those awful-looking farms. He also complained about the terrible goat barns up the road and said that the owner was a terrible man who did not even give water to pilgrims in the heat of the summer. He said that the goat herder up there in the hills is the winner of the whole area for the best goat cheese. I said, "I knew it. But where can I buy his cheese?" He just laughed.

⁂

Golinhac and the surrounding area all the way to Conques beyond were frequented by the members of the Carolingian dynasty. Louis the Pious (778–840), the third son of Charlemagne, took many of these small abbeys under his wing. They had been under the tutelage of the main Benedictine abbey in Conques. Golinhac was a stop for the rich and famous of the time, who donated funds and land. Walking along these very ancient paths, one cannot help but wonder who else passed by these stones. If only the stones could talk.

The *gîte* was kept by a warm caretaker. I had my own little cabin, which I shared with an older Italian who was very pleasant. I took a shower, changed my clothes, stuffed my shoes with newspaper to dry them, and headed for a nice communal supper. I was the only woman at a table of men—two Germans, a French man, a Swiss-Italian, and a Swiss-German. I could not figure out which language to speak. The retired French couples were eating at a different table. The French Vosges woman and Marie the Québecquois were cooking in their own dorm; I said goodnight to everyone on my way out.

The day had been quite long and everyone was tired after twenty miles of climbing and descending the steep terrain. Nevertheless, everyone loved to be out there, alone and walking all day, and could not wait to get up the next day and walk some more. Many were here for only a couple of weeks, and a few for the long haul. We all lived in our own time—our own true sense of time that depends on the sunrise, sunset, the weather, and other natural time clocks. We didn't listen to the news, talk on the phone (though some had cell phones), and rarely

*Abbey-Church of Saint-Foy in Conques*

*Abbey-Church of Saint-Foy tympanum*

*Abbey-Church of Saint-Foy tympanum detail*

saw a car or truck along these hidden paths—which was what we wanted. The longer we were on the road, the greater the inner peace that grabbed hold of us. Sometimes we would walk together—one or two talking or saying nothing—just enjoying the present moment and what was there. When we were tired of talking about the old problems back home, we kept quiet and allowed the wounds to heal. One listened and then quietly stepped up the pace, leaving the mourning pilgrim to his or her own thoughts and space for emptiness and healing.

> Compassion and respect allow us to know the solitude of another by finding him in the intimacy of our own interior solitude. It discovers the secrets in our own secrets. Instead of consuming him with indiscretion, and thus frustrating our own desires to show our love for him, if we respect the secrecy of his own interior loneliness, we are united with him in a friendship that makes us both grow in likeness to one another and to God. If I respect my brother's solitude, I will know his solitude by the reflection that it casts, through charity, upon the solitude of my own soul.

*Abbey-Church of Saint-Foy tympanum detail*

This respect for the deepest values hidden in another's personality is more than an obligation of charity. It is a debt we owe in justice to every being, but especially to those who, like ourselves, are created in the image of God....

If a man does not know the value of his own loneliness, how can he respect another's solitude?

*Leaving Conques*

It is at once our loneliness and our dignity to have an incommunicable personality that is ours, ours alone and no one else's, and will be so forever.

When human society fulfills its true function the persons who forms it grows more and more in their individual freedom and personal integrity. And the more each individual develops and discovers the secret resources of his own incommunicable personality, the more he can contribute to the life and the wealth of the whole. Solitude is as necessary for society as silence is for language and air is for lungs and food for the body.

A community that seeks to invade or destroy the spiritual solitude of the individuals who compose it is condemning itself to death by spiritual asphyxiation....

Solitude is so necessary both for society and for the individual that when society fails to provide sufficient solitude to develop the inner life of the persons who compose it, they rebel and seek false solitudes.

A false solitude is a point of vantage from which an individual, who has been denied the right to become a person, takes revenge on society by turning his individuality into a destructive weapon. True solitude is found in humility, which is infinitely rich. False solitude is the refuge of pride, and it is infinitely poor. The poverty of false solitude comes from an illusion that, by adorning itself in things it can never possess, pretends to distinguish one individual self from the mass of other men. True solitude is selfless. Therefore, it is rich in silence, charity, and peace. It finds in itself seemingly inexhaustible resources of good to bestow on other people. False solitude is self-centered. And because it finds nothing in its own center, it seeks to draw all things into itself. But everything it touches becomes infected with its own nothingness, and falls apart. Solitude cleans the soul, laying it open to the four winds of generosity. False solitude locks the door against all men and pores its own private accumulation of rubbish....

True solitude separates one man from the rest in order that he may freely develop the good that is his own, and then fulfill his true destiny by putting himself at the service of everyone else.[*]

༺༻

The changing scenery affected our minds and took all of our attention. The open sky and horizon were our rewards after climbing up mountainsides over stony paths and through thick forests on muddy paths. It was springtime, and the new vegetation was sending a message of renewal and birth. The great colors of spring—light yellow and cerulean blue—were healing for the pilgrims' wounded souls. At night the pilgrims would have serenity in their faces and an acute sense of being and knowing. Because we walk alone most of the time, our walking is a meditation. We achieve what the monks achieve in their monasteries—complete concentration and attention. We really don't have to talk to understand one another, and many things are left unsaid. Words become unnecessary. "If you go into solitude with a silent tongue, the silence of mute beings will share with you their rest. But if you go into solitude with a silent heart, the silence of creation will speak louder

---

[*] Merton, *No Man Is an Island,* pp. 245–247.

than the tongues of men or angels."* The people walking beside you become friends on the path. After a week of seeing your fellow travelers, you begin to look out for them. Their pains and sorrows become yours, and conversations often reflect this. "Did you see so and so? He had enormous blisters on his feet. Is he better?" "What has happened to so and so?" "Oh, he had to go home; he had only two weeks." We all bond together; we share picnics by the road, gruesome climbs, hot afternoons, coffee breaks, naps in the meadows, snacks in the tall pines, or simply a gaze into the valley we just left.

The next day, we began the day with a lively communal breakfast after packing our belongings. Our backpacks and walking sticks were lined up outside the restaurant. As we walked out of the old town together, we admired the ancient church and village. It was a talkative morning walk, and then each pilgrim went at his or her own pace, reflecting inwardly and singing—opera songs for the Italians, French songs for me, songs of Québec for Marie, and laughter from the German miner. We walked through pleasant, easy countryside, following an uphill and sinewy little road passing many farms. At the next, very scenic old town of Espeyrac, near a river, the old German and I stopped for a coffee break in a welcoming local restaurant before continuing on and chatting as we climbed a path into farm fields.

We met up with the other group of pilgrims having lunch in the next village of Senergues. I stopped again, because the place looked inviting, and the old German went on ahead. Marie, the German teacher, the French couples, and others were enjoying lunch by a quiet churchyard under a pear tree. When they went on, I continued alone owing to my many usual stops. I went along a forested path with lots of beautiful chestnut trees and then along a slippery, rocky, downhill path that tumbles into the city of Conques. I was puzzled because, according to my guidebook, I was very close to the town of Conques, but I couldn't see it. The path followed a ridge and a round mountaintop. I should

---

\*    Ibid., p. 256.

have been able to see the city, because I could see far into the other mountains and valleys. Nevertheless, the town was hidden from view. I passed another woman pilgrim and continued along the path going down. Finally, I was able to see this jewel of a town, tucked away in a special spot in between the mountains and flowing rivers, in a kind of secret little bowl. You just come upon it.

> In the rocky solitude of the Valley of the Stones, at the place where the site opens up to a kind of conch shell, where the gorges of the Ouche River join the valley of the Dourdou, someone called Dadou started his hermitage, next to the source of the Plo River in the 750s.... As soon as 801, Louis the Pious, son of Charlemagne, took under his protection the community of the Benedictines. It was also Louis who gave the name of Conques to the monastery.[*]

The pilgrims stayed at the Sainte-Foy Abbey, which was very well equipped to receive us. I deposited my backpack and went exploring the town and its historic monuments. It was full of tourist shops, galleries, a great bookstore (where I could have spent hundreds of dollars), restaurants, and outdoor cafés to linger in. The whole town had been renovated; it was a pleasure to wander the tiny streets and discover its riches. I decided to spend one day there to rest my legs. At suppertime, we all gathered in the enormous refectory, which had very large tables to accommodate sixty of us, which included pilgrims from many countries, numerous tourists, and tour travelers. The noisy supper began with a speech from the Catholic priest in charge, and the benediction of the pilgrims with the song *Ultreia* at the end. We were served by volunteers who had previously walked the Camino. The food was excellent and the company was even better. I sat with the Germans, Italian, French, Québecquois, and Spaniards and enjoyed the food in a brotherly atmosphere. That atmosphere *is* the heart of the pilgrimage. The servers knew it—their reason for serving—as did the priest.

---

[*] MSM, *Les Chemins de Saint Jacques de Compostelle*, p. 199.

Then, if that was not enough, in the evening there was a concert at the abbey church by a famous pianist. I went and listened to beautiful music in that very old church that had seen many kings, queens, and peasants for more than a thousand years. Everyone was captivated by the sounds resonating in the ancient stone space of the huge, tall church. It reminded me of the sublime sounds of the Harmony of the Spheres, which I had been allowed to hear after I attending Goenka's ten-day Vipassana meditation retreat course in India some twenty-three years earlier, when I was thirty-five years old.* I had not really understood what I was hearing until many years after, when, thanks to Anthroposophy, I could make some sense of those deep spiritual experiences.

> [Quoting Rudolf Steiner,] "What is called 'sound ether' here should not to be identified with what we call physical sound or tone, which is merely a reflection of what clairvoyant consciousness experiences as 'Harmony of the Spheres'"—etheric sound or tone weaving as a living power through the universe. In speaking of this "ether" and of "sound," we are therefore speaking of something far more spiritual and more ethereal than ordinary sound.
>
> Steiner describes how, although the sound and life ethers were withdrawn from our direct perception after the Fall, they continue to work into our astral body during sleep.
>
>> At the moment of going to sleep, the inner forces in the astral body and in "I" actually begin to expand over the whole solar system and to become part of it. From every direction, human beings draw into their astral body and "I" forces that strengthen our life during sleep, and on waking we contract into the narrower confines in our skin and pour into these what we have absorbed during the night from the whole solar system. That is why medieval esotericists, too, called this spiritual human body the "astral body"; it is united with the world of the stars and draws its forces from them.... What permeates the astral body during sleep when it is outside

---

\* I describe that and related experiences in my book *Deliverance of the Spellbound God*.

the physical and etheric bodies? It is the weaving life of the harmonies of the spheres, forces that can otherwise operate only in the sound ether. When a violin bow is drawn across the edge of a metal disc strewn with sand it produces the well-known Chladni sound figures; similarly, the harmonies of the spheres vibrate through human beings during sleep and restore order in what was cast into disorder during the day through our sense perceptions.

In a lecture in 1997, Manfred Schmidt-Brabant explained that many of the Templars had been "incarnated in the Pythagorean school, either directly as pupils or within its sphere of influence [where] the way the harmony of the world was taught and demonstrated, that access to it arises from what takes place between music and mathematics." In lecture 3 of his course on Matthew's Gospel (just quoted), Steiner also said, "In the Pythagorean schools, the power to become aware of the Harmony of the Spheres was understood to be the *reopening of a human being to the sound ether and to the divine life ether.*" When we consider this *karmic* connection between the Knights Templar and the Pythagorean school, we can understand that knowledge of the Harmony of the Spheres and the mathematics they might have experienced there laid a very broad foundation for their building work. The most lasting remnant we have of that work survives in the sublime architecture of the Gothic cathedrals. The dimensions of those buildings conform to the same laws as do the Harmony of the Spheres. Through the experience of those dimensions, the nature of the plain chant sounding through them and the accumulative power of their many colored windows, the effect on the astral body of the worshipper was of a similar nature to its night-time experience in the great cosmos.\*

☙

It is no wonder that this magical concert in such a powerful setting reminded me of those experiences from long ago; it all fit. I did not

---

\* Francke, *The Tree of Life and the Holy Grail*, pp. 66–67.

want to leave, so I lingered in the church until much later, finally going to my bunk bed.

The next day, the whole bunkroom awoke as usual and packed up. In thirty minutes the pilgrims who had become friends were gone. I was the only one left. It felt a bit sad to stay behind, but my legs needed a rest and I wanted to spend a little time in this historic village. The old German also decided to stay the day to rest, so we had coffee breaks together. I missed my new friends who had continued on; we had formed a strong bond, so I thought about them during the day. It was hard to resist following the gang. I had enjoyed our time together, sharing bits of our lives during the day and at night laughing at our adventures getting lost. It is strange how we become accustomed to a new family of people we barely know. Nevertheless, I would have had to leave them, because I was going on a different path than they were. I had to cross further southeast in order to get to the Somport Pass in the Pyrenees and into Spain. They were all going to Saint Jean-Pied-de Port Roncevaux Pass.

It was rainy—the perfect mood for enjoying a lazy day. I spent a lot of time looking at the magnificent tympanum of the Abbey and took many pictures. There were a number of tourists listening to their guides in their two-hour stop on the way to another five historical sites before being finished for the day. I found it difficult to recollect myself and plunge into that inner sanctum and peaceful space, trying to live in the time when this abbey was built. The inside of the abbey was cold dead stones and forgotten memories of the past. The music from the previous night had disappeared into those silent stones.

The tympanum, dated around the eleventh century and carved in local limestone, is the story of Paradise, Hell, the saints, Christ, angels, kings, the Virgin Mary, St. Foy, and Charlemagne, all painted in the stone architecture as an open book. It must have strongly impressed the pilgrims, reminding them of the eternal rules. There is something powerful in these stone storybooks—something very primal. The representation of Hell with many depictions shows a remarkable knowledge of man and woman. It has a very strong effect on the viewer; it grabs your attention and emotions in a powerful way. Nothing is forgotten, and it is much more appealing than the representation of Paradise. Even musicians who use their music for the wrong purpose are depicted, as well as thieves who steal from their feudal masters. The glutton and gourmand are both present, along with an amusing picture of a man ridden by his domineering wife. Scandalmongers have their tongues taken out; the miser is beautifully portrayed, hanging by the weight of his gold bag; and the monk who wrongfully falls in love, and his lover, are also damned.

The Christ in majesty was at the center, depicted in the simplest way. One can live in these pictures, just at a glance planting oneself in the moving story. There is no linear thinking; the picture is all there, all at once, taking hold of our attention. There is no intellectual, abstract thinking; it is very much a story as alive as it was in the hearts and minds of the artists. That is their greatness and their fascination to us who have become so cold, intellectual, and linear. Perhaps that is why this place is still one of the most popular sites in France. Thousands of people flock here each year to admire this tympanum. There is no wasted space in these stone sculptures; simple powerful gestures and symbols are minutely used by master stone carvers who were, without a doubt, *knowing* people. The Old and the New Testaments were alive in their souls.

> In the twentieth century, the link between human thinking and the etheric activity of a planet is not as necessary as it was in the distant past. Human beings have gradually freed themselves from their cosmic surroundings; they no longer submit to the rhythm of the Earth's life. The forces of the cosmos release them. This liberation is good inasmuch as it is part of the natural course of evolution, especially if it favors the development of another, fully conscious connection with the cosmos. However, it should be remembered... Bernard writing in Clairvaux... Benedict meditating on Monte Cassino, all the

great thinkers who became the pride and honor of Christian civilization after the disruption of the Roman order, all these individuals had a constitution of soul and spirit very different from ours. We can build a philosophical system without leaving our room on any street of any city, as Descartes did sitting by his stove in Poland, or Spinoza in his study at The Hague, but those who were alive between the sixth to eighth centuries were much more closely dependent than we are on cosmic events, the life and rhythms of the planet Earth.*

Then I saw the statue of St. Foy, a golden, wooden statue that reminds me a bit of idol worship of the past. It had a slight similarity to the black Madonna of Le Puy and Montserrat. It was golden and very ornate, encrusted with precious stones and jewels.

As I looked at it, I felt that there was nothing very Christian about the statue. The young girl was martyred in AD 303 at the age of twelve, when she refused as a converted Catholic to worship idols. Hundreds of years later, when having relics was the means to making a living for many abbeys and churches, the Cult of St. Foy came about—with a bit of the Black Madonna influence—to attract more pilgrims, and so it did. Conques became a center for pilgrims, and several kings and queens made the pilgrimage to Conques, thereby bringing much needed funds to grow the abbey and the village.

There's a little bit of a paradox here. Is her statue an idol? If not, what is it? It certainly looks like one; we cannot feel anything toward the young martyr by looking at this statue. Moreover, to top it off, the relics were stolen from Conques by monks. It seems that stealing relics was a favorite pastime of some bored, eager monks during the Middle Ages. Nevertheless, there is something deeply meaningful about these relics. Why a relic? What does it bring? Old bones, blood, stained garments, teeth, and hair?

---

\* Morizot, *The School of Chartres*, pp. 11–12.

We find this polarity (*di inferi* = *di superi,* or *Kabeiri*; lower gods = upper gods) in the respective forms of ancient worship. The light-bearing upper gods were worshipped in rites that had to do with light, sacrificial fire. Originally the priests cut out a grass rectangle and built the earth up toward the downward radiating light; this was the *primitive altar*—a term that comes from the Latin *altus,* meaning high, so that *altare* was the high place. On this altar the priest lit the flame, which together with the words of prayer rose toward the lofty regions of the light and its divine guardians.

In the worship of the lower gods, an approach to that realm was made again in the way the cult was ordered: the altar now was built downward instead of upward, as a more or less singular square hole in the earth in the shape of an altar. Such can still be found in old temple ruins in Greece and Asia Minor. It was closed by a decorated cover, but the bottom and sometimes the sides were left as bare, living earth; for the offering here was not fire that flames upward with its light to the heights of wisdom, but the warm, life-bearing blood of an animal that flowed down to the life-giving powers in the depths. Thus there were two kinds of altars—one raised, the other hollowed out of the earth like a grave, and on tables offerings for various divine hierarchies were given back by men what was their due.

This polarity of the upper and lower gods was observed in rituals that survived for a long time, and in some cases have done so to this day. For example, in the center of a Roman Catholic altar top there is still always an almost closed-over, small, level hollow containing relics, indeed bones, of some saint revered as a representative of Christendom. It is a late, barely conscious surviving form from early Christian times of the profound knowledge that Christ's table of offering must unite the altar and the grave in itself, because Christ, the cosmic Logos, unites all the heights and depths in himself.*

---

\*   From Roschl-Lehrs, *The Second Man in Us,* p. 91.

It rained all day. I think the next time I will not stay for a whole day, but perhaps leave later instead. Resting for an entire day breaks the rhythm of the journey. I was a tourist today, and tourism does not have much meaning. The pilgrimage is more "lets us walk together and share our joys and sufferings."

I had another communal meal just as delicious as the previous night. I got up early the next day for breakfast and was on the road with the old German pilgrim by 7:20. We started climbing and stopped at the little chapel facing Conques. There we rang the bell delightfully, and it sounded over the whole river valley and beyond, announcing that pilgrims were on their way to Compostella. It was a beautiful sound. I especially enjoyed this part—there was something rejuvenating and empowering about sounding these large bells. We climbed through a steep forest path, which was a hard way to start the morning. Then we reached rich farmland with spring green, soft hills full of beautiful and quite dignified long-horned, honey-colored cows having their morning breakfast, chewing their cud while lying peacefully in the grass.

The sky was dark and full of clouds, but we did not get rained on. We walked past farmhouses, small villages, old castles, churches, and chapels. We arrived in a newly built area where we saw a mine on our left, Decazeville, which has the largest opencast coalmine in Europe, dating back to Napoleon. We declined to remain there and walked on to Livinhac-le-Haut, a deserted town with no one to talk to at the *gîte*. It is one of those *gîtes* where you help yourself, sleep in your room, cook for yourself, and see no one—except the person who comes for ten minutes to collect ten euros. We bought some provisions and cooked supper, which we shared with another French man. We had an omelet, bread, endive salad, and chestnut crèmes in honor of all the chestnut trees growing in the area, and because—being French—it was one of my very favorite desserts. It was raining throughout the evening, and more pilgrims began pouring in. I had a good sleep, as I had my own room with four other empty beds; everyone was scattered throughout the hostel. We talked with the Breton French pilgrim about his adventures on a pilgrimage to Rome from Bretagne. He did not recommend it at all, since much of the walk is on regular roads with cars and trucks. He said it is extremely dangerous, and Italy does not have many pilgrims on the road, so there are very few pilgrim *gîtes*, making the walk exorbitant and an anachronism. He said that if he had known, he would have never gone. Walking in France and Spain is where it's at.

We got up early and had a communal breakfast with French pastries from the *boulangerie* next door. Then we all left quite early for Figeac, our next destination. It was a beautiful morning with fog resting in the surrounding spring green valleys that were dotted with cows. We climbed a bit, and the Breton left us because he was walking an average of twenty-five to thirty miles a day—not our pace. During the Middle Ages, pilgrims had to walk forty or fifty miles a day. They must have gotten into a rhythm, and of course they were more fit than we are today. Years ago, when I was younger, I did walk twenty-five or thirty miles a day, but the Breton was fifty-eight years old like me. Alexandra David-Neel was my idol during my twenties. I read *all* of her books and could not get enough of her "spiritual adventures." I even translated her two volumes of journals into English. She called herself a journalist of the spirit.

> I met the first *lung-gom-pa* in the Chang Thang of Northern Tibet. Toward the end of the afternoon, Yongden, our servants, and I were riding leisurely across a wide tableland, when I noticed, far away in front of us, a moving black spot, which my field glasses showed to be a man. I felt astonished. Meetings are not frequent in that region; for the last ten days we had not seen a human being. Moreover, men on foot and alone do not, as a rule, wander in these immense solitudes. Who could the strange traveler be?
>
> One of my servants suggested that he might belong to a trader's caravan that had been attacked by robbers and disbanded. Perhaps, having fled for life at night or otherwise escaped, he was now lost in the desert. That seemed possible. If such was really the case, I would take the lone man with us to some cowherds' encampment or wherever he might wish to go if not far out of our route.

But as I continued to observe him through the glasses, I noticed that the man proceeded at an unusual gait and, especially, with an extraordinary swiftness. Though, with the naked eyes, my men could hardly see anything but a black speck moving over the grassy ground, they, too, were not long in remarking the quickness of its advance. I handed them the glasses and one of them, having observed the traveler for a while, muttered, "*Lama lung-gom-pa chig da.*"

These words *lama lung-gom-pa* at once awakened my interest. I had heard a great deal about the feats performed by such men and was acquainted with the theory of the training. I had, even, a certain experience of the practice, but I had never seen an adept of *lung-gom* actually accomplishing one of these prodigious tramps that are so much talked about in Tibet.

Was I to be lucky enough to witness such a sight? The man continued to advance towards us and his curious speed became more and more evident. What was to be done if he really was a *lung-gom-pa*? I wanted to observe him at close quarters, I also wished to have a talk with him, to put him some questions, to photograph him... I wanted many things. But at the very first words I said about it, the man who had recognized him as a lama *lung-gom-pa* exclaimed, "Your Reverence will not stop the lama, nor speak to him. This would certainly kill him. These lamas when traveling must not break their meditation. The god who is in them escapes if they cease to repeat the *ngags,* and when thus leaving them before the proper time, he shakes them so hard that they die."

Put in that way, the warning seemed to express pure superstition. Nevertheless it was not to be altogether disregarded. From what I knew of the "technique" of the phenomena, the man walked in a kind of trance. Consequently, a sudden awakening, though I doubt if it could cause death, would certainly painfully disturb the nerves of the runner. To what extent that shock would harm him I could not guess and I did not want to make the lama the object of a more or less cruel experiment....

By that time he had nearly reached us; I could clearly see his perfectly calm impassive face and wide-open eyes with their gaze fixed on some invisible far-distant object situated somewhere high up in space. The man did not run. He seemed to lift himself from the ground, proceeding by leaps. It looked as if he had been endowed with the elasticity of a ball and rebounded each time his feet touched the ground. His steps had the regularity of a pendulum.

He wore the usual monastic robe and toga, both rather ragged. His left hand gripped a fold of the toga and was half hidden under the cloth. The right held a *phurba* (Magic dagger). His right arm moved slightly at each step as if leaning on a stick, just as though the *phurba,* whose pointed extremity was far above the ground, had touched it and were actually a support.*

We did not have such monk-trekkers here, but perhaps they will come, considering how popular long-distance walking is becoming in Europe; it could become another modern fad. This is very far from our way of walking. I have met several pilgrims who were trying to walk as fast as possible; needless to say, they did not see or notice many people or sights.

The scenery looked very much like Vermont in the United States, with pastures and farms nestled in the hills here and there. We trampled through the woods and muddy rocky paths. There were my favorite chestnut trees, and typical villages on top of a hill or on the side of a hill. We also noticed old towers with ominous shapes and a forbidding atmosphere. Through the forest path I made the wrong decision and we ended up down into a little quiet valley. There were great residences with well-tended ornamental and vegetable gardens, an old roman church, and a flock of sheep in the meadows. We asked for water at the house by the church. The aura was peaceful and happy; I would have lived there myself. We had to retrace our steps, but a nice woman took us back in her car to where we had made the wrong turn. Back on the road we approached Figeac and decided not to go to Rocamadour, which would have been another week, and avoided the noisy city. We took the path through the outskirts and headed for La Cassagnole,

---

\* David-Neel, *Magic and Mystery in Tibet,* pp. 200–203.

walking through busy suburbs full of cars; we had to be very careful on the narrow road. We passed the business park section, which was a dirty and disheveled countryside like all major cities. It was painful to walk through such abandoned sites—quite the opposite of the peaceful valley we had just walked through, which had given us the strength to watch disasters in the making. But we left the factories and slowly entered the gentle countryside again.

That day, we walked more than twenty miles, and the *gîte* in La Cassagnole was wonderful; the owner was a true servant of the pilgrims. We soon forgot the ugly surroundings of the city and enjoyed this little oasis tucked away by a tiny road between beautiful old stone walls. It was an artisan home, organically built, and still under construction, with herb and flower gardens. I had arrived in Charlemagne country. Of course this whole area is Charlemagne's country. He was always on horseback, crisscrossing Europe from Germany into Spain and Italy, but apparently he lived in this particular area. His third son, who was a twin, was born right around the corner from where we were staying, and one could see the remnant of the ancestral home-abbey in the meadow behind the trees of this *gîte*. A book on French kings and queens says that this son, Louis I, was born in Chasseneuil in 778. It sounds close enough to Cassagnole, but one never knows. When looking up the kings and queens, I became very interested in the queens of history. During my youth, history taught only about the systems of patriarchy, leaving aside most of the queens; as children we knew little of their existence—or perhaps I just had bad teachers.

Charlemagne had nine wives. He was born in 742, the oldest son of Pepin the Short and Bertha, about whom we will speak further. At age twenty-seven, Charlemagne married Himiltrude as *matrimonium ad morganicum,* meaning marriage for the morning gift; the marriage was primarily for his pleasure. In other words, the woman did not have royal standing and their offspring would have no rights after birth. Their son, Pepin the Hunchback, eventually went to a convent with his mother. His second marriage lasted only one year; she was banished at age twenty-six when Charlemagne became King in 771 and probably needed a more suitable wife, who would be Hildegard, the daughter of the count of Suabe, who was more important than the King of Lombard, the father of his previous wife.

Hildegard married Charlemagne at the age of thirteen when he was twenty-nine. She gave him nine children in twelve years and then died. When she was sixteen, she had her third son, Louis I, who was born up the road from where we were staying. He would become the king of France. The year that she died, Charlemagne, at the age of forty-one, married Fastrade, the eighteen-year-old daughter of the count of Franconia. She gave him two daughters and died at age twenty-nine. Soon after her death, Charlemagne at fifty-three married Liutgarde, who died six years later. His sixth wife, Madelgrade, whose age is not known—perhaps because she was considered underage—gave him two daughters.

Then at the age of fifty-eight in the year 800, Charlemagne was crowned emperor and married his seventh wife. At age sixty-four, he married wife number eight, a union that lasted two years. In the year 808, when he was sixty-six, he married Gerswinde, who was twenty-six years old. Charlemagne died six years later. He was such a powerful figure throughout that period that many leaders of those regions rushed to offer their daughters to the mighty king, thus sealing agreements between regions. More important, however, is the sad fact that most of his wives were very young women who died in their youth, often at childbirth.

It seems the caliphs of southern Spain and in the larger Arab world satisfied their needs through harems. The kings and queens of the West had convents and monasteries in which to place unwanted sons and brothers of kings. In one world, sensuality was accepted and cultivated; in the other, it was condemned. This was a different time in history, when marriage between men and women, especially those of high rank, had little or nothing to do with love; it was merely a merchant's bargain, often sealed when the children were infants. Some part of the country that could be gained was often the deciding factor for arranged marriages, with or without the blessing of the pope or bishops.

For the earlier Merovingian and Carolingian kings and queens, however, things were different; it was also about maintaining bloodlines, most often through the woman's lineage. When a line died out in the man's lineage owing to the lack of a male heir, the blood of the kings was reintroduced by marrying the daughters of a king's lineage. "Rudolf Steiner has told us that the forces of heredity work in such a way that they are in fact inherited through the males, while the woman rather works against heredity and, through what she gives, transmits forces to the children that are more universally human characteristics derived from the whole cosmos."* Charlemagne could not read, but he was a great warrior, pious, and a political leader. His task was to Christianize Europe, and he built an empire that his sons later fragmented, an outcome for which we can be thankful. Otherwise, we would not have beautifully distinct Germany, France, Italy, Spain, and the other European lands.

There is something else intriguing about Charlemagne, and perhaps that is why I have had a fascination with this great historical personality. Here is the legend of *Floire et Blanchefleur,* the grandparents of Charlemagne on his mother's side.

> Of Love will I tell you as well as I may
> And through this legend you shall learn
> How once there were two children
> Whom Love brought to grief.
> The two loved one another already,
> So the adventure relates,
> When they were not yet five years old.
> ........................

---

\*     Stein, *The Ninth century and the Holy Grail*, p. 212.

> Then to this loving pair
> A child was given,
> A lovely maid named Bertha of the foot,
> From this Bertha, as we find in the old books,
> And from Pippin, was born later
> Charles.
> ........................
> Know ye Floire was a heathen
> But Blanscheflur was a Christian,
> Yet this difference if you only believe it
> Divided them not in their lives,
> For Flore received baptism
> Through his love to Blanchefleur
> Who never knew doubt.[*]

The poet says that Flore inherited Hungary from his Uncle. The father of Flore is Fenix the King of Spain. He also came into conflict with a host of pilgrims who belonged to a Carolingian Count who, with his daughter, was taking part in a pilgrimage to Santiago de Compostella. This Count was then killed in battle so that his daughter, who was expecting a child and whose husband was dead, remained behind alone. This lady is the mother of Blanschefur. Taken prisoner by Fenix she came into his land. She disembarked at Naples and Fenix presented her as a gift to his wife, the Spanish Queen. She was lovingly received by the Queen and so it happened that the Queen of Spain bore her son at the same moment in which the Carolingian Countess bore a daughter, Blanscheflur.

> These two of whom I tell you
> Were both born on *one* day
> In *one* house, in *one* hour
> And what the legend says is well attested
> And *one* nurse brought them up both.

---

[*] Ibid., pp. 67–68.

It was on Palm Sunday that both of them came into the world. But Palm Sunday means "Blossoming Easter"—*paske florie,* as Conrad Fleck says. Therefore, they were called Blansche*flur* and *Flore*.... Of these two whom the legend names Flore and Blanscheflur, history knows at least Flore. He is Charibert von Laon.... The legend makes this Charibert to be the son of Fenix, King of Spain.[*]

The story continues with many challenges for the couple, but the story does not stop here; further on we will encounter other threads. So these are the great-grandparents of Louis the Pious, who was born around the corner.

❊

While walking with the old German miner I heard all about his life, which was most interesting. He started working in the mine at the age of fourteen, because he knew he wanted to be a miner from a very early age after a visit to the mines. His dad died during the war. At age twenty-four, after ten years of hard work in the mines, he was made chief of the mine. He was married four years later and at thirty-three had a son. His son was now a priest who was going to see the Pope in Rome the following week to celebrate his tenth year as a priest in Northern Germany. The old German miner worked very hard and played hard as well—he drove very fast in his yellow Mercedes. I learned much about the mines and was fascinated by this life spent underground. He said that, at one point in his late twenties, he once saw another miner who was enjoying himself walking around town with his wife. The German miner wondered why he could not do that. The fellow miner told him that it was no use trying to gather lots of coal just for oneself, being the strongest, and killing oneself in the process. I imagined him standing more than 6 feet, 4 inches, very strong, working like an ox, and being too exhausted when he came home to have any life of his own. The

---

[*] Ibid., pp. 68, 76.

*The vallée du Célé*

other miner said that he gathered just enough coal, and then helped his neighbor gather more coal, working in unison. From that day on, the German miner had a new life. He no longer worked selfishly, but more in cooperation with others. He had learned that brute strength is not what really counts. He said he learned to use his head and went back to school to study mining engineering.

We chatted about that and many other topics. He spoke of his son, who was extremely busy with his congregation, but very successful with young people. I told him jokingly that his son might be the next Pope.

In this quiet *gîte*, we shared a meal with a few other new pilgrims. One of the pilgrims, Brother Gabriel, was retired and had taught statistics at a Catholic university. He was going in the opposite direction toward Le Puy. He had started in Marseilles and had fallen, spending a couple of weeks in the hospital. He was a sweet, gentle, and lettered man who kept much to himself.

The next day we walked through very pleasant surroundings, trying to live in that old period of history. The paths had seen many knights,

*A village in the vallée du Célé*

queens, soldiers, and counts. They had seen little children play who later became kings. My eyes lingered on the quiet abbey, bathed in the soft, foggy morning light.

We arrived in Bedouer, a small town with a beautiful chateau overlooking the valley of Célé below. We stopped and had a coffee break in the old town. It was Sunday and many were at church, where we, too, paid a visit. We decided to take this *variante* route and not the pilgrims' route. In any case, in the olden days there was really no direct route; pilgrims went wherever they liked. If the path took them some days out of the general direction, it might have been because they wished to visit a particular church with some relic or other attraction. Many people had recommended this path for its pristine beauty and wilderness. We descended into the vallée du Célé, walked along the path by the river, and went through the woods. There was no one following us as we passed several villages on steep hills of the terrain sculpted by the serpentine river. It was quiet, and the old river flowed between the spring vegetation on its steep banks. It was getting hot, and the path

*Above la rivière Célé*

seemed to go on endlessly with no restaurant in sight. We had no food with us and were running low on water. The path crossed a little bridge over the river and climbed steeply on the other side. Then we saw what looked like a Romanesque castle that had been renovated. We hoped someone was living there, and then we saw an older retired man who offered us fresh water and chatted with us. They had moved here a few years ago from Paris and enjoyed the reclusive setting—as did we. He said that during the summer many pilgrims came through here, and that they always asked for water. He was planning to set up a little sandwich and drink stop.

After what seemed like a much longer walk than we had anticipated, passing richly renovated farmhouses, we arrived in the historic hamlet of Espagnac. It was Sunday, so the village had a festive atmosphere, packed with locals celebrating a family soccer event. Everything was closed, and the "hostel" was operated by the town. The woman working there directed me to a local farmer/gardener who was selling eggs. A little old woman took me to her cellar and I bought some fresh eggs. Then we went to the museum at the abbey church for a talk by a lively local, eighty-two-year-old historian. She loved her history, and I would have enjoyed talking with her for a whole week. She had stacks of books at the entrance of her home, and I would have loved to read them all. She was definitely no ordinary woman and had deep insight into the history of this famous women's abbey. The abbey had been constructed by a local bishop, who was a friend of the king of Portugal. It is called Notre-Dame-de-val-Paradis.

Here again is the Queen Blanche of Castile (1188–1252), wife of Louis VIII; she married at age twelve, and he at thirteen. They had eleven children, and their second son became the famous Louis IX (Saint Louis). Blanche was the aunt of the abbess here. Blanche of Castile was the granddaughter of Eleanor of Aquitaine, whom I mentioned earlier.

This beautiful setting was the home of aristocratic women related to kings of France and kings of Spain, as well as kings of England— *thanks again to Queen Eleanor.* Those learned women chose to live here (or were forced to live here), and so funding this beautiful place was not a problem. The cloister was self-sustained, having its own gardens, library, dorms, a great refectory and beautiful chapel, farmland, cows, sheep, an outdoor oven, and an artisan shop. The hundred *religieuses* who lived here ate in silence as the abbess read ancient religious texts. Men were not allowed within the compound, and it was surrounded by large fortress walls. Since it was on the other side of the river Célé, it was very difficult to access—a well-hidden spot for the seclusion of countesses and queens, women of fortune, and the faithful, such as the abbess, niece of Blanche of Castile, Queen of France. It had a beautiful octagonal steeple that dominated the cloistered abbey. However, much had been destroyed by fires during the Hundred Years' War. It had functioned without interruption until 1792.

After such a rich historical presentation, I walked around the gardens and admired the blooming irises. Meanwhile, one of the women heard of our plight (no food) and invited us for supper. We joined her in her home, the hostel, which she'd had to abandon owing to her poor

*Espagnac, the tower in which I got a room*

health and courageous fight against cancer. She served us a wonderful meal. Her two grandchildren came to visit, and we chatted for some time. She truly loved to serve the pilgrims. She had an enormous heart, and we said we would pray for her speedy recovery. We retired to bed in our tower bunk beds and woke early for a wonderful breakfast prepared by our host. Our visit to la vallée du Célé was well worth it, just to experience this very special hamlet of Espagnac, the warmth of our host, and its illustrious past.

※

The next misty, foggy morning, we crossed the ancient bridge over the river and followed the road very carefully to the next town. We met a group of underwater cave divers from England, who were ready to enter one of those carved-out tunnel caves, more than a mile in length along the river Célé. I thought they were very daring to enter these cold, dark waters perhaps to discover more Lascaux-type ancient caves or relics. We talked before going on our way, happy to be walking and breathing the wonderful air. We passed a little cottage owned by a former legionnaire who was not very talkative. We bought some food in Marcilhac-sur-Célé, and then headed for a path climbing the mountainside to a spectacular view of the river and cliffs. There we saw the unlikely sight of an old jeep driven by a very attractive woman and her husband along this narrow, rocky path. They were working toward an upcoming 160-mile World Cup horse-trekking event. I wished I could have stayed to watch those Olympic equestrian champions from all over Europe, Arabia, and other places compete in this very difficult event. The path was anything but easy; it was quite steep and rocky. The horses had to be extremely agile, strong, light on their feet, and quick. What a test of endurance! We saw the couple and their jeep all along our path, which took us past an ugly goose farm. Hundreds of geese, making lots of noise, were contained in a small compound. There was no grass, only dirt, and the family was not very happy to see us trampling near their farm. It was a public path, but we, too, would have liked to be elsewhere. Their dog followed us for at least two hours. After that experience, I will not be buying goose *pâté de foie gras* anytime soon.

We crossed into yet another valley, and the scenery became more desolate, with shrubs and not much farmland. We walked for several hours and arrived at the *gîte* in Espinières. "Horse Event" signs were everywhere. We saw castles, renovated old farmhouses, hills, rocky paths, thorny brushes, dry dirt paths, and good-smelling pine trees. The place was full with kids on a geology fieldtrip and wealthy, dirt-biking tourists. We had a bunkroom for ourselves, as well as a great communal supper of duck, soup, salad, fresh bread, dessert, coffee, and local wine—not exactly a pilgrim's diet.

The people in this particular place did not really like the pilgrim crowd; they were graduating to the more affluent weekend tourists. They were proud of the fact that they were fully booked and were not terribly happy to see us. Their attitude was, *So what if you are walking across Europe? Don't expect us to lower our prices or make changes for you. If you don't like it, leave and sleep out in the grass.*

We left early the next day after breakfast. It was another misty morning, and the walk was again very quiet; not a single pilgrim was on this out-of-the-way path. The earth turned very hard, limy, calcareous, and, again, full of thorny brushes. I decided to visit the famous caves of Pech-Merle, which were a few miles out of the way; it was worth it. The old German miner had to be cajoled into it—after all, he had spent his whole life underground, so why not see this subterranean site?

The path took us down into the village of Cabreret, surrounded by cliffs carved by the river Célé, which met the Sagne, a smaller river. We climbed steadily to the top of the Rochecourbe cliffs to reach the Pech-Merle caves. It took longer than I thought, but we arrived there fifteen minutes early and signed up. The old German miner finally decided to join me for this tour, along with a group who had arrived by bus.

Happily, I had brought my sweater and hat; it became cold as we stepped steadily down into the large caves. The whole area through which we had been walking for the last four days, in the upper-Pyrenees region of the Quercy and Perigord, shows visible signs of human habitation in these caves as much as 10,000 or 15,000 years ago or more.

I had never before seen such an ancient sight, and I had not really planned on seeing these famous caves. I seemed like a real gift that I did not miss it by joining all the other pilgrims who chose the more common route. Because I am a painter, it was a special experience to live with these 10,000-year-old majestic paintings. The old German miner loved being underneath the earth and said he missed going into the mines. He caressed the stones very gently, looking for veins and signs of coal along the dark, sinuous path leading to the enormous caves. He barely looked at the art. He said it was a hoax and would not even consider that it was real. I was getting very excited about the enormous paintings, but he would not hear it. I learned a lot about his work as a miner and his passion for the rocks. I said I would go visit him at his home to see his enormous rock collection.

I admired the paintings in silence, and tried to keep all of my pores opened so that even my skin could take in the sight; my senses were working overtime to grasp what lived in the painter's mind, body, and soul. It was clear that they did not think as they painted, so I shut my brain and intellect and breathed into the silence. This was not an easy task with so many people around me, including the old German skeptic. It must have been painted by shamans and priests during a ritualistic ceremony. They painted with charcoal from the fires used for light, and fire was sacred at that time. They used local iron ore ground into powder, and white calcium powder that they blew or spat onto the wall. The artists painted symbolic horses, cows, bulls, bison, Aurochs, mammoths, Ibex, fish, bears, and their own hands. Only the animals were depicted on a large scale. There was no difference between the painters and the animals; the painter was what he painted and lived what he painted. They lived in the world of movement and animals. Their consciousness was a very dreamy one, similar to the present-day consciousness of children. Their depiction of the human being was a stick figure, like that of a three- or four-year-old. They must have had a magical kind of life, still living in a paradise where the Gods were forever present and revered. The large animals were their neighbors and, thanks to their sacrifices, could be eaten. Looking at these masterpieces, there was a lot of love, care, worship, and awe coming out of these paintings. They must have been painted at very special times of the year, perhaps in the summertime when food was plentiful and the surroundings were full of plant life, making them even more dreamy and united with nature.

In his book "The Healing Wisdom of Africa," Malidoma Somé gives an inkling of the frame of mind out of which these paintings were born. These ancient forms of consciousness are still alive in the elder African Priests and Shamen when they direct initiation ceremonies:

> Ritual is the most ancient way of binding a community together in a close relationship with Spirit. It is a way of communicating with forms of consciousness and beings from countless worlds. It has been one of the most practical and efficient ways to stimulate the safe healing required by both the individual and the community....
>
> What is a ritual? Every time a gathering of people, under the protection of Spirit, triggers a body of emotional energy aimed at bringing them very tightly together, a ritual of one type or another is in effect. In this kind of gathering people primarily use nonverbal means of interacting with one another, thereby stimulating the life of the psyche....
>
> Ritual is a dance with Spirit, the soul's way of interacting with the Other world, the human psyche's opportunity to develop relationship with the symbols of this world and the spirits of the other.
>
> Symbols are the doorway to the ritual. Just as our bodies can't survive without nourishment, our psyche cannot sustain themselves without symbolism....
>
> The symbolic and the spiritual are not far apart. In fact, in (our language) Dagara (in Burkina Faso, West Africa), there is no word that directly translates as *symbol*. There is no word for symbol other than the word *spirit*, because there is an assumed indivisible connection between Spirit and symbol. Beings that live in other dimensions are so intimately linked to us that they are referred to by name....
>
> For the Dagara, and other indigenous people, it is inconceivable that the human mind could capture something that does not already exist somewhere. The human capacity to imagine is an example of our connection with remote fields of energy. If human

consciousness is able to capture, and thereby understand, these realities, then imagination and visionary consciousness are linking us to other types of realities, directly or otherwise. If modern consciousness is, for the time being, unable to interact with other intelligences in the time-space continuum, the modern psyche nevertheless maintains a great attraction toward and relationship with other dimensions and types of consciousness.\*

Finally, we saw ancient footprints molded in the mud, of a small child who, without a doubt, had played there. By then the incredulous old German miner was beside himself with disbelief, but I was becoming increasingly enchanted with the cavernous setting and ancient icons.

> People in ancient times saw something true to reality, where people now see only strange and fantastic myths. In ancient times, people knew that when they looked at an animal in the physical, sensory world, it had a clearly defined outline. However, they were not interested in such definite outlines; rather, they wanted to understand the life that moved everywhere in a flowing stream. They felt this was not possible in sharply defined pictures or concepts, but only in fluid, changing, and metamorphosing images. This is how things were presented in the mysteries.\*\*

> The Lemurians (beings from a very distant prehistoric period, before the Atlantic deluge) did not have dwellings in our sense, except in their latest times. They lived where nature gave them the opportunity to do so. The caves they used were altered and extended only insofar as necessary. Later they built such caves themselves, and at that time they developed great skills in such construction.... If the Lemurian was a born magician, such talent was developed into art and insight. Only those who, through all kinds of discipline, had acquired the ability to overcome themselves to the greatest extent could be admitted. For all others, what happened in these institutions was the most profound secret. Here one came to know and control the forces of nature

---

\* Somé, *The Healing Wisdom of Africa*, pp. 141–150.
\*\* Steiner, *Earthly Knowledge and Heavenly Wisdom*, p. 5.

through direct contemplation of them. However, the learning was such that in human beings the forces of nature changed into forces of volition. Such people could thereby execute what nature accomplished.... The activities of the Lemurian humanity towered high above everything the animal world can produce through instinct. They even stood far above what humankind has since acquired in the way of arts and sciences through memory, reason, and imagination. If we were to use an expression for these institutions that would facilitate our understanding of them, we could call them "colleges of will power and the clairvoyant power of the imagination".... What has been described here was true of only a small part of humankind. The rest lived their life in animalism. In their external appearance and in their way of life, those animal people were quite different from the small group. They were not especially different from the lower animals, which resembled them in form in certain respects.*

⁂

It was time to head back up, single file, into the fresh warm air. The old miner reminisced about his days in the mine as we put our backpacks on and headed out through the thorny brushes, pines trees, and calcerous soil, walking on *top* of what we had just seen. I said that we should not venture across, but instead use the path as we could fall into one of these caves. The path wound down the cliff-mountain into the deep valley of the Célé, which was going to join the larger Le Lot River near the town of Bouziès. We stopped for lunch at a restaurant packed with sightseers from a bus tour, all wearing their fine clothes. We made quite a scene in our dirty shorts, shirts, backpacks, hiking sticks, disheveled hair, and sweaty and dirty faces, as well as his large cowboy hat and my baseball cap. The whole dining room stopped eating and glared at us, so we opted to eat outside; it was a bit chilly but more comfortable and we did not want to be confined to a room full of tourists. It was too early for food, so I just had a coffee. I wanted to walk up to the

---

\* Steiner, *Cosmic Memory*, pp. 74–76.

famous town of Saint-Cirq-Lapopie, a medieval town built on top of the cliffs overlooking the Lot River—an eight-mile detour. I left my backpack at the restaurant and ran into town, while the old German opted to continue on.

The walk was spectacular along the cliff and flowing river. I climbed the steep path up the cliff and arrived in the ancient city. The town was full of fantastic scenery: an old fortress, a beautiful church, ancient fortress walls, and castle ruins. There were lots of tourists, studios, and artisan shops, but I had no time to linger for coffee. I had to run back to the restaurant and head toward Pasturat, eight miles away. It was around 4:00 o'clock, and there was no time to waste; darkness would come soon. I did not have a very detailed map of the area (the old German had the good map), so I asked the restaurant owner for directions. He said that if I walked along the old train tracks I would come to a bridge across the river, and from there it would be easier to get to Pasturat. The old German was walking on the right side of the river on a busy and dangerous road that was narrow and had little room for hikers when the trucks and cars drove by. I chose the train tracks on the opposite side.

It was a pleasant walk. From the road, I bushwhacked through the fields to the train tracks, where it was even more deserted. It was a bit mysterious, and absolutely no one was there. I could see the wide, muddy river far below. I encountered an old peasant who lived nearby. He said that it would be easier to walk on the path just below the tracks, as it would lead me to my destination. I thanked him—the train tracks were not comfortable to walk on, but the path was under a canopy of thick trees with the noise of the river. Here it was a quiet walk. It was getting late, so I had to pick up my pace. Strangely, however, I was not tired; I had covered more than fourteen miles, five at running speed (no backpack), and had another long seven-and-a-half miles to go. I chose to stop counting and forget the miles, since it made no difference. I would just walk until 7:00 o'clock; there would still be light, and that was it. At three miles per hour it would be fine.

The path became wider, and I entered a small valley with a lot of large gardens with workers in fields of asparagus. The path indicated a sharp left and led up the mountain, but it went in the opposite direction of where I wanted to go, so I kept going on the path along the River Lot valley. A mile or two later, I saw the train-track bridge I was supposed to take, but I decided to stay on my nice, quiet path. Why not? It was a nice path. It went on past a couple of homes, and then it became very small and kind of unused. I considered turning back but had come a long way; I thought it was just as well to keep going.

Some distance further, the path stopped at the bottom of a cliff. Not willing to admit I had taken the wrong path, I headed to the left up the mountainside, where there was something that resembled a path, but was probably no longer such a thing. Of course, there was no way I would head back; I just kept telling myself to keep going. Then the paths were everywhere. Which way, left or right? I was in the middle of the mountains, the main path had disappeared, and I was following goat paths and other traces I recognized as wild boar. They live in these wild places, and I had seen a lot of traces of the animals scratching the ground for food. Goats don't do that, but wild boars do.

Now I was beginning to panic; it was getting dark, and I had no clue where I was going. Going down to the right was a cliff overlooking the river. The path I had encountered pointed to the left quite a ways back—at least three miles—and it did so for a reason: to circumvent the mountain cliffs so that hikers would walk above them. Nevertheless, I was too stupid and had no map, so I kept climbing.

The weight of my backpack suddenly disappeared, and I was running up the path, in one direction and then another, hoping not to meet one of those wild boars. I don't know where the energy was coming from—perhaps fear of being lost and stranded with no food and little water with wild boars at nightfall. Then after great effort on my part and what seemed like an eternity, I suddenly came to a clearing. What joy! It was a narrow strip of farmland. Then I knew I had gone in the right direction. I went through several meadows—always up—and finally found the correct pilgrims' path with its familiar markings, which was on top of the mountain. I was elated and didn't care how much longer I would have to walk; at least I was not lost. I walked on top of the mountain now past beautifully restored stone homes and gardens. The path went into the woods, into the valley, and ended on a small country road with some traffic. I finally arrived in the village of Pasturat. I had walked about twenty-three miles.

The old German had arrived there quite a while earlier and had reserved a bed and supper for me. He'd had a very difficult time on the main road with the traffic, but now we could relax. There was another couple from Austria, but they were very quiet and not willing to talk much.

I really enjoyed the shower. As for the food it was simply lousy considering what I had to pay. I am a good cook, so when someone gives me a bowl of hot water, old bread, salt and pepper, and a piece of fried onion, I know I have been had. We also had a cup of boiled rice with a bit of sausage, but no salad or vegetable—all for about eighteen dollars. The stores were closed and we had a bit of old food, but I was still hungry since I had not eaten since breakfast. Otherwise, I would have skipped supper and eaten the next day. Pilgrims are definitely taken advantage of in some places; people throw some old food on the table and charge exorbitant prices. I was disgusted.

Breakfast was no better, so we started our walk early, going up and down paths through a pleasant forest, still on top of the mountains. We followed the meandering River Le Lot, which headed toward the larger city of Cahors. We had to go only about ten or eleven miles—a short day.

We arrived at the top of the small town of Arcambal, where a dog chose to follow us, and then we descended and walked by the River Le Lot and made a picnic of some old food in the valley. We saw lovely villages on the other side of the river, and then crossed a huge highway, *autoroute* 20. Along the path in the valley were lots of crops growing under plastic, mainly strawberries and asparagus.

Next to the path was a collection of plastic trash, barrels, and buckets that, according to the signs, had contained every kind of chemical and pesticide you could imagine, and it drained right into the big river. I certainly avoided the white asparagus salads being served in the restaurants. I decided to eat only bread and cheese, though not goat cheese. I had to find artisan cheese. Looking at these sights was a wake-up call. We kept on walking on the path that left the gardens, and then we saw a family who was picnicking. We asked them if they could keep the dog for a while in their gardens. We did not want to have the dog in the city. He kept following us and we could not get rid of him. They agreed to keep him for a while, and we went on. The path entered a thick forest and then we arrived in the suburbs of Cahors. The town was a bit puzzling because the river makes a "U" around the city, and we could not figure out how to get to the center. After another couple of miles, we reached the center and stayed in the *foyers des jeunes,* or young workers' dorms. It was filled with noisy, young Africans, Arabs, and French. I was too tired to look for something else and decided to stay despite the noise. Here we rejoined the regular pilgrims' path.

I took care of downloading pictures and emailing my family, who might have thought I'd disappeared. I had supper with the old German, and we were ready to part ways. Later that evening, I was still hungry and, to my delight, found a Moroccan restaurant that served great vegetarian couscous and hot steaming mint tea. I chatted with two French-Moroccan women and took a walk on a famous fortified bridge built in the early 1300s. I climbed the centuries-old, worn-down stone steps and took in the views and the river while contemplating the soldiers who had stood there over the centuries. Then I headed for my bunk.

❧

Cahors was definitely a city of the south. It had a southern flavor that announced the Mediterranean atmosphere and its many shades of skin, warm weather, and the atmosphere of Africa, Spain, and Arabic lands that suffused the air. "If you wish to portray something historical, then ask yourself, 'What do I first have to become to be able to portray it?' It was a path of becoming, of work on oneself that Steiner showed us."*

From the beginning of the twelfth century, Cahors and this region of the Quercy suffered major wars between the Plantagenet kings of England, Queen Eleanor and her sons (allies of Duke Raymond of Toulouse), and allied rebels against the kings of France—wars over land and, of course, Rome. Cahors had seen many kings run through her streets. This area was strategic because the boundary there between the two emerging powers of the future: France and England. The via Podiensis goes right along that line.

> Seventeen years after the first crusades, an immense army assembled near Lyon, the day of the Ascension in 1226; they took the road toward Provence in southern France, and came down toward Avignon. Let us imagine "fifty-thousand men on horseback, riders as well as squires, and a much greater number of foot soldiers," followed by a numerous crowd of cutthroats, merchants of all sorts, blacksmiths, carpenters, tailors, monks, prelates, and prostitutes. Even if the facts given to us by the historians are a bit dubious, one understands that the cities "taken by terror" chose to open their doors at the arrival of this boisterous human tide. Even when those cities were entered peacefully, the small market towns had to withstand deep prejudices. Did they then open their doors because it was the king of France who was coming...or is it that the specter of death and pillage preceded that formidable armada as the wind precedes thunder?
>
> Raymond of Toulouse found himself alone facing that powerful coalition as an instrument of Rome.
>
> Henri III Plantagenet (the king of England) was dying to come to his aid and to take back the territories...conquered by Louis VIII, but he was dissuaded by the menaces of the Pope and the reticent attitude of some of his Dukes....

---

\* See Tautz, W. J. *Stein: A Biography*.

Around October, Louis VIII decided to return to France. He left Humbert of Beaujeu the task of governing "Occitanie" in his name. But on October 29, on the return journey, he took ill in Montpensier and died on November 8, 1226, at age thirty-nine, leaving his wife Blanche of Castile to govern with her twelve-year-old eldest son, Louis IX (Saint Louis)....

As France was without a king until 1236, it was of no surprise that the papal inquisition was created in 1233. Rome had free range to establish *l'ordre de l'eglise toute puissante*....

The inquisition was created in 1233 and in April 1234, the council of Beziers reinforced the canons published in Narbonne in 1227; every Sunday, all the heretics and their culprits were excommunicated; they were taken hold of and presented to the bishop in their place of residence; the priests had to keep a register of all who seemed suspect. Those suspected victims were not allowed under any circumstances to become bailiffs or public officials.

In each diocese, the preachers opened a church tribunal that convened, interrogated, and condemned the suspects. In Cahors, before 1233, it was the bishop Guillaume of Cardaillac...who assumed the role of inquisitor. He reconciled with Guillemette of Sapiac, who in her youth had become a "perfect" [dressed as a heretic] for two years. When she fell back into heresy, because she continued to entertain such heretics as Guiraud Abit, Perfect Deacon of the region, and the Perfect Jeanne d'Avignon and their friends. She was condemned later by Pierre Cellan to carry a cross for seven years and had to accomplish a pilgrimage to Le Puy, Saint-Gilles, St. Jacques de Compostela, St. Sauveur, Saint Denis, Saint Thomas, and finally Rome....

Terror was induced and instilled in "a context of extreme moral and physical coercion, and arrest." It is easy to imagine the constant worry of people whose neighborhood could at any time overthrow their quiet life due to informants and false accusations, all this committed with impunity since the witness remained anonymous. "No one could find out what kind of stories were circulating on one's account, neither the interest which the accusing party could benefit from such accusations or the fanatical zeal used to compromise them.".... For a long time the inquisitors praised such methods, which consisted of creating a permanent psychotic and informant atmosphere forcing people to betray the *"parfaits,"* their parents, their friends, and their enemies, even if they did not have ties with the heresy. The excuses were not lacking, and one knows the laying of waste and havoc which this system perpetrated at the heart of the society, including harm to the "little poor people" without defense but also to the social network of the noblemen, who were the main supporters of Catharism.[*]

The movement toward "individualism," like many other phenomena of modern civilization, has long ago shifted its center of gravity outside the walls of the Church. Once it was felt as the peculiar glory of the Christian religion. In the Dark Ages, heresies that attempted to explain away the significant paradox of Christ's simultaneous divinity and humanity were hunted down with the utmost rigor, and it is probable that a vivid sense of the dignity of the individual human soul was at the bottom of a good many actions which now seem to us like the very stultification of such a conviction. This great inner world of consciousness, we may suppose, which each individual was now felt to control in some measure for himself, was a thing to fear as well as to respect. It gave to every single soul almost infinite potentialities, for evil as well as good; and even the wisest heads seem to have felt that civilization could only be held together as long as all these souls maintained a certain uniformity of pattern. Thus, while the influence of Christianity had ensured to all men—not merely to a small slave-owning class—a modicum of personal liberty, it deprived them in the same breath of that dearest of all possessions, freedom of thought. The grim meaning gradually acquired by the Latin word *Inquisition*, meaning inquiry, still signifies to us the ruthless pains that were now taken, for the first time in the world's history, to pry into and endeavor to control that private thinking life of men which had suddenly acquired such a vast importance in their eyes. The still grimmer *auto da fé* began life as a Spanish phrase meaning simply "an act of faith."[**]

---

[*] Bordes, *Cathares et Vaudois*, pp. 127-128 136-137, 150 (tr. M-L. Valandro).
[**] Barfield, *History in English Words*, p. 133 -134.

*Leaving the Massif Central region of the French Camino*

Another dimension I noticed began to emerge, but now it had become more real. Pilgrims had been forced to make these walks, many without shoes, and with a cross sewn onto their clothing, barring them, of course, any employment; it was *mort sociale,* or social death. Heretics were thrown out of their towns, their belongings were stolen, and they were forced to live in a "Catholic" social milieu. The pilgrims were called *Croises*. Walking these paths, one ponders the sufferings such people had to undergo as the price of freedom; we can walk in a mood of thankfulness toward the thousands of persecuted who walked the path and even lost their lives in the process. Perhaps many of the people walking now are returning to their former battleground. The whole region, from Le Puy to Spain, is stained with the blood of those martyrs.

These paths are indeed ancient, full of unknown invisible crosses. Cruel fighting during the age of knights was concentrated in this area.

From Figeac to Moissac, not one hamlet or castle was left untouched. It was a kind of free-for-all as kings changed wives, wives died and left young kings in power, and divorced wives married other royalty. Nobles were free to do as they pleased in their little fiefdoms; Rome was vying for power; abbots wanted their monks and priests to clean up their monasteries; and cutthroat armies fought for money and land. Meanwhile, the population had access to written sacred works (the Bible in particular), which led to the possibility of a purer (Cathar) life without the mediation of the "Holy Church," leading to the freedom of individual self-reflection. Saint Thomas Aquinas was born in 1226 and would ascend the peaks of pure thinking.

In the middle of that turmoil, troubadours were discovering love for those ladies tucked away alone in castles; their noble husbands had gone to the Crusades, leaving them the opportunity to celebrate the many facets of *amour*.

> The medieval lyric, as it gradually loses its exclusive preoccupation with ecclesiastical subjects, becomes more and more concerned with woman, and concerned with her in a new way. Through the poetry of Italy, where the Renaissance was already stirring, the troubadour literature of France, and that strange "Rose" tradition (*roman de la Rose*)...there grew during the thirteenth and fourteenth centuries a small special vocabulary defining the landmarks in that new region of the imagination which the poets, and even the scholars, of Europe were just discovering; we might call it the region of devotional love. Indeed, it was more than a vocabulary; it developed at one time into a sort of miniature mythology, for the various conflicting elements in a lady's disposition which the lover had to meet with and overcome....
>
> *Anguish, beauty, bounty, charity, comfort, compassion, courtesy, delicate, devotion, grace, honor, humble, passion, patience, peace, purity*, and *tender* are further examples of this new vocabulary of tenderness which came...from Latin through Early French....
>
> If there are occasions when a single word seems to throw more light on the workings of men's minds than a whole volume

of history or a whole page of contemporary literature, the Middle English *lovelonging* is certainly one of them.

A new element has entered into human relationships, for which perhaps the best name that can be found is *tenderness*.*

> Sweet handsome friend, I can tell you truly
> That I've never been without desire
> Since it pleased you that I have you as my courtly lover;
> Nor did a time ever arrive, sweet handsome friend,
> When I didn't want to see you often;
> Nor did I ever feel regret,
> Nor did it ever come to pass, if you went off angry,
> That I felt joy until you had come back;
> Nor...**

As we walked on those paths, we saw numerous abandoned castles. Not much is left of them: a lonely tower seen in the distance or a pile of rubble with a single wall standing above a meadow, making a nice silhouette against the farmers' field and blue sky. Sometimes we heard that farmers helped themselves to the old stones to build a home. The scene was enlivened for a moment in my imagination by images of troubadours, perhaps on a horse riding across the land.

> The perfect equestrians: While wearing helmets on their heads, the top part of the body is covered with a coat of mail, and hands and feet protected by iron gloves and socks, knights protect themselves with their shields. Their weapon *par excellence* is the spear, but they also carry one or two swords, as well, the longest of which is tied to one's saddle. All of this is extremely heavy and cumbersome. Therefore, going into battle a knight has three available horses: a heavy workhorse for battle, a palfrey for covering territory, and a beast of burden. Knights were also assisted on the road and battleground by a squire and two or three foot soldiers.... They liked to wear their colors on their

---

\*   Barfield, *History in English Words*, pp. 128–130.
\*\*  Bogin, *The Women Troubadours*, p. 193.

shield and tunic, which covered the coat of mail, and carried a small flag on their spear. In this way, they identified themselves and recognized their adversaries in battle.*

---

The next morning, after breakfast in the communal dining room, I began my day by visiting a North African shop to buy fruits, bread, cheese, and other road food. The shop's owners had lived in Chicago for a few years. I talked with them about my pilgrimage and then moved on.

I chose the shorter route, which crossed a well-known bridge and then climbed a cliff. The old German took the other route. This path was a hard climb but worth it; I could see the whole city from above. Only a few pilgrims were on the path. It took four hours just to walk the next five miles to the next town, where everyone was resting—removing their shoes, filling water bottles at the fountain, and eating lunch on a lawn shaded by large trees behind an old church. It was a hot day. Not far away was an old *hospitalier,* built for pilgrims by the Knights Templar around 1286. It could be seen from a distance. There were numerous hospitals for pilgrims on the path.

> Naturally, wherever something great and noble arises—as it did among the Templar knights—much that does not belong, perhaps even immorality, becomes attached to that greatness and nobility. There were, of course, knights who could be accused of all sorts of things, which cannot be denied. Nevertheless, there was nothing of this kind in the spirit of the foundation of that order; what the knights had accomplished for Jerusalem stood first, as well as what could be accomplished for Christianizing the whole of European culture. Gradually, the knights spread out in highly influential societies over England, France, Spain, parts of

---

\*   MSM, *Les Cathares,* p. 164 (tr. M-L. Valandro).

Italy, and Central Europe. They spread everywhere. Every knight developed to the highest degree complete penetration of the soul with a feeling and experience of the Mystery of Golgotha and of all that is connected with the Christian impulse. The force of this union with the Christ was strong and intense. True Templar knights no longer knew anything of themselves; when they felt, they let the Christ feel in them; when they thought, they let the Christ think in them; when they were filled with enthusiasm, they let the Christ in them be enthusiastic. There were probably few who had worked this ideal to a complete transformation.... Something quite remarkable and powerful had thus entered the Templar Order—though they knew nothing of the rules of the Christian initiation other than sacrificial service.*

I walked for another six miles through the quiet scenery, past farms and meadows, and then I entered Lascabane, a great old village, and headed enthusiastically toward the *gîte* for a well-earned shower. Then I saw a sign that read "No Room, Filled Up." The French pilgrims and travelers were at it again, using cell phones to make reservations. Those who arrived earlier but had not called ahead had to move on. I was disappointed, because I had to walk another six or seven miles, and it was hot. I asked around and hitched a ride, hoping they would know where I could find a place to sleep. People said that everything was full for miles around. An older couple took me to a tiny enclave of old homes about two miles down the road. There I was welcomed by an older woman, who said that she had room, but offered me a nice cup of coffee.

As I was chatting with her and drinking the hot brew, we heard that someone else had arrived and was sitting on the other side of the road. I stepped outside and saw the old German, who had also come through the previous village. He had arrived before me in the village and kept walking, while I hitched a ride. I was happy to see him. He was sweating profusely, and I was worried about his health since he had heart

---

\* Steiner, *Inner Impulses of Evolution*, p. 116.

troubles. The woman then told us that she was driving to the next, larger town of Montcuq ("mount ass"). That town had a larger *gîte,* so we waited for thirty minutes or so, drank our coffee, and shared our adventures of the day, and then the woman took us in her car to the next town four miles away. The old German was clearly very happy with this turn of events, as I was.

We ended up at the well-known *gîte du Soleillou,* which had been a dream. It was designed especially for pilgrims, with a large communal dining/living room, a large collection of books (for us), and of course wonderful food. Jacques, the owner, welcomed us with his homemade *syrop de lavande* drink, the most delicious drink I've ever had (I managed to get the recipe from him). The place was full of pilgrims. There were twenty-two of us, including an Australian couple, several French couples, Germans, and others. We enjoyed the evening with lively conversations from all directions, and I stayed up looking through their many books.

After a great breakfast, we headed out. I started out walking with the old German, but soon lost sight of him owing to my usual stops. Besides, he had to walk a longer day than I did—he was headed for Lourdes and a train back home to Germany. It was time to part. I walked uphill through a quiet forest and was surprised by a *cavaliere* on an early morning ride. I also visited a beautiful old castle, Château de Charry, where they raise horses. The surroundings suggested wealth and reminded me of former times.

The path continued up and then down, as I missed signs and got lost for a while until I heard a faint call. I looked up and saw a couple, arms raised and yelling at me to go on the right road. I had to retrace my steps for a couple of miles and was soon back on the right track, which had me climbing again through fields to an old farmyard, where there were drinks and some welcome walnuts for us. I chatted with the North African-French who worked there before continuing on through more valleys, up and down, through farm country and several picturesque fortress-villages. I saw the usual large, mustard-green fields, very soft color to the eyes, and a great expanse of blue sky. Then I saw in the distance a large, old castle city; it appeared to be near but was not. One had to cross several large hills before reaching the walled-in, medieval city of Lauzerte. Part of the terrain was calcareous, and one began to feel the warm Mediterranean climate. Growing all around was lavender roses, fig trees, orchards of plums and cherries, and vineyards. Sheep grazed quietly in the fields.

To reach Lauzerte required a long, hot climb; it seemed remote. After reaching the city center, I left my backpack at a café to look for the *gîte d'etape,* but found none. The town was a bit strange. There were few pilgrims, and I discovered later that none of the group pilgrims from the previous night had made the long, hot climb to the city. After a lunch of tomatoes, cheese, bread, coffee, and chocolate éclairs and a couple of hours of rest, I decided to go on. It took forty-five minutes to find my way out of the city, and I was a bit flustered under the hot sun as I headed uphill to the next town. I calculated that I had another six or seven miles, so I hitched a ride for a short distance.

A young woman gave me a ride up the hill, where I continued on my own path, ignoring the regular path, which I could not find in any case. After a couple of miles, a farmer on a tractor gave me directions, and I found the path again, meeting up with other pilgrims. Again I climbed into meadows, following the other pilgrims; it was more of a cross-country walk than following a path. Many frogs were singing in their ponds. Then I saw a beautiful *cavaliere* on a large, black Belgian mare, and of course I had to stop for a chat. We stopped at the next farm at the top of the hill, where I took pictures. It was at least ninety degrees, and she had no hat on, but the woman seemed to be enjoying the day. She was sixty-one and truly a very attractive person, like the *cavaliere* I had met earlier.

Two French weekend pilgrims arrived, and we all talked for a while in the shade. The rider explained to us that a couple of years earlier she had sustained a serious injury when a horse kicked her in the liver. Nonetheless, she continues to ride because horses are her life. There

*Pilgrim on a Belgian mare*

was a great deal of dignity and elegance in the woman, and I wondered who she might have been in another lifetime.

We walked on and I found a lovely *gîte* in Figue le Haut, outside the town of Durfort-Lacapelette. There was room, and the couple who had showed me the correct path was staying there, as well. We all took advantage of the hot weather to do some laundry. In the evening we ate a fantastic communal meal of curried chicken. Solange, our host, told us that they managed the farm with outside help from the West African country of Gabon to help them pick grapes, and the helpers stay with them. They have the problem common to most rural areas; the young people leave the farm for the city.

The next morning, I was off bright and early without breakfast and instead went to the local bakery for fresh chocolate croissants. In the next town, I stopped at a *gîte* and had hot tea and breakfast outside. The road was pleasant again, and it would not be a long day (about ten or eleven miles), leaving most of the day to visit the famous medieval city of Moissac. I decided to follow the road all the way. It was a small country road, lined on both sides with large platane trees, which have smooth bark and look a little like the tall Eucalyptus trees of Ecuador. I had to be careful of trucks and cars, but took the risk; I did not feel like climbing again and walking out of the way. I was being lazy.

It was another nine miles or so before the suburbs of Moissac came into view, with beautiful gardens in small yards and quiet paths. The city was big, and I chose to stay at the local monastery up the hill, which had been turned into an international center. It was yet another climb to the old monastery overlooking the ancient city, but I would not miss it.

A room had been reserved for me by one of the women I had met on the road the day before and worked there; she had insisted on calling ahead for me. The room was in the basement; everything else was full, because there was a popular zazen weekend workshop scheduled. Important Zen teachers and pupils were there from all over France for the retreat. When I arrived they were in their meditation room, and the familiar sight of the shoes outside the hall entrance welcomed me to the monastery. I thought it was a great use of the former Catholic monastery, and it reminded me of my former Buddhist meditation retreats of some thirty years earlier. Instead of the Benedictine monks of eight-hundred years ago, we have the modern Zen male and female monks moving about. I think we have come full circle. Buddha rejoins the Christ, but few realize it.

Being very French, some of the Zen monks enjoyed, more than the meditation itself, the way they looked in their beautiful outfits. Take the uniform away, and they will have a more difficult time. The French are very much into the correct outfits for hunting, cycling, driving, motorbiking, and even walking—and now meditation.

Then the participants came out for a snack, and I invited myself to speak with the monks in their black and white outfits. Many of the men had shaved heads. I asked if I could participate for a session, and they gladly agreed. I put my shoes with the others by the door, and one "very knowledgeable" female monk reprimanded me because my shoes were not set up neatly enough. I thought, *Why don't you tell the others who also threw their shoes outside the dojo?* Never mind, maybe she resented my intrusion. One teaches by *example*, not by telling others what to do. If she had simply taken her shoes and put them beside mine very neatly, I would have gotten the message and been more careful with my actions.

I sat with them for a session and benefited greatly from the quiet, focused, dense atmosphere. I had not sat for many years, but had no problem being quiet and still. I was thankful to be there with these serious meditants—distinguished outfits and all. I think my long walks had something to do with it.

I wanted to have a conversation and share with them some of my experiences as a walking meditant, and listen to their experiences in sitting meditation, but time did not allow it. There were many very intelligent, awakened faces with whom to speak, and perhaps we spoke anyway, at night, when we all went to sleep and shared the same space in dreamland. The Zen group reminded me of these words by a *Taoist* master. They come from a different background, but the feeling is similar.

> For *Taoists*, to walk is to live in a state of mind in which time no longer exists, "to vomit one's intelligence," and to go through obstacles without getting hurt. To walk like an autumn leaf falling from a tree, going where the wind takes you, without knowing whether it is the wind that carries you or if you carry the wind yourself....
>
> *Taoists* go to wild, inhabited places to look for spiritual energies; while walking in those places they impregnate themselves with supernatural forces. From these walks, they return with magic plants, talismans, and whole scriptures, most inspired by those wild, secluded places....
>
> To walk, in the eye of a Taoist is to participate in the thousand transformations;... to walk is to change with change—to inhabit the *tao* of the universe, to follow the movement of its waves.*

---

\* Jourdan and Vigne, *Marcher, méditer,* pp. 74–77 (tr. M-L. Valandro).

## A Troubadour of Nature on the Via Podiensis

❦

Getting hungry, I went to visit the medieval city in search of a restaurant. I had ample time to visit the Benedictine Abbaye Saint-Pierre de Moissac, the tympanum, and the twelfth-century cloister, and to stroll in the ancient quarters. It was going to be market day, and I also had to email home.

I signed up for the museum walk of the cloister founded in the 630s. It was destroyed by the Arab invasion and rebuilt with the help of Charlemagne and his son Louis the Pious. It finally became an important center during the eleventh and twelfth centuries, thanks to the pilgrims. Today, people come to visit the sculptures—stories in stone carved on 116 columns, 76 capitols telling stories from Apocalypse, and stories of the Bible and saints. I took many pictures of these breathtaking scenes. I was spellbound by the masterpieces, which could make the stones come to life, depicting ancient stories with simplicity of form and ancient symbols. The many visitors were deeply quiet, absorbing the magical stone stories with reverence and awe. Our guide was a very knowledgeable raconteur. Later, I sat at a café facing the tympanum of the abbey church and quietly looked at this apocalyptic stone story.

> This is dated to the period before 1130. It contains one of the earliest Romanesque tympana, which has a large-format, figurative relief. The theme is Christ enthroned and crowned, in strict frontality, with scarcely a hint of motion, his left hand resting on a book and his right hand raised in a gesture of majesty and blessing—a form that inspires fear and seems to know no leniency. In this enthroned Christ, one senses the judge of the last day judgment, meting out punishment with unswerving severity.... It depicts a vision of the Apocalypse in which Christ is surrounded by the four beasts—lion, calf, man, and eagle—and by the twenty-four enthroned elders.[*]

---

[*] Schutz, *Great Monasteries of Europe*, p. 132.

# LE TYMPAN DE MOISSAC

ILLUSTRE CE TEXTE DE L'APOCALYPSE DE SAINT JEAN:
JE VIS: UNE PORTE ETAIT OUVERTE DANS LE CIEL.
AUSSITOT, JE FUS SAISI PAR L'ESPRIT. ET VOICI: UN
TRONE SE DRESSAIT DANS LE CIEL, ET, SIEGEANT SUR
LE TRONE, QUELQU'UN. UNE GLOIRE NIMBAIT LE TRONE
DE REFLETS D'EMERAUDE. TOUT AUTOUR, VINGT-QUATRE TRONES SUR LESQUELS SIEGEAIENT VINGT-QUATRE ANCIENS VETUS DE BLANC, PORTANT SUR LEUR TETE DES COURONNES D'OR. CHACUN TENAIT UNE HARPE ET UNE COUPE D'OR PLEINE DES PARFUMS QUI SONT LES PRIERES DES SAINTS. DEVANT LE TRONE, COMME UNE MER LIMPIDE SEMBLABLE A DU CRISTAL. AUTOUR DU TRONE, QUATRE ANIMAUX: LE PREMIER RESSEMBLAIT A UN LION, LE DEUXIEME A UN TAUREAU, LE TROISIEME AVAIT COMME UN VISAGE D'HOMME ET LE QUATRIEME ETAIT SEMBLABLE A UN AIGLE QUI VOLE. ILS NE SE DONNAIENT DE REPOS NI LE JOUR NI LA NUIT, DISANT: SAINT! SAINT! SAINT, LE SEIGNEUR, DIEU DE L'UNIVERS CELUI QUI ETAIT, QUI EST ET QUI VIENT.

*A sign at the Abbeye Saint-Pierre de Moissac*

*The tympanum of the southwest portico*

*Bas-relief of the rich man and Lazarus: Abbaye Saint-Pierre de Moissac*

What captured my attention in the tympanum were the eight rosettes, on which stood the twenty-four music-playing elders surrounding the Christ. Here we have the Christ with the book, or word, and the musicians with their instrument sending the tones into the world, and these eight rosettes showing the activity of the sound in matter, the way a drop falling into water forms a shape. Here it reminded me of the "drop picture" research of Theodore Schwenk.

> The experimental technique is based upon the following principle: The water specimen under study is contained as a thin layer in a level, round glass bowl, and is then brought into motion by a number of drops of distilled water falling into it at regular intervals, in the course of which currents are set in motion. A homogeneous solution of the water sample, to which glycerin has been added, is used as a neutral, inert schlieren agent. The patterns formed are rendered visible by means of a schlierenoptical device adapted from Topler by Theodor Schwenk, and these are photographically recorded....
>
> The flow pattern that comes into being in the sample after a drop has fallen into it remains almost unchanged for the few seconds before the next drop enters. The pattern changes somewhat with the entrance of every further drop, so that the characteristic changes are continually occurring.... Single delicate vortices radiate in all directions from the center of the bowl where the drops strike; they form a *rosette that develops from drop to drop as the leaflike vortices spread out, multiply and undergo differentiation*....
>
> What is at work here is not some anonymous force or other; individual beings of various hierarchies and elemental kingdoms are involved and active in them (as said by Rudolf Steiner)....
>
> These flow-forms tell us in a physically perceptible way about the cosmic origin of the formative forces, confirming Steiner's indications that fluid substances such as water "stand under the influence of the whole planetary system," and that the forces of various planets "take effect from the part of the heavens where these planets stand."*

---

\* Schwenk, *Water: The Element of Life*, pp. 196, 232.

Those sculptors were true masters and could still feel the *power of the word*. How better to portray this than the Christ, the four beasts, the book, the word, twenty-four elders with instruments, music, and tones—all sitting on eight rosettes and formed in stones.

The hundreds of columns in the cloister also showed a wealth of such lively forms: water, quiet waves, stormy waves, various rosettes—flower forms reminding us of a world livelier than our mineral-earthly world with its physical laws. Here was sculpted the world of the life forces, or etheric world, teeming with life, where these biblical stories have their home—the world of eternal life with different laws. It is the world which defies our earthly laws, where healing comes from. The sculptors portrayed that world using as many symbols as they could find; I noticed only a few of them. Isn't this why pilgrims are on the road—to glimpse that world?

༄

I sat with some pilgrims for refreshments and then headed for my basement bed along with six others, but not before a stroll in the surrounding gardens. Everyone had gone to bed; the Zen meditants were also calling it a day. Back in my basement, there were more pilgrims I had not met. Sleeping near my bunk was a middle-aged man with a golden-cross earring.

The next morning, I had a quiet breakfast with some of the new pilgrims, one of whom was a blue-eyed, middle-aged, slightly heavyset woman from Québec. She was traveling with a nineteen-year-old Indonesian-Dutch man from Holland, and the three of us shared stories. They had met on the path and were enjoying the Camino.

After breakfast I looked at all the shoes beside the meditation hall, put on *my* shoes, and started my walking meditation. Heading out, I joined several pilgrims on the road looking for the way out of the city. It was easy; we had to walk by the canal along the Tarn River. It was a quiet walk and flat for a change. We were not used to such easy terrain. I read somewhere that, because of the ups and downs one walks every day, if you walk from Le Puy to Santiago (I had already done the second part) it is the equivalent of climbing Mount Everest twice. Up the mountain, down the mountain, up again, and so forth, all day, every day.

I walked with a French woman and, after a few hours, we decided to go off the path. We found a small restaurant and I grabbed a cup of coffee and pastries. The inn was very cozy and was preparing for its Sunday customers. The woman decided to stay and eat a steak and *pommes frites* lunch, but I went on. For me, it was too early to eat so much food.

I found the path again and crossed over a river that merged with the larger Garonne River. To my unpleasant surprise, two looming, gargantuan chimneys were spewing steam in the distance on my right. Nuclear energy is big in France. They do not have their *"grosses têtes"* engineers for nothing. The towers—new "cathedrals" of the West—spoiled the scenery, and one could not avoid the view; it would probably be in sight for at least two days. I thought of hitching a ride, because I did not want to be so close to these enormous centers of uncanny power. Nevertheless, I walked on, while two pretty, young German women passed by, going in the opposite direction with handsome horses and a lively dog. They seemed to be having fun, which was not so easy for me.

The Parisian watercolor painter and his wife were also walking. I passed them, as well as fields, farms, meadows, hamlets, a lonely quiet church, and then a quiet bridge over the Garonne that led to a lovely, hilltop town. It was an arduous climb under the scorching sun. The town had a great square with a few artisans selling their goods. I bought a large bottle of cider and some vegetables. Then I sat under a well-restored, circular, medieval market hall surrounded by a square with arcaded shops. Many people were having lunch there. I talked with a young couple with two children; they wanted to know if it was difficult to walk like this. I replied, "No, just get your backpack and head out. It would be great for your two kids." Then I headed out again in the unbearably hot weather; it must have been over ninety degrees. I am not at my best in great heat; I prefer cold weather. I looked at my guidebook and decided to stop at all the villages along the way regardless of how long it would take. It was simply too hot to keep walking without the breaks.

I discovered a little restaurant packed with Sunday outers in a small village off the path. I ordered lemonade with cassis and ice and watched the old folks and families eating while they watched me. Then as I was sipping my drink, who should appear at the door? A big head peeked inside—a huge donkey with his owner, a pilgrim in his late seventies. He got some water for the poor old soul and then continued on. It was love at first sight for the restaurant customers.

After that refreshing stop, I walked another three miles to the *gîte* in St. Antoine.

> This village takes its name from the religious order of the Antonins, who set up a hospital (the present chateau) for people suffering from ergotism (a disease known as "St Anthony's fire"), which was very prevalent in the Middle Ages. It was contracted by consuming cereal products (such as rye bread) contaminated by the ergot fungus, and resulted in a gangrenous condition of the hands and feet.[*]

As I entered the old town, I saw a young man of about nineteen sprawled on the sidewalk in the heat—a long-haired, bearded pilgrim, lying with his head on his backpack. I greeted him and asked him what he was doing out in the heat. He told me he was waiting for someone and that he was from Belgium. I told him, "Why don't you go into the *gîte*? It would be more comfortable." Seeing that he was so young and traveling with a tent, I realized that he probably did not have much money. He reminded me of my son, who often travels with no money just for the fun of it. I told him that I would pay for his bed if he did not have any funds.

---

[*]   Raju, *The Way of St. James, France*, p. 111.

The *gîte* was quiet—just a place to sleep, without much atmosphere. The woman keeping it was providing beds just for money. No books, no conversation—just sleep. I was instructed to eat in the kitchen, as the dining room was only for the pilgrims who wanted to eat *her* supper and breakfast.

I told her that there was a young man outside and that if he came to her *gîte* I would pay for his bed. I couldn't leave him out in the heat. She understood; she gave him a bed and did not charge him much. We had supper together and he slept with us that night. He was walking all the way to Santiago, sleeping at night in his tent.

Most of the pilgrims were interested in walking as fast as possible to the next stop so that they could get the best beds. They did not seem to enjoy the journey—its villages, scenery, people, sights, and food. The house was full of people hurrying—hurrying to nowhere. Most of these pilgrims had gone on the same route I had, but had not stopped so often. I had been getting upset because those pilgrims always arrived before I did and had more time to relax; they always looked at the last arrivals with disdain and often made fun. I wanted to tell them, "Forget your pride. Keep your own pace. Let others run."

The man with the donkey was also staying there. His donkey was happy to be eating wonderful green grass and was making a lot of noise. He was a great distraction for everyone.

I walked to the old church, which was quiet and cool; this was pinned on the door:

> Je marcherai sous le soleil trop lourd,
> sous la pluie à verse ou dans la tornade.
> En marchant, le soleil réchauffera mon cœur de pierre;
> la pluie fera de mes déserts un jardin.
> A force d'user mes chaussures,
> j'userai mes habitudes.
> Je marcherai et ma marche sera démarche.
> J'irais moins au bout de la route
> qu'au bout de moi-même.

*Je serai pèlerin.*
*Je ne partirai pas seulement en voyage.*
*Je deviendrai moi-même un voyage, un pèlerinage.*
—Jean Debruynne

I will walk under the sun too heavy,
under the pouring rain, in storms.
While walking, the sun will warm up
my heart of stone;
the rain will turn my desires into a garden.
By wearing out my shoes
I will use up my habits.
I will walk, and my walk will become initiative.
I will reach the end of the road
less than the center of myself.
I will be a pilgrim.
I will not only go on travels.
I will become myself a journey, a pilgrimage.

I hoped that many other pilgrims would read this.

I was happy to leave our quarters. The whole new gang left with the donkey and his pilgrim master, and we had to prod the donkey along by touching him on his rump so that he would move along. The owner said that sometimes he would cover only ten miles or less, because the donkey refused to continue. It was a hell of a lot of work. We all walked together, each taking turns encouraging the donkey to keep moving. We told jokes as we walked in the early-morning hours past farms and ponds.

Our group arrived in the hamlet of Flamarens, which had an old castle under renovation, with beautiful old stone walls and flowers. The castle seemed more refined than most architecture of the Middle Ages. We stopped to admire the elegant lines of the spacious, kingly residence and took a lot of pictures.

We were walking over rich humus, though still-calcareous, earth. Much of the garlic consumed by the French grows in this rich farm country. Garlic was introduced here by Crusaders returning to southern France.

One finds excellent cooking in the Gascogne region, and plums form the basis of its rich Armagnac *eau-de-vie,* which also includes wheat and corn, which had been imported from the Americas in the 1600s. Corn replaced millet, which had been cultivated in that area since antiquity.*

> This vast territory between the Atlantic Ocean, the Mediterranean, and the Pyrenees took the name of Vazconia, which became in turn *Gascogne.* By the way, it is the Vascons, which refused to be dominated by the Carolingians kings, who united their forces with the Sarrazins and murdered in Roncevaux Charlemagne's Frankish army whose military chief was the famous Roland....
>
> The French province extending north of the Pyrenees on the shores of the Atlantic is called *Gascogne* or *Guascogne,* which again means "land of the Basques." Thus we arrive almost as far as Bordeaux in reconstructing the ancient home of the oldest nation of Europe. This conclusion, drawn from linguistics facts, is easily supported by archaeological evidence: the Franco-Cantabrian caves, which, like the American Indian *kivas* and many caves in early epochs, were mystery centers and religious gathering places. More geographical evidence is offered by the name of the *Biscayan* or *Viscayan Gulf,* marking the extension of the territory once peopled by the Basques up to the northwestern tip of Brittany and France, to the English Channel.**

The countryside was peaceful (not always the case), with many meadows and large farms. We walked through many miles of farmland and saw numerous abandoned *châteaus.* I especially liked a one that had only an old tower standing among ancient stone piles on a little hill, surrounded by an expanse of rich fields. Long ago, it must have seen more than a few visiting troubadours.

The whole gang, including the donkey, stopped in a refreshing town called Castet-Arrouy, where we all went shopping for lunch. I

---

\* See TopoGuides, *Sentier vers Saint-Jacques-de-Compostelle via Le Puy,* pp.24–25.

\*\* Wadler, *One Language,* pp. 40–41.

ate by a churchyard, not far from an old Gallo-Roman well. Afterward, we all walked along the main road. It was another very hot day with little shade to linger under. I was so sweaty and dehydrated that I hitched a ride for a couple of miles, because I wanted to spend more time in the old city of Lectoure, where I could find a "hot bath"; it was either walk and get there very late or hitch a ride and enjoy the "spa" town. The decision was easy; my aching back needed the hot mineral baths. A tourist couple gave me a ride to the entrance of the old city. This important city had nine hospitals at one time. It was built on a hill and now dominates the scenery. I found the very welcoming *Gîte d'étape l'Etoile Occitane,* a health and beauty spa. It was started by a young woman who had traveled worldwide and wanted to help the pilgrims. It was youth-oriented, brightly painted, and looked similar to places I used to stay at in Katmandu or Ecuador rather than in France. We felt at home in these clean, sun-filled rooms, with a great library of magazines. In the evening, we prepared a communal supper for the gang. The donkey stayed at a farm down the road, and the donkey's owner was happy to rest. He slept next to my bunk and wore so much cologne that I couldn't sleep. The heavy scent wafted from his bunk and engulfed the whole room. Meanwhile, having arrived before everyone else, I had spent two or three hours at the spa swimming from one pool to the next with my new friends.

A group from a psychiatric center was having a day outing at the spa. They were a boisterous group, and one man was especially lively. I was told by the caretaker that the only thing the man wanted was to have blue eyes. He would sing Frank Sinatra songs to us in English. I told him that in his next life he would have blue eyes, so not to worry.

There were also some very sad looking women who were not handicapped but must have had very sorrowful lives. They had nothing physically wrong, but perhaps had nervous breakdowns, depression, or drug use. One of them looked like a former drugged-up farmer's wife. Another was a very pretty thirty-year-old who seemed to have no mind at all; she stared into the infinite with a vacuous look in her beautiful, crystal-clear, blue eyes. It may have taken a lot of drugs to achieve this. Her companion was just the opposite; she didn't stop talking. There were about twenty people exhibiting various mental challenges. We all enjoyed the hot waters until our skin started to resemble stewed prunes and it was time to leave.

As I sat there watching these suffering human beings, I was reminded again of the "Washing of the Feet" scene. My knowledge is to be put in the service of others who have sacrificed themselves so that I can learn. How much do I owe for my knowledge? How many beings have I stood on to acquire knowledge? This knowledge transforms itself into caring and selfless love for others who have sacrificed themselves so that I can know. It is extremely painful to know the price of freedom. When one can witness the birth of responsibility toward the other, the true meaning of the Christian message "Love thy neighbor" is revealed.

> When in dark and anxious hours
> Almost fails the heart in us;
> When by illness we are bowed
> And our soul is gnawed by fear;
> When we think how dearest loved ones
> Suffer under grief and care;
> When deep clouds our gaze are shrouding
> And no beam of hope shines through;
>
> Oh. Then God bends down unto us;
> Then to us his love draws near;
> Then we long for passage over;
> There his angel for us stands;
> Brings the cup of life renewing,
> Murmurs courage and heart to us,
> And we do not ask in vain
> When we pray for loved ones' rest.[*]

---

[*] Novalis, *Spiritual Songs*, p. 73.

With these somber thoughts by Novalis, I went for a walk around the medieval town of Lectoure—its fortress walk, old churches, ancient buildings, and delicious pastry shops. Our host had mentioned a Carmelite cloister for women that, to my amazement, was still functioning. I found the cloister tucked away and hidden on a side street. I entered the ancient cloister courtyard and rang the bell, wanting to visit their bookstore. After a while, a tiny, ancient nun came to my aid. She appeared to be a foot shorter than I am (5 feet, 2 inches). She was dressed in the traditional long, black habit with no hair showing—only white encircling her face. She was very kind and told me I could go inside the small chapel to attend evening prayer. I went in, and another older woman was there. Other than the two of us, it was deserted. Twelve of the cloistered Carmelites were singing, but they were separated from us by a large iron wall or gate through which we could see. There was not enough sunlight for us to see the sisters clearly; it had been specially designed this way, so that the sisters would always be in shadow. They looked at us from the side. It was truly an ancient sight; the women had abandoned their ordinary lives to live in seclusion, as it had been for hundreds of years.

It was a peaceful life, dedicated to prayer twenty-four hours a day, all year. The sisters did not see anyone and never left the cloister. They were indeed completely separated from our everyday life. It seems extremely tempting to join such a quiet life of prayer, away from the twenty-first century and its problems. Here was a little oasis of peace, contemplation, and a life dedicated to Christ. At the end, I left the little chapel and returned to the cloister. The old woman let me into the shop and I chatted with her, telling her that I was a pilgrim. She said one of their latest sisters had knocked at their door a while ago, saying, "Please, I need a place to stay in the name of God." She was from East Germany and walking to Compostela. Passing by, she decided to come to the cloister. She never left. The other Carmelite sisters are from all over the world, including Spain, Germany, France, Scotland, and Ireland. There were only twelve of them. I thought it would be great to live in such a huge place with only twelve other people.

The bookstore—one of my favorite kind of places—had a lot of intriguing books, and I bought a few. One was by Thérèse de Lisieux, the famous Carmelite sister and a favorite in their cloister. Here are some of endearing passages from her *Manuscrits autobiographiques, Sainte Therese de l'Enfant Jesus*. This passage is from a letter written by her mother describing her ninth and last child, Thérèse, born in 1873.

> Our dear little girls, Céline and Thérèse, are angels of blessing, good-natured angelic souls. Thérèse brings much joy, happiness, and glory to her sister Marie; it is unbelievable how proud she is of her. It is true that she comes up with extremely rare and wise statements for her very young age [she was 4], and she teaches Céline, who is twice her age. Céline was saying the other day, "How can you explain that the Good Lord can be in such a tiny wafer?" The little one replied, "It is not so astonishing because the good Lord is all powerful. But what does it mean that the good Lord is all powerful? It means that he can do whatever he wishes."\*

In this passage Thérèse had just had a premonition, a vision in which she saw her old, old dad, near death.

> Oh My lord. Why is it to me that God has chosen to give this Inner Light? Why has he shown to such a little child such stupendous things that she could not possibly understand, and if she could understand them, it would bring intense suffering and death. Why?... Here is one of these great mysteries that we will understand only when we are in Heaven and that will bring us eternal admiration."\*\*

---

\* Thérèse de Lisieux, *Sainte Thérèse de l'Enfant Jésus: Histoire d'une âme écrite par elle-même*, p. 38 (all tr. M-L. Valandro).

\*\* Ibid., p. 62.

Here, Thérèse is eight years old and living at "the Pensionnat" with her sister Céline:

> The poor little flower had been used to plunge her fragile, tender roots in a "chosen earth" made exactly for her, so it seems extremely hard to see oneself amid all kinds of flowers, having very rough and not so delicate roots, and to have to find in this very common ground the necessary nectar for her sustenance....
>
> The good Lord gave me the grace of having known the outside world just enough to hate it and to remove myself from it....
>
> One day, one of my teachers at school asked me what I was doing during my day off when I was alone. I answered her that I would go behind my bed in the empty space there, which was easy to close off with a curtain, and would think. She said, "But what do you think about?" "Oh, I think about the good Lord, about life, about eternity. *I am thinking.*" The good nun had a great laugh at my expense, and later she reminded me about the time when *I was thinking*, asking me if I still *thought*. I understand now that I was in deep prayer without knowing it and that even at that early age the good Lord was teaching me in secret.
>
> Because I was so small and weak, the good Lord was coming toward me and teaching me in secret all about his Love. Oh, if great minds and scientists who had spent their whole life in deep studies had come to examine or to question me, they would have been astonished to find out how much a child of fourteen could understand about all things, such as perfection and secrets, which all of their science could not discover, because to have such knowledge one must be poor in spirit.[*]

This is from a conversation between Thérèse and one of her older superior sisters about sharing her inner life. She was fifteen and recently cloistered:

> "My little one, it seems to me that you have nothing to say to your superiors." Thérèse replied, "Why, dear Mother Superior, do you say that?...' The sister said, "Because your soul is extremely *simple;*

---

[*] Ibid., pp. 65, 87, 89, 125.

but when you have become perfect, you will *be even simpler.* The nearer one comes to the Good Lord, the simpler we become." The good Mother Superior was right; however, the difficulty I had in opening up my soul, whereas it did come from my simplicity, was nevertheless a veritable martyrdom to share. However, I understand it now, because while remaining simple I can express my thoughts with enormous ease....

One night, after the death of Sister Geneviève, I had a very appeasing dream. I dreamed that she was writing her will, giving to each sister something that had belonged to her. When it came to my turn, I thought that I was going to receive nothing, because it seemed there was nothing left to give. But sitting herself up, she told me three times in a penetrating voice, "To you I give my *heart.*"[*]

Her memoirs also touch upon the serious topic of accepting such a young soul into a cloister. She had a very difficult time being accepted; she had to travel to Rome with her father to meet the pope and ask permission to enter the cloister. Here we see that entering the cloistered life was taken very seriously by Church authorities, who knew the dangers of such a life.

ΟΤΟ

I left the Cloister, leaving a bit of myself in there. Twelve women were praying for all of us all day, all week, all month, and every year for life, without interruption. I would in turn always send them some warm thoughts; every little bit helps.

The next morning we all packed up and had breakfast together in the sunny room. Then we all said good-bye to our charming host outside. It was a party in honor of the donkey, waiting there and ready to go. The old man had to get up at least an hour-and-a-half before the rest of us to fetch the donkey and put on the saddlebags, which hung on either side. The donkey was tied to a post by the *boulangerie,* giving

---

[*] Ibid., pp. 177, 196.

*Fellow pilgrims leaving the hostel in Lectoure*

out his loud "hee-haw, hee-haw," and waking up the whole neighborhood. It was still around 7:30 in the morning.

I had not looked at the map to get out of the city, so we went in a kind of procession, one couple, the donkey and his master, and myself. The donkey had to go over some stairs, which he managed, but then we got lost. I chose to go another way as the little group was arguing about which way to go. I went in the opposite direction, down along the fortress walls on a dirt path with three other French people, who had gotten the right directions. We crossed the river and climbed past meadows, forests, and old manors. I was alone again because of my numerous stops; the others had gone on ahead. I arrived in the town of Marsolan, a hilltop town with an old church. There used to be an ancient castle there, but nothing is left of it. The view of the surrounding hills is enchanting and quiet. It is a good place for a rest under shady trees.

After a while, I walked down into a valley, and after a few miles on the path a former commanderie appeared. This ancient pilgrimage path is dotted with numerous *commanderies des hospitalières de*

*Saint Jean de Jerusalem,* where pilgrims used to stay to receive free treatment when they were sick. This particular one is now a private home. St. John is everywhere on this path in France. We could not go a half a day without encountering a hospital built by the Knights Templar or by the St. John *Hospitalières.* It is no wonder the Cathars and Bonhommes, who loved St. John's Gospel, retreated to these remote places.

After crossing another little bridge I decided to walk up to the ancient town of La Romieu, taking the small, sinuous climbing road instead of the path. The other pilgrims did not take that road; they all bypassed this ancient hill town. It was a quiet, hot walk past old stone homes and vegetable gardens, old farms, green meadows, and forests. Then at last one could see the tall tower of La Romieu from a distance. *L'Arromieu* means "the pilgrim" in the Gascon language. It came from Rome—pilgrims walking to Rome.

> Among much that originated soon after the Crusaders won their first successes, we see the founding of the Order of the Knights Templar in 1119. Five French knights united under the leadership of Hugo de Payens, and at the holy place where the Mystery of Golgotha occurred they founded an order dedicated entirely to the Mystery of Golgotha.... In each moment of their lives they were to think that the blood coursing in their own veins did not belong to them but to their great spiritual mission. Whatever wealth they might acquire belonged to no single individual but only to the order....
>
> At the close of the thirteenth and beginning of the fourteenth century, when the Templar order—not the individual knights of the order—had attained great prestige and wealth through its activity and had spread over western Europe, we have a human personality ruling the West who can actually be said to have experienced in his soul a kind of inspiration through the moral, or the immoral power of gold.[*]

---

[*] Steiner, *Inner Impulses of Evolution,* pp. 111, 113.

This town of La Romieu became an ecclesiastical center with an abbey–cloister and a sumptuous palace which has left no trace except an enormous tower, when Arnaud d'Aux, born in La Romieu, became acquainted with very influential men such as his friend and cousin Bertrand de Got, the Bishop of Bordeaux, who would be named the future Pope Clement V by Phillip IV the Fair, King of France (1268-1314). As Bertrand de Got's personal helper, and later next in power after the Pope, Arnaud d'Aux, Bishop of Poitiers, built himself this residence. Pope Clement V trusted him with important delegations to England with King Edward, and with the king of France. From the English king who owned this area, he collected a lot of funds to build his little "empire" in La Romieu. He also had the most unfortunate task of presiding over the trials of the Templars and thereby, one would assume, acquired much more wealth.

> A highly gifted personality, Philip IV the Fair, who was equipped with an extraordinary degree of cunning and the most evil ahrimanic wisdom, had access to this inspiration through gold. Phillip IV, who reigned in France from 1285 to 1314, can really be said to have had a genius for avarice. He felt the instinctive urge to recognize nothing else in the world but what can be paid for with gold, and he was willing to concede power over gold to none but himself. He wished to bring forcibly under his control all the power that can be exercised through gold. This grew in him to be the immense passion that has become famous in history. When Pope Boniface forbade the French clergy to pay taxes to the state, this fact—in itself very important—led Philip IV to make a law forbidding anyone to take gold and silver out of France. All of it was to remain there, such was his will, and only he was to have control of it.... He sought to keep gold and silver for himself and gave a debased currency to his subjects and others. Uproar and resentment among the people could not prevent him from carrying out this policy, so that, when he made a last attempt to mix as little gold and silver as possible in the coinage, he had to flee, on the occasion of a popular riot, to the temple of the Knights Templar. Driven to do so by his own severe regulation, he'd had his

treasures deposited for safety with them. He was astounded to see how quickly the knights calmed the popular arising. At the same time, he was filled with fear because he had seen how great was the moral power of the Knights Templar over the people, and how little he, who was only inspired by gold, availed against them. The knights, too, had by this time acquired rich treasures, and were immensely wealthy, but according to their rules, they were obliged to place all their riches of the order in the service of spiritual activities and creative work....

Phillip the Fair undertook to bring the entire Church completely under his control, thereby making Church officials mere security for the kingly power in which gold ruled. He then caused the removal of the Pope to Avignon [1309–1377].... Pope Clement V, former bishop of Bordeaux, resided in Avignon and was a tool completely in the hands of Philip the Fair. Gradually, under the activity of Philip's powerful will, he had reached the point of having no longer a will of his own but used his ecclesiastical power only to serve Philip IV, carrying out all that he desired. Philip was filled with a passionate desire to make himself master of all the wealth available at the time....

Plots were made, instigated by Philip IV, together with his vassals who had been summoned to make investigations against the knights. Although they were innocent, they were accused of every imaginable vice. One day in France, they were suddenly attacked and thrown into prison. During their confinement their treasures were seized....

It is one of the saddest chapters of human history, but one that can be understood only if one sees clearly that, behind the veil of what is related in history, are active forces, and that human life is truly a battlefield....

Thus it came about that Philip the Fair, Philip IV of France, was able to succeed in convincing his vassal, Pope Clement V—it was not difficult—that the knights had committed the most shameful crimes, that they were the most unchristian heretics. All this the pope sanctioned with his benediction. Fifty-four knights, including Jacques de Molay, were burned at the stake. Shortly afterward in other European countries—in England,

Spain, then right into Central Europe and Italy—action was also taken against them....

Humanity was not yet ripe to receive the impulse of wisdom, beauty, and strength in the way the knights desired....

But what lived and worked in the Knights Templars could not be eradicated....

What now came from the souls of the knights who had been murdered in this pitiful way and who, before their deaths by burning, had to undergo the most frightful experiences that anyone can suffer, was to become for many others a principle of inspiration. Powerful impulses were to flow down in humanity.... The cosmic wisdom that these Knights Templars possessed has entered many souls....

So it continues.... The wisdom lives on that could only enter the world amid sufferings, tortures, persecutions, and the most frightful offences. Nevertheless it lives on in spiritual form.*

Philip the Fair died November 29, 1314. His sons have left a bad aura in the history of France. The wife of his eldest son, King Louis X, was imprisoned and strangled by order of her husband, leaving Louis X free to marry Clemence d'Anjou, who gave birth to a son who died a few days later. Louis X died at age twenty-seven. King Philip V (Philip the Fair's second son) also had his wife imprisoned, and she spent the rest of her life in the Tower of Nesle facing the Louvre. Philip V died of dysentery at age twenty-nine. Philip the Fair's third son, King Charles IV, had his wife imprisoned at the Chateau-Gaillard after the Pope annulled her marriage, and she ended her days at Abbaye de Monbuisson. King Charles IV then married Marie of Luxembourg, who died giving birth to a short-lived son. Charles IV died at thirty-four, leaving three daughters and his eighteen-year-old third wife, who also died very young.**

Thus ended the sorrowful fate of Philip the Fair's sons and Kings of France. In history, this episode is known as the "battle of the

---

\*    Ibid., pp. 111–122.

\*\*   Wenzler, *Mémento des rois de France*, pp. 104–112 (tr. M-L. Valandro).

daughters-in-law" or the *Tour de Nesle* affair (so named for the prison tower). Philip the Fair's love of gold spread an evil spell over his own sons and a thick fog of unrest over the whole kingdom, as we see from history. Because of the chaos and the economic crisis emerging from the removal of the stable banking system of the Templars, France experienced famine, revolts, and violent repression of the Jews—all heralding the Hundred Year's War and the bubonic plague, which would kill half of Europe's population.

Philip the Fair was consumed by his greed for gold; this is a fact. Recently, the Vatican has published many papers about the trials of heretics in a book, where it is clear that the Pope was only doing Philip the Fair's *will*. Here this quote of Rudolf Steiner is highly relevant, especially nowadays.

> About no other period in evolution could we say, with regard to the inner necessities of evolution, that *clarity* of thinking is just as essential as eating and drinking are to the maintenance of physical life.... Previous times enjoyed a heritage from the days when spirituality pervaded the more atavistic inner life of human beings. Now, for the first time, we must actively *strive for spirituality*—if we desire it....
>
> In their souls, human beings *increasingly resemble their thoughts*—what people consider knowledge. This will seem strange to modern minds, but is nevertheless true.... To regard Darwinism as the only valid view of the world, to believe the only possible truth to be that human beings descended from animals—repeatedly thinking, *I descend from the animals; I descend entirely from forces that produce the animals*—such thoughts, today, tend to make the soul resemble its self-image. This is an important matter. When the body is left behind, the soul is confronted with the sorry fate of perceiving its resemblance to its own thought.
>
> All that we need is compassion for our fellow human beings, who need [anthroposophic Spiritual Science] because these thoughts are creative powers in the life of the soul; it is ordained that, *in the future, what human beings consider themselves to be they will become*.... The Gods were bound to make it possible

for human beings to become what they make of themselves....
Thoughts will gradually have to be understood as a concretely
real force of the soul, not merely to be the miserable abstraction
produced so proudly by the modern age. People living in earlier
times were still linked, by an ancient heritage, with the spiritual
world. Although for many centuries now, atavistic clairvoyance
has almost entirely ebbed away, this heritage still lives in the
feeling and in the will. But the time has come when everything
that is *conscious* must become a real power....

Thoughts in our age are destined to become powers in more
sense than one. They work as powers of thoughts as such, so that
after death the soul assumes an increasingly stronger likeness to
what, in the body, it imagines itself to be.*

❦

After a long climb in the heat and arriving in La Romieu, I was ready for a rest but instead went to the tourist office. I was the last one to visit the abbey-church museum before closing, so I wandered through the ancient walls alone. The ancient church was silent; the abbey was "silence in stones," cool and quiet under the arches leading to a courtyard; there was only silence. The sumptuous castle was gone, and the church was empty except for a dubious couple. The abbey was also empty. It was an enormous compound for such a tiny hamlet. The church had a kind of tower attached to it, and one wondered whether it was a church or a palace; it seems the architect could not decide. It was more a fortified castle than a church. Perhaps the famous bishop needed protection.

I exited the large abbey as they were closing the doors and sat in the shade of a tree near the church. I ate a lunch of what was left in my backpack—bread, cheese, ham, dates, pastries, and juice; I didn't want to carry it further. I met another French pilgrim, Yolande, and we chatted while enjoying our well-earned half day off. Then we decided to move to the large town square with arcaded shops on one side. We

---

\* Steiner, *The Archangel Micheal*, pp. 69–74.

sat at a café, sipped coffee in the cool shade, and exchanged stories for two hours while the sun blazed. As we were talking we heard the familiar sound, "Hee-haw, hee-haw"—our friends had arrived. The old man hitched the donkey at the door of the Mairie and came to have lunch at a table near us. The donkey kept making noise, and all of a sudden someone came to the old man and told him to "move that damn beast that was soiling the steps of the 'sacred Mairie.'" The old man trudged along and moved his beloved donkey down the road where more amiable companions would not mind his presence. I was glad I was not staying in this very unsympathetic town.

At our table, we kept talking while being entertained with all the "donkey business." Things had gotten back to normal; the old man enjoyed his well-earned lunch, and his beloved donkey was happily munching on grass in a nearby, friendly garden. The donkey, with his enormous ears, was truly teaching us some lessons.

> How should we think of the relationship between human beings and animals? The theory that people descended from the apes is like saying that perfect arises from imperfect. They don't necessarily descend from each other at all; they could be brothers with the same father. One evolved, and the other devolved. This is also the way we can view the relationship between human beings and apes. In Atlantis, the human form was still apelike. In Lemuria, the soul took possession of a body that was even less perfected, and that body evolved. However, the apelike forms have degenerated partly to become the present-day apes. Thus, apes are degenerated corporal brothers of humankind. The human race branched during the Atlantean epoch; one branch evolved into modern human beings and the other devolved into today's apes. Likewise, all the animals that live around us are human beings who were expelled and degenerated. The ascent of beings is not possible unless other beings sacrifice themselves. The higher expels the lower so that it can become still higher. Later on, the expelled ones are compensated.*

---

\*   Steiner, "Theosophy and the Gospel of St. John," p. 24 (unpublished).

It was time to leave, because I would have another long afternoon—a seven-mile walk to the next larger city of Condom. As I left the town, the old man was busy entertaining several older female tourists who *just loved* the donkey. I wondered if he was wearing his cologne.

I decided again to follow the road; otherwise I would have had an additional twelve miles to walk, which would have been too much—though, in retrospect, a lot better. The road went through hills and past many farms, forests, little rivers, and old villages. In one such village, an English woman emerging from her old farmhouse gave me water from her beautiful spring on the roadside. I also had pleasant conversations with local farmers on their tractors, and asked for directions. The quiet road soon joined the hell of a large highway. There was no room for pedestrians, and one had to run along the road while watching for traffic to avoid being hit. It was stupid of me to choose this road, and I was very nervous for the rest of the afternoon.

I finally arrived in the city and—exhausted from my crazy adventure—sat on a bench at the city entrance to collect my wits. I found the next communal *gîte*. It was a large, monastery-like, and deserted, but I was too tired to find something else. I took a shower in the filthy bathrooms and then went out for supper. In a narrow alley, I walked to a little Italian restaurant full of people, and the owner found me a tiny table. Other pilgrims came and we enjoyed a great dinner under the stars until it was time to hit the sack.

At around 11:00 o'clock, an older couple came into the room where another pilgrim and I were sound asleep. With no warning, they turned on the light and woke everyone. They had absolutely no remorse and no concept of disturbing others; I was furious and I told them so. They had sneaked in without paying because it was late and there was no one there to collect payment. The couple appeared quite affluent, and the next day they did not speak to any of us but kept to themselves. I had seen them in the church back in La Romieu and had wondered what they were doing there. They wore nice designer clothing, so I had thought to myself that they might be the kind of people who were on the lookout for antiques to take or buy. Old statues, relics—anything is game. Now they were in my bunkroom. I do have a great imagination.

The next morning I awoke a bit late because I had to do some banking around 9:00 o'clock. So I visited the cathedral of Saint Pierre and went shopping for breakfast. After my quiet breakfast, I visited four banks, none of which could exchange my dollars for euros. *"Madame, c'est trop compliqée. Mon ordinateur ne me permet pas de faire cette transaction."* Great. So I continued on, having wasted my time. By this time, all the pilgrims I knew had left to go on toward Santiago. I lost track of the donkey and the old man.

I headed out of the city, crossed the bridge, and walked on through the suburbs, which lasted quite a while. The path went through more farming hills, forests, quiet woods, mustard-green fields, and freshly plowed meadows. One could see the hills in the distance and the vast sky. I met another pilgrim, this one from Pierrelatte, in the Rhône valley, where one of my aunts lives. He had retired from working in an atomic energy plant. He was about forty years old and seemed a bit different from the other pilgrims. Prior to leaving on his pilgrimage, he had received a letter from his local bishop saying he was a "formal" pilgrim. He was very Catholic. Most pilgrims I have met are not religious at all. He seemed a bit temperamental but became a bit more talkative as we walked on. Then he went on ahead, as I had my usual stops.

After about four miles from Condom, I took another path to visit a village fortress completely enclosed within the tall walls of Larressingle. It used to belong to the bishops of Condom and dates from the 1200s. No one was there, since it was so early. I wandered around the well-preserved fortress. The little chapel was cozy and suited to a prayerful mood. It was a secluded little compound, built for the Church clergy. I had imagined that it might have belonged to some fancy count and his educated lady who would entertain troubadours, but none of that. Forget my fanciful ideas.

As I left the fortress, a huge tourist bus pulled in. I was safe and they wondered what I was doing with my enormous backpack in the middle of Nowhere, France. I am sure the guide must have told them about us pilgrims. Because we travel mostly on hidden paths, tourists would not see us most of the time. They saw us only in larger towns, but without our backpacks. Also, we leave too early in the morning for tourists to see us depart. They sleep late.

The road wound quietly down to the River and crossed an old, abandoned bridge. Further along was another castle, belonging to former Marquis de Montespan, who exiled himself here after Louis XIV stole his wife, Françoise-Athénaïs, Marquise de Montespan (1640–1707), as one of his many favorite lovers and the mother of the two "royal children" acknowledged by the king. French history becomes enormously interesting when one walks through it. What else will I find by walking the old pilgrim roads of France?

The soft path crossed more hilly farmland surrounded by stone walls and shady trees. After a couple of hours I came upon a farm *gîte* that looked inviting, so I stopped to have a look. A woman had renovated the whole place with great taste. It was a pilgrims' spot with a terrace where one could linger and look at the sunrises or sunsets, so I gladly stopped to enjoy the gardens and sculptures. She was a great cook and served me a reasonably priced lunch of eggs, spinach, salad, and coffee. I would not starve today. The next town was another couple of hours away.

Then I climbed to the old bastide of Montreal-du-Gers. It is built on a former Celtic rocky peak and is one of the oldest fortress cities of this area, dating back to 1289. I walked to the town-center square with its arcaded shops, cafés, and an old church. It felt good to take off my backpack and sit to have another coffee break; it was still very warm. I enjoyed the warmth and the protected atmosphere of the old city. This area has seen numerous wars, because the king of England, who owned the Quercy-Lomagne, and the king of France were always fighting over territories. Here the people from the surrounding towns were gathered under one roof, so to speak. More than 350 such fortress towns and cities were built in the Middle Ages, and many are still standing. One could close the doors, and invading soldiers could not enter unless they laid siege to the fortress, which happened all through the Middle Ages. Meanwhile, the sun was shining, and there were a few tourists meandering through the quiet, narrow, and ancient streets. I visited the old church and then headed out. A small street took me out of the fortress and descended very sharply down a cliff to the river Gers.

I went on and again decided to visit another famous site a couple of miles away, and spend the night at the nearby Gîte Ferme du Soleil. More farm fields and vineyards were appearing. The *gîte* was a working farm, and the farmer's wife was happy to entertain pilgrims and to share her many stories. She gave me a room all to myself in a comfortable trailer, which I enjoyed; I never thought a trailer could be so great. There was a shower and everything, as well as a night-light for reading. I left my backpack and walked to an ancient Roman archeological site. In the past week, my mind had felt like a rubber ball being bounced around in history. From 25,000 years ago in the caves up to now and everything in between—how amazing human beings are! It is not for nothing that this path is called *Via Podiensis,* meaning "path of power," especially when you truly immerse yourself in it, which is difficult to avoid. Perhaps I was getting a little too much of it and needed to rest.

I followed a path behind the farmhouse and past a messy unused cow barn, with dirty stuff everywhere, lots of old chemical barrels, and bad-smelling barns—not a very promising farm. I was a bit disgusted to see such a terribly run operation, poisoning the land for miles around. A large compound still being excavated came into view. It was evening by then, so there were not many tourists around. I saw the previous night's couple who had turned on the dorm lights late at night. They did not even say hello.

This place is called "La villa gallo-romaine de Séviac," and I loved it. It was a total change from the dark spaces of the barbaric medieval castles. What happened? Here are vast spaces, open to the sun, beautiful mosaic rugs on the floors and walls of the residences, and fantastic baths with the most amazing roman engineering system for hot water, called *hypocaust*. It was built on a hill for sunshine, better water circulation, and dryness, which was what their engineers had wanted. Of course, the slaves kept the place running, with a separate wood-burning system for warming the water in the large pools. It showed the life of wealthy Romans in their *maisons de campagne* not far from the city of Eauze (ten miles away), where they probably worked as politicians. We see the influence of the warm climate of Italy transplanted here. Moreover, with the abundance of castles in the area, we see perhaps the influence of the Nordic people—the cold, the fighting spirit—in contrast to the Roman civil life. In this villa there are several large gathering rooms for entertaining and of course large pools, which I am sure were full of friends, leisurely enjoying one another's company and good food, massages, and body oils. Perhaps that is why we like the life in Italy; it is more civil. I walked through the spacious property and thought we could still learn from this warm-water system and their baths. I cannot go to a place with hot baths without stepping into them.

> The operation of one's properties allowed the owner free time to lead a golden life with much idleness, as we can see from a description by Paulin de Pella, who in AD 45 at eighty years of age nostalgically remembered his life at [his villa] in Aquitaine: "I wanted a practical house with very spacious apartments—one next to the other—arranged for the needs of the different seasons, with a well furbished brilliant table, lots of furniture for different uses, beautifully handmade silverware, and artists' works of various styles. My mind was lulled by the customary do-nothing lifestyle, the familiar rests, and the many advantages this home provided."\*

The Romans lived well, the rich ones that is, and ate well; they had wines from Gaza, oils from Africa, oysters from the coasts, and salted fish from Spain or Africa. They also enjoyed the arts, artistic objects

---

\* From Fages and Gugole, *Visiter la villa de Séviac* (tr. M-L. Valandro).

in ivory or wood, silver dishes, and marble and bronze sculptures. In this domain there was weaving, pottery, ceramics, and so on, making products that could be sold in the markets.

My head was spinning from one era to another. Such different minds, cultures, interests, and impulses were all meeting here in this very important area of Europe. No wonder there was bloodshed for thousands of years. Africa and the Middle East were meeting the German Goths and the Normands. There did not seem to be any continuous thread to follow. Influences came from all directions, making it hard to grasp what was what.

> The Roman world, which the Christian impulse followed in its greatest westward development, was permeated in its spiritual understanding with an inclination, a fondness, for the abstract. The Romans tended to translate perceptions, observations, and insights into abstract concepts. However, the Roman world was actually decaying and falling apart as Christianity spread gradually toward the west. In addition, the northern people were pushing from the eastern part of Europe into the west and south....
>
> Entirely different destinies would have befallen Christianity—it would have become entirely rigidified—had not the northern people come pushing into the west and the south. Those northern people brought with them their own natural talent, a predisposition entirely different from that of the southern people, the Greeks and the Romans.... Among the earlier Romans, and even more among the earlier Greeks, there were always those from the mass of people who developed themselves, passing through initiation and learning to see in the spiritual world. Such vision, in its last phase, is preserved in the theology of Dionysius the Areopagite.... The whole tendency of the older theological mood predisposed the soul to see the events in the world *inwardly*.... First to see the spiritual and then to admit to oneself that the sensory world can be seen only if one starts from the spiritual....
>
> To begin with, however, the people coming from the north had nothing of this older theological drive that, as I said, was so strong in the Greeks. The natural abilities of the Gothic people, the

Germanic, did not allow such a theological mood to arise directly and unmediated in the soul.... Those people were themselves still at an earlier, more primitive stage of human development. They—the Goths, Lombards (Germanic tribes, Anglo-Saxons, the Franks, and so on)—still brought some of the old clairvoyance with them.... The northern people did not see the spiritual world from the *inside*, so to speak, as the southern people had. The northerners saw the spiritual world from the *outside*....

What does it mean to say that those peoples saw the spiritual world from the *outside*? Say, for example, that they saw a brave man die in battle. The life, which they saw in this man spiritually from the *outside*, was not an end for them. With his death, they could follow him (still from *outside*, spiritually speaking) on his path to the spiritual world. They could follow not only the way that man lived into the spiritual world, but also the ways he continued to be active on behalf of humankind on earth.[*]

This is the deeper aspect of South meets North. In the atmosphere when warm currents meet cold currents we get tornadoes and bad storms. It is no wonder this region is full of movement—tragic happenings and unsettled territories.

I walked around until it was time to return and eat supper at the farm *gîte*. I'd had a full day and my mind was beginning to feel a bit bruised from all the roman villas, abbeys, cloisters, bishops, palaces, medieval castles, fortress-towns, saints, cloistered nuns, cathedrals, pilgrim hospitals, old bridges, Templar hospitals, and caves. Perhaps it was time for a little rest and seeing nothing. But I had another hundred miles before reaching the Pyrenees (which one could see from here on a *very* clear day) and crossing into Spain. There, the biggest castle of them all awaited me: the "third" *castle of the Holy Grail*. But, since it is *invisible*, I might just walk right through it.

I stepped into the communal dining room, where other pilgrims were awaiting supper. There were a couple of French men from Lyon, a

---

[*] Steiner, *The Mystery of the Trinity*, pp. 13–15.

Swiss woman, and an old couple from Burgundy. As we ate, I noticed the older couple had a very familiar accent when they spoke French. It was exactly the accent of my many French aunts and uncles scattered throughout parts of Burgundy, Corsica, the Alps, the South, and so on. It turned out that old couple lived in a little town near Montbard, which is a very special place to me. Moreover, one of the four knights who formed the original Knights Templars was Hugo de Montbard.

When I was young, between the ages of two and five, I used to visit my father's aunt and stay there for vacations. She would spoil me, and I have great recollections of spending time there. There was teatime, chocolate left on the stove every morning of Easter vacation, and exploration in her old attic, where I found old dolls, perambulators, and books. I would sleep in the bedroom of my aunt's daughter and read Bible stories she had lent to me. I was very young, but I could read already, and I lived into whatever I read. I still remember those biblical stories (which I didn't understand at all), and I could actually smell their atmosphere; they have remained in my mind to this day. I also remember wandering with my uncle in her vegetable garden and strawberry patch and being fascinated by the *Myosotis*—the tiny little blue flowers (forget-me-nots) that told me their secrets. The house was near a railroad and the large factory where my uncle worked. I wanted to follow the train tracks and just keep going. They were fascinating; if I could follow them until the very end, where would I be? I was especially fascinated by the abandoned areas of the garden, probably because of the elemental beings who were left undisturbed there.

Talking to the older woman here was like talking with my great-aunt. This couple was amazing; they were seventy-eight, and three years ago they had traveled the Camino on bicycles, from Vezelay Bourgogne all the way to Santiago on the Via Lemovicensis. They shared many stories. Now she could not walk well. He could still walk for a few hours at a time, so she went by car as he walked parts of the Camino.

Supper consisted of vegetable soup, *pâté* and *jambon*, pork, potatoes, rice, salad, cheese, ice cream puffs, red wine, after-dinner liqueur, and herb tea. Many great stories of the Camino were told around the table. This was not exactly a pilgrims' meal but a banquet. Then we all retired.

❧

In the morning, our host prepared a great breakfast and we all went on our way. It was quiet, and an early-morning fog surrounded the hills and farms. I walked on the road for a while, being careful because it was also a busy highway. After a few hours, I decided to hitch a ride; I did not want to walk twenty-five miles. I had to keep up the pace if I wanted to arrive in Jaca, Spain, on time to catch my flight back home, and I wanted to get to the main city and find a bank that would exchange my dollars. If I got there at lunchtime, the bank would be closed. So I got a ride for a couple of miles to the city of Eauze, and once again I could get no funds. I still had some Euros, which might be enough until the end of the trip. I just could not buy any more books and ship them home. That was extremely expensive.

Eauze was a large and lively city. I stopped, of course, at a pastry shop for French pastries; I had to get my fill before returning to the United States. On this trip, unlike my Spanish Camino trip the previous year, I was not starving. I did not look "skeletal" but, on the other hand, the lighter you are, the faster you walk.

I shared tea on a busy terrace with the couple I'd met two nights earlier. They had been with the gang and the donkey, but had gone their own way. The café owner had a special pilgrims' book, which I enjoyed reading and signing.

The pilgrims' path passed the house of Jeanne d'Albret (1528–1572). Now we can again deepen our knowledge of French history—not through the kings, but through the women. When women enter the picture it gets complicated. Perhaps that is why the historians tend to mention only the men. Jeanne d'Albret was an important figure in history, both because her mother was Marguerite de Navarre, a great writer, and because her son was King Henri IV.

Going back a bit further back in history, we find that King François I (1494–1547) was raised to be a king by his mother, Louise de Savoie. His sister was named Marguerite.

> Although Marguerite was first born of Charles d'Angouleme and Louise de Savoie, Marguerite de Navarre grew up in a household thoroughly dedicated to the formation of her younger brother François as the future king of France. Louise de Savoie's ambitions for her son began before birth, when she sought the counsel and intervention of François de Paola. The hermit and presumed miracle worker assured Louise not only that she would produce a male heir but that her son would become king of France....
>
> After her husband died prematurely in 1496, Louise had to strike a compromise with Louis d'Orleans to retain custody of her two children, since, at nineteen, she was under the minimum legal age for guardianship. He agreed to become honorary guardian of Marguerite and François, allowing Louise to remain with her children at Amboise.
>
> Since King Charles VIII had died childless in 1498 (his wife was Ann de Bretagne), his successor, King Louis XII, had still produced no heirs (his wife being the same Ann de Bretagne), and the education of young François took on added importance for those charged with his care. But Louise de Savoie saw to it that her older daughter was educated alongside François in French, Spanish, English, Hebrew, Latin, and some Italian and German, as well as philosophy, theology, literature, and history.
>
> This broad and egalitarian education surely contributed to the role that Marguerite would come to play in her brother's court after he ascended to the throne. François had become enamored of the "new learning" and with the lively renewal of art and architecture that he encountered during several visits to Italy. He invited to France such renowned painters as Leonardo Da Vinci and Andrea del Sarto and began the redecoration of numerous beautiful chateaux in the Loire valley, as well as of his crowning achievement, Fontainebleau.*

---

\*    Thysell, *The Pleasure of Discernment*, p. 6.

Marguerite's second husband was King Henri d'Albret of Navarre. She had a daughter, Jeanne d'Albret, whose house I had just walked past. But that is not the end of the story; there is much more. Marguerite's brother, King François I, of course, was given a wife. As we know, it was all about acquiring land, possessions, and so on, so the former king of France, Louis XII, had no sons but married off his daughter Claude, of course, to his "relative" François I, brother of Marguerite de Navarre.

Claude was perhaps a miracle child. Historically, she is known as *la bonne reine,* the good queen. Her health was fragile, she was lame and unattractive, but she gave the king seven children, one of whom would be King Henri II.

*La bonne reine* Claude's mother was Anne de Bretagne, who was very important because of her land holdings. She was made to marry Charles VIII in 1491. She was fourteen, and he was twenty-one. At fifteen, Anne de Bretagne gave him one son, who died at the age of three, and from the age of seventeen to twenty, she bore four children, all of whom were dead at birth. Her husband Charles VIII (the king who invaded Florence) then died by hitting his head on a low door lintel in the castle in Amboise.

After that, in 1499, she was made to marry again, this time to the king's cousin, the new king, Louis XII, one year after the previous failed birth and the death of her husband. Now twenty-one, she immediately gave birth to Claude, a lame, limping, poor child, and then at twenty-six another stillborn child. Again, at thirty-three, she bore yet another dead child, and at thirty-five her final stillborn child. Anne de Bretagne died two years later, leaving Claude, her only daughter, who was then fourteen years old; at fifteen, she married François I, the brother of Marguerite de Navarre, whose daughter was Jeanne d'Albret.

Looking at the life of that poor soul, one wonders today at such criminal, calculating, unthoughtful, and brutish treatment of a child bride. It is European history seen from the eyes of its women, both peasants and queens. This is just one example from 1,400 years of French and other European kings. Of course I am judging from the perspective of my twenty-first-century-female frame of mind.

> The emblem, crest, or symbol for Ann de Bretagne was the ermine, whose fur is used to make pure white coats. The crest for Claude de France was a swan. Those who mediate between the lofty being who guides humankind and the people are always associated with great individualities and are always known by the specific name "Swan," which denotes a particular stage of higher development.*

Of course, the Queen did not choose the emblem—it was done in earlier history. Nonetheless, there was still some truth behind the choice of these symbols. Claude de France being called "The Good Queen" also has a higher meaning. What is important here is that women were as highly developed as the men were, but women were far more hidden. Thus, it was much easier for them to accomplish a great deal. Reading about those women showed me how barbaric those times were. I should forget the history I was taught and rewrite history as seen through the eyes of those women martyrs. Of course, the kings also did as they were told by their fathers, uncles, ruling mothers, popes, caretakers, and so on.

Coming back to Jeanne d'Albret, daughter of Marguerite de Navarre, she had a son, Henry of Bourbon, who became King Henri IV in 1594, when he converted to Catholicism. Marguerite de Navarre, sister of François I (and married to the unfortunate Claude), had a grandson, Henri IV. Marguerite, because of her education, became a learned theologian and could converse with most thinkers of the time. One of her books was *Heptaméron,* published posthumously in 1558 (Boccaccio had written *Decameron*). She must have known her brother's wife, Claude, the poor, unattractive, limping Queen, and their children, as well as the stories of Claude's mother, Ann de Bretagne

---

\* Steiner, "Theosophy and the Gospel of St. John," p. 189 (unpublished transcript).

(discussed earlier), who had eight stillborn children as the wife of two kings. This extremely intelligent woman knew only too well the state of affairs for women, and her book, *Heptaméron*, makes for a very captivating story.

⁕

The group had gone to be healed by the waters at a spa much further south, at the foot of the Pyrenees. It is supposedly in the town of Sarrance, which I would walk through about ten days later.

> A novella collection, ostensibly modeled after Boccaccio's Decameron, the *Heptaméron* is a collection of seventy-two tales (the author died before completing the work) framed by the story of a group of travelers who are surprised by a flood in the Cauteret Mountains. Stranded in a monastery until a bridge can be repaired, they decide to relieve their boredom by listening each morning to meditations on Scripture by the eldest woman among them, Oisille, and by sharing stories with each other in the afternoons....
> 
> Pleasure is a central theme in the *Heptaméron,* and the tales and discussions wrestle with a proper understanding of sensual pleasure and its relationship to the spiritual life. In the prologue, the eldest of the *devisants,* Oisille, suggests that the group share her greatest pleasure, meditating on Scripture, but Hircan is more interested in a pastime agreeable to the body: "In that way we will spend the day happily": ... *et ainsy passerons la journée joyeusement.* Parlamente [Hircan's spouse] understands the kind of pleasure to which he is referring, however, and suggests that they not choose "pastimes that require only two participants" (*passetemps ou deuc seullement peuvent avoit part*)...; the agreement that Parlamente negotiates calls for them to begin the day as Oisille suggested, with Scripture readings and meditations, and then to retire to the meadows to share their "true stories." Thus, storytelling itself takes on an aspect of sensual pleasure as the compromised activity between spiritual and bodily delights. Juxtaposed with the morning scriptural meditations,

the sensual pleasure of storytelling becomes an integral part of the group's spiritual growth.

While the tales and discussions exhibit a wide diversity of opinion about the value of sensual pleasure, there is no doubt that the group's pleasure in hearing the Word increases each morning. In the prologue, Oisille is the vehicle through which the Word is heard. *"Oisille"* as diminutive of *oiseau*, or bird, suggests both the dove that served as a messenger of God to Noah when the flood had abated and the dove traditionally used in Christian imagery for the Holy Spirit.

As the *devisants* listen to the Word as interpreted by the Spirit, their regeneration as a community becomes obvious. For the first two days, they do not register any particular reaction to the scriptural readings or Oisille's lesson. But, on the third day, after Oisille has spent more than half an hour preparing her lesson, they are drawn to her words more than on the previous day, since "if it had not been for one of the monks coming to call them to mass, they would never have gone at all, for they were so deep in contemplation that they had not heard the bell...."

At the beginning of the fifth day, Oisille's sermons are compared with food. Her spiritual meal is "so nourishing that it sufficed to fortify both body and soul"... and the "whole company was very attentive"....

The sixth day marks a real turning point in the spiritual formation of this little community. Not only does Oisille get up early to prepare the reading, but the others also rush to begin their contemplation.... She moves from readings in Romans... to John, a book that is "full of Love".... They found this such sweet nourishment....

By day seven, the group is so enthused by the spirit that "they almost forgot their story-telling venture".... On day eight, Oisille keeps the group longer than normal, hoping to finish the Epistles of Saint John before having to leave.... In this final prologue to the existing text, the relationship between Oisille and the Spirit is named explicitly, "so well did she deliver the reading that the Holy Spirit, full of sweetness and love, seemed to be speaking through her mouth....

Clearly, the frame story suggests not only spiritual development among the *devisants* but also the presence of the Spirit in their midst...inflamed with this fire.*

Now we can read some of the stories that the group tells in the afternoon after having received their spiritual "nourishment through the Words." These stories show that none of the storytellers shies away from facing evil; all is told in its gruesome truth.

When Oisille decides to tell a story about the Franciscans to illustrate their hypocrisy and false teachings, she does so with the intent that the others not be taken by the hypocrisy of "men who consider themselves more religious than others.... Oisille cautions her hearers about deceptive teachers by using the biblical reference to Satan transforming himself into an angel of light to confuse others by the "outward appearance of sanctity and devotion"....

Oisille's tale concerns a man who respects the Cordeliers ["roped" monks] too much. He asks a friar for advice on whether he may lie with his wife without sin following her confinement for childbirth. The friar tells him sternly to abstain from this pleasure but the monk seeing an opportunity for himself, counsels the man the Church's "holy theology" has some provisions of mercy. He may, if he is secretive about it, go to his wife but not until after two o'clock in the morning so as not to disturb his wife's digestion. The friar, of course, goes secretly to his wife earlier than two o'clock and then flees before the man gets into bed with his wife. Realizing they have both been deceived by the friar, the husband names the evil deed and declares that it was "our fine father confessor who came to your bed and performed his good works!"....

The story of a poor man and a lady-in-waiting, Paulina. The two fall in love but are prevented from marrying by their different stations in life; their love for each other continues, but both finally

---

\* Thysell, *The Pleasure of Discernment*, pp. 10–59.

enter the religious life in the hope that their love of each other will be converted to love of God....

A young man named d'Avannes is "adopted" by a childless man, but d'Avannes falls in love with the man's wife. The love is reciprocal, but since the relationship is not possible, the young man goes off to live a sensual life with another woman who takes her marriage vows less seriously. Tired and sick from his wanton living, he returns to the honorable woman and her husband to be nursed back to health; the woman's health suffers, however, because of the tension she feels between love and honor. On her deathbed, she declares her love to the young man but maintains that her love of her husband and of God remain in her heart as well. The husband hears of her loves and her faithfulness from d'Avannes himself, but it only increases his love of his wife....

When a gentleman marries a much younger woman but ignores her [and has an affair with another woman] so much that she is led to have several affairs herself, she presents a defense that explicitly delineates the power between men and women in her culture: "Suppose that what each of us has done is weighed in the balance. There are you, a mature man with experience of the ways of the world, who ought to be able to tell right from wrong. There am I, young and with no experience of the violence and the power of love. You have a wife who wants to be with you, who admires you and loves you more than life itself. And what have I got? A husband who keeps out of my way as much as possible, who hates me and despises me more than if I were a chambermaid."

She also reminds him that the man she has taken as a lover is under bond to no one but that her husband's mistress is also the mistress of the King, his best friend. She challenges her husband about who is more deserving of punishment: she, the rejected young innocent wife who despaired of his love, or he, the experienced older man who betrays his young wife and his friend the King as well....

An Italian duke has his wife's servant girl put to death when he discovers that she has been carrying letters from his son to a young woman he does not want his son to marry.... The people we usually think of as being the greatest and most subtle speakers are punished by being made more stupid than the beasts.... In this tale a frozen lump of excrement is passed off as a "sugar loaf," in order to get revenge on the one who thinks he has received something free of charge. It of course begins to thaw, and the cheapskate becomes the object of much ridicule. The *devisants* laugh about the trick as well, but Oisille turns the discussion to language. There are some words, she says, that do not "smell," but there are other words, words referred to as disgusting, which have such an evil odor that the soul is far more disturbed than is the body smelling something like the sugar loaf in your story....

The very men who speak for the Church and require the language of vows to sanction marriage are themselves the ones who break those vows for others by their sexual liaisons with married women. She notes that the "doctors of the Church maintain that spiritual language is greater than any other.... Yet the "spiritual language" of Church rites does not itself hold up to scrutiny. The language of the confessional, as well, is tainted when "women who are rather quiet and timid derive much pleasure from sinning with a man they know can absolve them.*

In this little *aperçu* into the world of Marguerite de Navarre, we can see that she was trying with her enormous knowledge, scholarship, to help the stature and the lives of women as well as the lives of men in her days. She was a theologian—I would say a high priestess. She was "allowed" such writings because her brother, her protector, was the king. Her daughter Jeanne d' Albret was a Calvinist, which is why this city of Eauze did not care much for her or her son, the future king Henry IV. No need to mention that in France, only a man can become king, the famous *"lois salines,"* unlike their neighbors in England, Scotland, and Spain where a woman can also be a queen.

※

---

* Ibid., pp. 54-120.

It was time to get back on the road, I had more than fourteen miles to go before reaching Nogaro. The walk was quiet through rolling hills, farms, and vineyards, with signs of major pesticide use and huge advertisements for wine placed in the fields. I took a picture of a huge ad in the middle of a vineyard and a big tractor below the sign spraying chemicals on the growing grapes. I hurried by as fast as I could, not wanting to inhale this "growing cocktail."

The path then continued past some fisheries with large ponds built many centuries ago by the monks of various abbeys.

> Another reason for the inexorable and triumphal rise of the Cistercians was surely that the order had an army of specialists in agriculture and forestry and possessed well-equipped estates everywhere—the so-called granges. Their agriculture benefited from the unusually mild climate of the period. Food could be guaranteed, with the help of large fishponds. This may have moved many to enter the monasteries....
>
> The Cistercian order from the start prohibited donors from setting up an administration that might have influenced the monastery's development. The protectorate was either a *defensio specialis* with the king or a *defensio imperialis* with the emperor. Because Cistercians, at least according to their charter, could only settle in unpopulated seclusion, donors liked to employ them to colonize land: they cleared forests, drained swamps, and made great stretches of land arable for such tasks. Many conversations were required for such tasks. Frequently they were twice as numerous as the monks, sometimes more than three times....
>
> Sites on mountains, large rivers, or lakes, at the sea or on a small island were all scorned. A Cistercian monastery in a remote river valley, surrounded by hills, fields, forests, always offered the charm of peaceful, idyllic landscape, an inviting *locus amoenus* (delightful place) that offered a retreat from the world. The desire for isolation had its unpleasant side, however: when the Cistercians were granted a nearby village, they would ruthlessly drive away the farmers living there or, if necessary, use them as paid laborers.

Already in the twelfth century this caused some of the population to hate the white monk. The complaints multiplied.\*

⁕

There is not one part of these ancient pilgrim's paths that has not received the touch of the working monks.

A couple of miles later, leaving the large fishponds behind, Manciet came into view at the top of a hill. It was home to a former commanderie, with St. James Hospital and a chapel built by the Spanish Knights of Santiago. From there I walked with two pilgrims. I had last seen the former French nuclear reactor worker and the young Belgian lying on the ground on that very hot day. We walked chatting together over rugged terrain, muddy fields, and pretty scenery, enjoying nature. Then I walked a bit faster and went on ahead to visit the little église-hôpital Ste-Christie. I left my backpack by the road and went along the small path to the old site. It was abandoned with a beautiful small, quiet chapel. I went inside and sat looking at the peaceful setting, which had clearly been used by many pilgrims through the centuries. It used to belong to the Order of the Knights of Malta.

Two pilgrims came in and enjoyed the special atmosphere of the place. We all sat and meditated for a while, and then it was time to leave. I had not seen that the path continued on from the chapel, so I had to retrace my steps and retrieve my backpack, which took some time. The others waited patiently for me.

We walked out of the area and noticed a beautiful stone Maltese Cross as we left the commanderie. We walked up and down again through many fields, and finally arrived in Nogaro (from *nogarium*, meaning "walnut grove"). The *gîte communal* was just outside town, and we all settled there in the large, round bunkhouse. The others who had arrived earlier stayed in their own little rooms. The weather was changing fast—ominous clouds and dark indigo sky; rain was coming,

---

\* Schultz, *Great Monisteries of Europe*, pp. 39–40.

and the young Belgium pilgrim was going to be out in a tent. We told him don't bother; just come in and sleep here, no one will notice.

I went shopping for supper, and we all cooked a wonderful meal together, which we ate outside just before it started pouring. Then we had some tea and shared stories with other pilgrims who were walking with their cars; they walk, and a car follows with their belongings. The only bad thing is that they get to the *gîte* before us; they don't carry anything, so it is easier for them to arrive early and grab the beds. I could feel tension between the pilgrims with backpacks and the ones touring with all the comforts of home. The young Belgian sneaked into the *gîte* later when it began pouring.

The next morning, the bad weather was gone. I had to wait until 9:00 o'clock for the post office to open and send some heavy books home. So I went to visit the beautiful local church. Two older women dressed in black were setting up the church and bringing in beautiful flowers, and they turned on the light inside. The church St. Laurent has some of my favorite carvings on the pillars. They were very old, powerful symbols carved in stone that I could stare at for hours. It also has a strikingly simple tympanum that held my attention for quite a while. There used to be an old cloister next to the church, and a hospital for pilgrims was not far. I left my backpack in the church and went to the post office, where many familiar little delivery trucks awaited their daily tours. I had been accustomed to seeing them all over the country roads delivering mail. One of the mail carriers complained, in the usual French manner, that he was underpaid for such difficult work.

I walked out of the city on the small country road that went uphill, chatting with other women by the road, then looked back at the beautiful *"clocher"* from a distance.

I had taken the wrong road, misled by some workers, so I added at least three miles to the morning walk. I turned back and found the right road. It was a pleasant walk and the road was not busy. I could look at the changing architecture as I headed south; the homes looked different—some beautiful old brick, estates like farms or monasteries, many abandoned, and others being renovated. There were lots of stone and iron crucifixes along the road, which crossed a river, went into the woods, and passed more farms, fields, and vineyards. Then I entered a very thick forest. The forest was very still and quiet; it was easy to meditate and enjoy the seclusion. I stopped around lunchtime and sat in the middle of the forest on some mossy ground to eat.

I continued on the beautiful, dark mossy path, and a few minutes from where I had lunch I saw the young Belgian, the Québecquois woman, the young Dutch-Indonesian man, and a German girl sitting protected from the elements and having lunch in a little hut built for pilgrims. I thought if I had waited five minutes I would have had lunch with them. Nevertheless, I went on because we still had a whole afternoon of walking before reaching d'Aire-sur-l'Adour.

We went over more winding roads and crossed paths, farms, and fields. Then there was a little bench by a farm, where a farmer dressed in typical "working blue" came out of his house with his dogs. I asked him if this was the right direction. He said yes, and that there was a shortcut just down a bit that would save a couple of miles and was quieter. I said, *"Je vous remercie, au revoir."* So I went that way. The other way was not as enticing; it followed a former train track for most of the way. More fun to go through hamlets here and there and, of course, the wonderful chance of getting lost, which I was getting used to by now, having already gotten lost once that morning.

The road was indeed quiet and easy to follow. After a few hours, I arrived in a beautiful old hill town with a shady spot for rest. I asked a mail carrier if there was a place nearby for coffee, and he suggested a couple down the road who offered coffee to pilgrims. I saw their lovely little cottage with a pilgrims' shell (a scallop) in the front, so I knocked on the door. A sweet old woman answered the door and invited me in. I removed my dirty shoes and sat at their kitchen table. Her husband was there, too, but he'd had a stroke and could not walk. She prepared a nice cup of coffee and showed me postcards that pilgrims had sent to her. We chatted, and she said she liked to offer coffee to pilgrims and enjoyed meeting people from all over the world. I stayed for quite a while, enjoying their company, and then left. As soon as I left, the German girl arrived in the village, and I suggested that she get a cup of coffee. She went in and I continued on. I was very thankful for the hospitality.

France is not very enthusiastic about us pilgrims. Often one sees cars with drivers eyeing us on the road and wondering, *What the hell are these people doing; can't they travel like everyone else? They are just a bunch of tramps.* I have to admit that some of us do look like tramps after a month on the road. The German pilgrims, however, are always very sporty and chic, with the latest light hiking clothes, latest backpacks, and latest everything, while some of the French, especially those just retired, are *super* chic. They don't want the very efficient hiking clothes in navy blues, red, or white, as do their friendly neighbors the Germans; they want "the look," as well. I have to say that I was envious, because their clothes never looked like mine, but always proper, very light, greenish beige, and quick-drying. I got some of my clothes at the second-hand store in my little Midwestern town—the kind of clothes that gets donated because Grandma died. I am probably wearing someone's old grandma clothes. However, I throw them out after the walk. My clothes cost me a grand total of twelve dollars. Some of those super-chic French shirts, pants, vests, or shorts cost what I paid to fly across the Atlantic. Nevertheless, I am not doing bad; like the German, I have an excellent backpack and a great anorak. In any case Spain was much more *accueillant*, or welcoming, to us tramps than France was.

The road left the hill town and descended gradually into a rich valley that was home to several farms. Finally, I arrived on the outskirts of d'Aire-sur-l'Adour, in the town of Barcelonne-du-Gers. As I arrived in this little town, I saw the young Belgian and the French former nuclear worker. We were looking for a place to rest, and I found a

*Our wonderful host in d'Aire-sur-l'Adour*

café-bar that had the funniest sight. A beautiful dog was standing behind the counter—yes, standing—with his paws on the counter, no one else was there. I sat and looked at my *garçon de café,* ready to order a coffee. The other two pilgrims came in and laughed like hell at the scene, and then the owner came out of the kitchen. I jokingly asked him if this handsome *"garcon"* would take my order. We all sat there and enjoyed our last leg of the journey. They had taken yet another path, different from mine, and now we had another mile or two before reaching the old city.

We walked along the busy highway, joking, and finding amusement in the looks people gave us. Perhaps people don't see many pilgrims around there. I have to admit we made a sight: the young Belgian with long, black curly hair flying in all directions, a huge beard, a big wooden walking stick, a funny hat, backpack, underwear hung out to dry on his backpack, and big hiking shoes; the former nuclear worker with a crewcut, walking stick, large backpack; and me with a baseball cap, muddy clothes and shoes, and walking sticks.

Finally, we crossed the old bridge and entered the old city. The main street was full of people, mainly tourists enjoying themselves at the cafés or talking together in the streets; it was a joyous atmosphere. It took us a while to find the town center, and then we all went in separate directions. I was looking forward to a shower and then seeing this ancient city.

I went to the local *gîte* and saw the usual French couples already there, showered, and set up in the best bunks. The owner said that there was no room available. The Belgian came in and was told the same. The whole town was full—no room to be found anywhere, and I did not want to stay at an expensive hotel, which would probably be full anyway.

Meanwhile, the church would be blessing the pilgrims at 5:30, so we decided to go and be blessed by the old priest. We arrived there— the young Belgian, the Québecquois woman, the Indonesian, and me— with no place to stay, feeling dirty, tired, and grumpy. The French couples also arrived to be blessed, refreshed after showers; thanks to their cell phones, they had beds.

We all stood to be blessed, with much talk about brotherly love. I was feeling furious about the French pseudo-pilgrims and their bloody cell phones, but got a hold on myself. The four of us went to the priest in his little office, and he issued another pilgrim credential to me; the one I had was full with no more room for stamps. In Spain, one cannot stay in pilgrim hostels without that booklet to prove that one is actually a pilgrim, allowing the pilgrims to pay only eight to ten euros each night. In France the document is not necessary, but they also charge double the price.

The priest wanted to help us out, and an older assistant started making phone calls. After an hour or so, the priest and assistant were tiring of us and wondering when we would leave. Then they received a call and the four of us had a place to stay only fifteen minutes away. We thanked them profusely and left the church in the direction of our new host.

When we arrived, a tiny woman, about four feet tall, answered the door. She appeared to be in her eighties and said yes, she had room, and let us in her beautiful old home with several bedrooms. We could stay wherever we pleased. How charming; we each had our own room. Then she asked us what we would like for supper. I told her it was really not necessary to feed us all, but she insisted; so we all said in unison, "Whatever you have is fine." Dinner would be served at 8:30. The young Belgian went for a dip in the cold pool and then helped our host set the table.

The woman's husband was more than six feet tall, a big guy was just as gentle as his wife. They had both been in the army, and now he was retired from his business. They were part of the Catholic Church group that volunteered to help pilgrims. Together, we enjoyed a lively supper at their gracious table. It was a great meal, with cognac, tea, coffee, and ice cream for dessert. The old man was also a historian; he showed us to the famous Gothic church, and his wife insisted we see the famous crypt in the church basement. We all went to the church across the street around 11:00 for a private showing.

> Former cathedral built in the twelfth century, Gothic church, built where there was the Benedictine abbey of Sainte-Quitterie.... Vast roman crypt where one can notice ancient roman slabs from a temple dedicated to the god Mars.
>
> Sainte Quitterie, according to tradition, is not far from the Roman walls of Aire, near a hill on which Sainte Quitterie is said to have been martyred. She was a gothic princess whose radiating

power reached Spain as well as Portugal.... The white marble sarcophagus in the crypt containes her relics.*

According to another source: "She was the daughter of the Governor of Galicia and Lucitania; she would have been martyred in Aire under the reign of the Roman Emperor Commodus (AD 176–192). Many Spanish towns confirm as well that she was martyred in Aire."**

༄༅

We walked everywhere and admired many stone-relief works. Our generous guest showed us the acoustic in one small area used to read the scriptures. There we experienced perfect acoustics like I had never heard; one would have thought there were microphones. If you spoke in a little spot at the middle of the tiny basement chapel, the sound seemed to come out of the wall. We were mesmerized by the unearthly sound, coming it seemed from heaven—from the periphery. The builders certainly knew sacred architecture and music. Bernard de Clairvaux was known to be an expert in acoustics, and his students or he might have had something to do with building this jewel. Aire-sur-l'Adour was a famous pilgrimage center even at that time.

Then we looked at the white marble sarcophagus hidden under drapes. I removed them and then, of course, put them back. It was an incredible work of sacred art, sculpted with biblical scenes that appeared smooth, cool, and eternal. The little church had many secrets, and never mind the old Mars god worshipped here more than 2,000 years ago. It is said that this city D'Aire-sur-l'Adour was a famous roman city, and then became the residence of Alaric II, king of the Visigoths in the fifth century, until he was defeated by Clovis, king of the Franks, in the Battle of Vouillé in 507.

---

\* TopoGuides, *Sentier vers Saint Jacques de Compostelle via Le Puy, de Moissac à Roncevaux* (GR 65), p. 79 (tr. M-L. Valandro).

\*\* *Les Chemins de Saint Jacques de Compostelle* (ed. MSM editions), p. 214 (tr. M-L. Valandro).

Looking up all those old kings of the fourth and fifth centuries to learn about their wives, I found my mother's maiden name. I had wondered where on earth that name had come from; now I know it is a very old name from Burgundy and the Franc and Merovingian kings. I asked my mother, who has the memory of an elephant, but she had never heard of where the name came from. She said "Oh, that name has always been there." *I guess so,* I thought—at least since AD 400. but my mother was not interested and didn't care about the old Frankish and Merovingian kings; she preferred her mother's side and was not fond of her father at all, because her farmer father had made her work much too hard in her youth, cutting wood in the forest with a team of Belgian horses, working in the fields, milking cows in the barn, attending to her mother and thirteen siblings.

"Besides," she said, "your grandmother was an aristocrat, with a "de" in front of her name [though she didn't mean it that way], whose family owned a large *filature* (spinning mill) in the north of France as well as in Belgium. They lost it all during the war, when the factory-estate became a center of the German occupation." Then she threw in "Did you know that your great-aunt and her husband were *francmaçonnes?* They paid for our wedding in Tunisia before you were born." (I attended the party; my mother was four months pregnant with me—the reason she left Dijon.) Walking these paths, I am discovering much more than I thought I would.

⁕

We walked back to the old house and slept well until morning, when we discovered that our host had prepared a great breakfast for us. She said, "You must excuse our dusty home, but we just returned yesterday from a long trip to Vietnam." They love traveling. Her husband had been in the Vietnam-French ("Indochina") War during the 1950s.

After saying our goodbyes, I decided to join the other pilgrim route called "Via Tolosana," the path of Toulouse just to the south. I was tired of the cell phone crowd and wanted to rejoin that road in any case. So I went to the center of town to catch a bus toward Pau, where the Via Tolosana passes through about twenty-two miles away. I wandered around the busy town, had some coffee, and bought more food. While I waited at the bus stop, I noticed dozens of buses passing through. I had never seen such a commotion. The large buses were filled with people, so I asked what was going on. Someone said, "Oh, this is one of the stops on the way to Lourdes, which is southeast just down the road. All these buses are making 'rest' before Lourdes."

Then I noticed all the priests in the front of a bus talking to the religious tourists; they had come from all over France. People with nametags were taking care of the old people who going to Lourdes. There were many double-deck buses filled with people who were lying down, very sick, and unable to walk being cared for by nurses dressed in white. Some buses were filled with handicapped people, who also had lots of helpers in special uniforms. It was a real mess with so many buses; there was no room to turn them around, which caused traffic jams. I told myself that I should have gone to Lourdes (but that will be on my next walk—from Arles through more Cathar/Bonhomme country). Someone told me that Lourdes is the most popular pilgrimage city in France; hundreds of thousands visit it every year. It brings millions to businesses there—saints join capitalism, and perhaps between the saints and capitalism, some are healed.

My bus arrived, and after a while we pulled off the highway, into a village, and then back onto the highway. At the crossroad, whom do I see? The tough-looking French pilgrim with a little golden cross on his ear on his way to Lourdes. He had slept on the bunk next to mine in Moissac. A coincidence? We acknowledge each other, me through the bus window, him from the road. I said goodbye. After a few days of walking, sleeping, eating, and brushing your teeth with the other pilgrims, you get to know one another even if you don't talk. He was heading for Lourdes and I for Spain. It was a moving moment; we were brother and sister pilgrims sharing the same path. We never had

*Henry IV of France, Castillo de Pau*

*Buses lined up to take tourists to Lourdes*

a real conversation because he stayed to himself, walked alone, and did not socialize. I detected a bit of tragedy in him, so I did not have my usual conversation: "Oh, where are you from... blah blah." It would seem inappropriate. So here he went alone, probably not sharing his life story for good reasons. On this path, "when two or more are gathered in His name" lots of things happen without words. Such was that moment.

I sat in the front so I could see everything. In the distance, I could see the far-away splendor of the Pyrenees, and I thought to myself, *I have to cross those snowy peaks in just a few days.* The power of my legs never ceases to amaze me. I am forever thankful that they carry me everywhere, but those mountains certainly looked majestic, gigantic, and daunting. The climb was coming—not that I hadn't climbed already. The weather was changing. It was cloudy, rainy, and thundering—not the best weather for crossing a high pass.

The bus left me in the center of the huge city with quite a history. I found a small hotel in the center, left my backpack there, and started visiting the area. I went straight to the museum and "new" castle. This city is King Henri IV's country, for he was the King of Navarre.

❦

Henri IV, the son of Jeanne d'Albret, was married to another exceptional woman, Marguerite de Valois. Like Henri IV, Marguerite was also a writer. She was the daughter of King Henry II of France and Catherine de' Medici. We can also recall that the mother of Henry II was the tragic Claude (whose life I mentioned) and that his father was François I. We can see why the Pope did not want an alliance between Marguerite de Valois, who was Catholic, and Henri IV, a Protestant. They were second cousins (their grandparents were brother and sister), as mentioned in previous stories.

Marguerite de Valois the writer left us her memoirs, which give some insight into her life with King Henry IV. Here, the Queen complained of being treated badly when she wanted to celebrate the Catholic mass (Jeanne d'Albret had forbidden the Catholic faith in the Bearn province), being in Protestant territory:

> And to make my life more miserable [she and the king were both twenty years old] since the departure of Dayelle [one of the king's lovers], my husband the King was chasing after Rebours [another lover], who was really a girl full of malice. She did not care much for me, his wife, and was doing everything in her power to do me harm....
>
> During these very trying times, my faith in God helped me tremendously. He then took pity on me in my tears and allowed that we should leave this "little Geneva Pau" [referring to the non-Catholic state], where good fortune caused his lover Rebours to fall ill and remain behind. Out of sight, out of heart—my husband the king lost his affection for her but started running after Fosseuse, who was much prettier, a child of fourteen, and all goodness. We left, heading for Montauban, and passed by the little town of Eauze. The night that we arrived, my husband the king fell ill with a great fever and headaches that lasted a week.

He had no rest, night or day, and constantly changed beds, from one to the next. I was such a good companion, serving him day and night; the king my husband found my help so great that he told everyone about it....

Now they are living in the King's domain Nerac, a region I just walked through north of Montreal-Larressingle.... During all this time, the King was "serving" [having sex with] Fosseuse, who was totally dependent on me, was behaving with such honor and virtue that if she had kept on behaving thus nothing bad would have happened to her or to me....

After a relative peace [between Catholics and Huguenots] my brother went back to France in order to gather his army [one of her brothers, the duke of Anjou had just gone to England to see if he could marry the famous Queen Elizabeth], and Henry IV, my husband the king, and I returned to Nerac, where as soon as we got there, Fosseuse puts it into the king's head that she needed to go to Aigues-chaudes [warm healing baths] in the province of Bearne. She probably wanted to cover up her pregnancy, or get rid of what she had. I pleaded with my husband the king to excuse me from accompanying him there, as I had sworn to myself never to enter into those territories unless they were Catholic. He really insisted on my going and went into a rage. He told me that his "girl," as he called Fosseuse, needed to go to the waters there for her stomachache. I told him that I was not opposed to her going there. He then said that she would not go without me; that it would be the source of some bad thinking where there was none; the king became even more upset that I did not want to take her there. Finally, he had to accept it, and she would go with two of her friends who were Rebours [another lover of the king] and Villesavin and a maid....

After a month or five weeks, the King my husband came back with Fosseuse and her other companions....

The pains of labor came one very early morning before sunrise, while she was sleeping in her quarters with her ladies; she called for my doctor and told him to tell the king my husband that she was in labor. We were sleeping in the same room but in separate beds as was our custom. As the doctor told him the news, the king my husband became very much alarmed, not knowing what to do, being afraid to be discovered on one hand, or on the other that no one would come to her help. He truly cared for her. He finally decided to confide everything to me, and pleaded with me to go and help her out, knowing very well that whatever happened I would be there to do whatever he wanted me to....

I had her promptly taken out of the ladies' quarters, and put her in a room far away with my own doctor and ladies to help out, and had her very well taken care of. God willed that she only had a daughter, who died at birth. Having delivered, she was taken to the ladies, quarters, where even though everything had been extremely discrete, we could not prevent the news from spreading throughout the castle about what had happened. The king my husband, having come back from his customary hunting expedition, went to see her as was his habit.... She begged him to send me over to her quarters, as I used to do to check on them when they were sick, thinking by this action to get rid of the damaging rumors. The king my husband came into our bedroom and saw that I was back in bed, because I was tired from having gotten up too early to help her out. He told me to get up and go see Fosseuse. I told him that I had already done so when she needed me, but that at this time she no longer needed me; and besides if I went there, I would discover that more than pretending that nothing had happened, everyone would be pointing fingers at me. He got extremely angry with me, and this made me even more upset. It seemed that I did not deserve this kind of treatment for what I had done for him this morning.*

Henry IV, King of Navarre, became the King of France after Marguerite de Navarre's brothers, who all became kings one after another and then died, left him the sole heir to the French crown. Henry IV abandoned her for his many lovers and finally had the marriage annulled. She was left alone, scorned by her mother Catherine de'

---

* *Mémoires de Marguerite de Valois* (Y. Cazaux, ed.), pp. 175–190 (tr. M-L. Valandro).

Medici, her former husband, and everyone else. Her oldest sister had married the King of Spain, who had also died. Finally, she was shut up in a tower north of Le Puy in a deserted part of the Auvergne, where she spent many years before being allowed to return to Paris and to the court. There she resumed her dialogue with her former husband, Henry IV, now married to another Marie de' Medici. Marguerite de Navarre loved his children and visited them often from her large estate. She died surrounded by quite a "literary court."

Marguerite de Valois had traveled through much of the countryside I had walked through during the past week or two. I had stayed in many beautiful castles owned by Jeanne d'Albret, and her son Henri IV.

In front of the great museum dedicated to Henri IV, there is this enormous statue of him, and of course nothing is mentioned of his outrageous behavior toward women. As we see from her diaries, he ignored his wife Marguerite de Valois and had many lovers vying for his affection and trying to give him an heir. As mentioned, he was eventually married at the age of forty-seven to the young Marie de' Medici, age twenty-seven, who gave him six children. Henri IV would be assassinated in Paris by a teacher-turned-monk.

After staying for a while in the beautiful museum and the bookstore, I walked throughout the old city, visited the large cathedral, returned to my little hotel, and later went to a North African restaurant for delicious couscous. However, the service was not very nice. I am blond with blue eyes and was thus treated to racism and nastiness. The waiter first served the others in the dining room full of local French-North African customers and ignored me. Nevertheless, I remained, wanting to see how long he would make me wait. The North Africans are not well treated in France, so here in the south it is their domain and they return the treatment.

Of course, the waiter could not know that I had lived in Morocco and Algeria throughout my childhood from the age of six to twelve, or that when I returned to Burgundy, France, where I grew up, and to Nantes, where we ended up living, I was treated as *"pieds noirs,"* a derogatory term for those who left the North African colonies (Algeria, Morocco, and Tunisia) and returned to live in France between 1956 and 1962. I was offended when this treatment was given to me by the teachers at the *lycée* where I went to school, because it was not true. I had lived there for only part of my childhood, from twelve to thirteen. Comments such as, "What the heck did they teach you over there" and "You can't really come to this *lycée*, which is for well-taught students." It was as if to say, "How could you ever know anything 'over there' in North Africa?" I remember my mother being *"en larmes,"* in tears, at the office of the *lycée*, because they would not accept me in the school. They finally took me in. My mother, who had been prevented from becoming a doctor because of the family situation (fourteen brothers and sisters), was not going to accept their refusal. I was extremely upset myself, because I loved school and knew then that my life would include studies, as it still does.

Nevertheless, the more difficulties one encounters, the stronger one gets. I learned at an early age about the nastiness of some people, in whose minds the truth does not matter. The funny thing is that, throughout all those years in North Africa when I did the shopping for my mother, I was always treated with kindness by the shopkeepers. I walked everywhere with little concern. I never received the outrageous treatment that I got in France from classmates and others.

So all these memories came back to me, and I simply ignored the waiter's obvious nastiness toward me. I was as pleasant as could be, praising the food and so on. He even made me wait another thirty minutes for the bill. As I left, however, I told him sarcastically, *"Vous êtes extrêmement occupé,"* and left him no tip.

Then I went into a café sweet shop, which was again full of well-dressed French-North African kids and their families—a hangout for well-to-do young teenagers. The North African owner, a hip-looking guy, also completely ignored me because of my Anglo appearance. Here the hatred was even more blatant. I said to myself that France is in for some real problems if nothing is done about this situation. I did not leave and ignored their treatment. I ordered some sweets after the man got tired of making me wait. It didn't bother me, because I was having fun listening to the teens' conversations. They were all planning to go to Morocco, in this case, to visit relatives there for the summer, some by land, some by plane, and so on. But there was a total breakdown of civility—simple hate that was not nice to see. It was clear that these kids had grown up in France; they were well dressed and handsome kids, but their allegiance was to their North African countries, and I suspect they do not feel at home there either; rather, they are caught in the middle. They are not religious and want nothing to do with that, thanks to their "liberated" sisters and mothers. It is simply racial tension. Before I left, refusing to accept their racial attitude, I engaged the owner in a conversation: "Why don't you have an internet café in here? It would be helpful to the tourists." He answered that he would think about it, realizing that I was from somewhere else, perhaps from the U.S. and not part of their racial situation, and that throwing hate at me would not get him anywhere.

That evening I decided not to walk around but just enjoyed the private room and watched the news on television. The next morning, very early, I took a taxi out of this large city directly to the pilgrim's path. The outskirts of cities are usually dirty, and this was no exception. Walking by the river, I saw big dumps and I did not feel very safe. No one was around, but the countryside improved, with farms and forests, and I arrived in the small village of Lescar for tea, where again the man working in the café would not pay attention to me or serve me; this place was full of men, no women.

This area does not see many pilgrims. Again I said to myself, "What is going on here? Am I so disturbing to look at?" Then a sweet old man, who was sitting with another man, asked if I was walking the Camino, and I said yes. He said that he belongs to the organization that takes care of pilgrims in the area. I wonder what would happen if no one took care of the pilgrims. He had walked part of the path with friends and loved to walk. When we said good-bye, he showed me the way out.

Except for that helpful old man, I was happy to leave that unwelcoming café.

I went on through beautiful forests of steep paths made muddy by the previous day's rainfall. I arrived in the very pretty town of La Commanderie. It was time for lunch, and I saw a promising restaurant. Being Sunday, it was full of families enjoying the excellent food. I asked if I could have lunch and if I could sit in the other, almost empty dining room, because my shoes and clothes were full of mud. They were extremely kind and served me a very special lunch, because I told them I had not eaten since my couscous lunch the day before. The cook, a woman, came to chat with me. She said she would prepare something special. I said that it was not necessary—any food would be great. She disappeared into her big kitchen.

I was brought a meal fit for kings—no, for queens! Curried chicken, salad, vegetables, *mousse au chocolat,* and coffee. In the end, I was so full that I was not fit to walk, so I decided to stay in the pilgrims' *gîte* next to the beautiful old chapel-commanderie. In ancient times, this was a very busy road for the pilgrims arriving from the southeast, for whom they also had a large hospital.

The couple who owned the inn returned, and we chatted for a while; they wanted to go to the U.S. I have found that, whenever I receive bad treatment in one place, the next place is sure to make up for it. This has been consistent throughout my walk.

Back at the *gîte,* which was opened by now, there were two French pilgrims also heading south. One was from a city in the south near Toulouse. He was originally from Spain but had moved to France at an early age; now he was walking back home. He said, "I am not a pilgrim at all. I'm just walking back home to visit my relatives, and the path goes right by my house in Spain." He showed me a picture of the luxurious and perfect bed-and-breakfast he owned with his partner, another French man. He had another 650 miles to go. The other French man—small, skinny, and in his seventies—had enlisted as a professional in the French army and had been a parachutist, legionnaire, or something like that. He had lived in Africa, where he'd had businesses. He talked about his African friends and the racial character of many of his fellow soldiers who were in Africa only to make a quick buck and return home. He said that he cared more about doing something right. He seemed to love Africa and probably missed his life of adventure there. We shared a simple supper, though I was not very hungry after my sumptuous lunch.

The commanderie had been renovated; the yard was full of beautiful stone monument crosses called *"stele"* taken from the local cemetery. All the designs were different. I wanted to take a lot of pictures, but my camera's memory was full, so I took mental pictures. Then a downpour came that lasted all night. Good, I thought; tomorrow the weather should be sunny.

The guys got up very early, at six o'clock—too early for me. They set out on the road, and I chose to take the path. We were going to climb quite a bit that day, starting up toward the Hautes-Pyrénées. The path went through old mountain forests, beautifully quiet, and serene. No one was around. There were no villages or farms, just a winding, rocky, and steep path. The path had beautiful ochre mud-clay encrusted with beautiful little stones, telling me that glaciers had been here. It was very muddy and slippery because of the rain. I can see why they eat wild boar around here; it is a place for deer and wild boar. I had admired beautiful tapestries at the museum in Pau depicting scenes of wild boar hunts.

I arrived at a crossroad on top of a ridge and had no clue about where to go from there. Luckily, a car arrived and the driver pointed me in the right direction; I would have gone the opposite way. I reached a solitary hamlet with a few people going into their gardens, and farm fields. I was on top of the ridge and by now out of the forest. From there, I could see the beautiful, snowy peaks of the Pyrenees spread over the southern horizon. I was very upset because, from now on, *no pictures*—no more memory in my camera. The path took me along the fringe of many farm fields of rich, red earth, while still seeing the fantastic mountains on the horizon. I had glimpsed the men on the main road, and we arrived in Oloron-Sainte-Marie at the same time. I was tired from the steep up-and-down paths.

Oloron-Sainte-Marie is a very old town, built by a fast-running river of icy water from the high peaks. The town had several beautiful old bridges and old churches, including the the *cathédrale Sainte-Marie d'Oloron,* which I could not photograph, of course.

I found a pilgrim *gîte* in a former convent, where I had my own room and where the two French pilgrims also stayed. We made plans to eat supper together at a well-known and inexpensive local restaurant. I lingered at a local café, watching people and buying my usual pastries while chatting with local merchants. Walking around the charming old city, I had the panoramic background of the Pyrenees in the distance. I could have stayed here much longer and I planned on coming back to this quaint, deserted *vallée d'Aspe,* next time with a camera and a car.

I spent quite a while admiring the cathedral's tympanum, just as incredible as the one in Moissac and Conques. But I preferred this one, being in my opinion more original and poignant. It depicted Christ being taken from the Cross, surrounded by two circles. The inner circle: "One of the best-known sculpted arches seems to be occupied by an abundance of people whose main occupation is the acquisition of the best and richest earthly nourishment."[*] I saw wild boar hunters with enormous clubs, a butcher, makers of wood wine barrels, a grape gatherer, a thinker or king, a fish seller, salmon fishermen, a duck cook, a baker, a ham cook, a coffee grinder, an omelet cook, and so on, all in simple and charming detail. Everyone who came to the church was portrayed in this grand panorama of earthly life.

The second, outer circle depicts the 24 elders and musicians.

At Sainte-Marie, the elders are all seated, crowned and with beards, mustaches, and bare feet painted in ochre. Contrary to

---

[*] Sernin, *La cathédrale d'Oloron-Sainte-Marie,* p. 64 (tr. M-L. Valandro).

the depiction of the common people below, those portrayed above are kings, dressed in majestic clothes, with radiant, inspired faces. They have power and wisdom. In the high circle there is no place for useless agitation, but only great peaceful calm, sweet music, and heavenly scent.*

This tympanum entices because of the master sculptor himself and the *joie de vivre* that comes through his work.

For us, the [meaning] of the sculpted arch depicting the feverish preparations for a banquet and the happy people full of life and taste is perhaps the portrayal of miracles through the images, but especially the manifestation of the feast that awaits "the chosen ones" in the Kingdom of Heaven. As for the "fallen ones," we find them being devoured in the mouth of the monster located in the keystone of the vault.

This particular master sculptor loved life and people. He must have been a *bon vivant*. Nothing about the art of gastronomy escaped him. He knew everything about butchering pigs and making wine barrels. He loved theater, mime, acrobats, and troubadours. In addition, music was his great specialty. With the elders, it was normal to depict the whole range of musical instruments.

It is not necessary for church iconography to be negative, revengeful, and moralizing.**

This last comment is the one I liked best, because this tympanum is so positive, delightful, and lively. One feels invited to come into the church for a celebration, not for gloom—for partaking in a sacred meal together as we enter the joyful archway entry, it surrounds the apostles as they take down Christ's body from the Cross, with the Moon and Sun on either side.

Experiencing this tympanum I am reminded of Rudolf Steiner's words about Wagner and his colossal masterpieces.

---

\*    Ibid., p. 70.

\*\*   Ibid., pp. 84–85.

On Good Friday 1857, he [Wagner] was sitting in the retreat, "the sanctuary on the green hill." Looking out over the fields watching the plants come to life, sprouting from the earth, an inkling arose in him of the power of the germinating force emerging from the earth in response to the rays of the sun: a driving force, a motivating force that permeates the whole world and lives in all beings; a force that must evolve, that cannot remain as it is; a force that, to reach higher stages, must pass through death. Watching the plants, he felt the force of sprouting life, and turning his gaze across the Lake of Zurich to the village, he contemplated the opposite idea, that of death—the two polar concepts to which Goethe give such eloquent expressions in his poem, "Blessing Longing."

> And until you truly have
> the dying and becoming,
> you are only a troubled guest
> roaming o'er the dark earth.

Goethe rewrote the words in his hymn to nature saying, "Nature invented death to have more life; only through death can she create a higher spiritual life."

On Good Friday, as the symbol of death came to face humankind in remembrance, Wagner sensed the interconnection of life, death, and immortality. He felt a connection between the life sprouting from the earth and the death on the Cross—the death that is also the source of a Christian belief that, ultimately, life will be victorious over death and become eternal life. Wagner sensed an inner connection among sprouting life, spring, and the Good Friday belief in redemption, the belief that eternal life springs from death on the Cross. This thought is the same as that contained in the quest for the Holy Grail, by which the chaste plant blossom striving toward the sun is contrasted with human desire filled nature....

Looking toward the Cross, Wagner saw the blood flowing from the Redeemer, the symbol of redemption being caught in the Grail chalice. This picture linked itself within him to awaking life in nature. These thoughts were passing through Wagner's soul on Good Friday of 1857. He jotted down a few words.... "The blossoming plant springs from death; eternal life springs from Christ's death"....

The path to the Holy Grail is portrayed as a cleansing of the sinful blood of lower desires until, on a higher level, it is as pure and chaste as is the plant calyx in its relation to the sunbeam. Only those who are pure in heart, unworldly, and untouched by temptation, so that they approach the Holy Grail as "innocent fools" filled with questions of its secret, can discover the path.*

⁕

Again the tympanum represents, masterfully and joyfully, these ancient books carved in stone. The walk was worth it just to discover this treasure. I walked there several times and met many Spaniards who had driven on the main highway through the huge tunnel between Spain and France. A young Spanish couple with a small child was, like me, in awe of this work.

There is such joyfulness in the partakers of the feast, it is *present*; their earthiness disappears, and their joy remains as the body of Christ is taken down from the Cross, watched over by the female Moon and the male Sun. The master stoneworker must have been a member of the sacred brotherhood who still *knew* the truth, otherwise one could not have worked with the symbols in such a powerful way. Here we have death and joy right next to each other. The powerful words of Judith von Halle speak about the Feast:

> The spiritual-physical process of nutrition...based on the ingestion of spiritual food...lies at the foundation—even if buried deeply—of every existing human being and will play an ever larger role in the future development of the human being. This will be made clearer by means of some references to the story of the Grail. Spiritual Science refers to itself as a "science of the grail" and has, as a result, a special relationship to everything connected with the Grail....

---

\*    Steiner, *Supersensible Knowledge*, pp. 191–192.

The Grail story can be traced back to Joseph of Arimathea and Nicodemus, who asked Pilate for permission to take the body of Christ down from the Cross and to lay it in the grave, which was granted them. In the French Grail tradition, the Grail is the chalice used at the Last Supper and at the same time the vessel in which the blood from the Savior's wounds was collected. It is sufficient here to draw attention to the fact that the blood that was collected did not flow into the Earth, but was received and looked after by human beings. In this Grail tradition, a direct relationship to the events of Golgotha is established through the blood in the chalice. For Wolfram von Eschenbach, the Grail is a stone whose power is renewed with each Good Friday by a small white host brought to it by a dove. Both Grail traditions therefore are clearly connected with the Mystery of Golgotha, and... it is understandable that the Grail would be unthinkable without the Resurrection of Christ, the Easter event. This can be especially seen in the properties that the Grail possesses. The Pheonix burns to ashes on the Grail stone, but the ashes rapidly restore him to life as though he were born again, and he shines radiant and beautiful.

Wolgram von Eschenbach then emphasizes that the Grail has the same effect on humans. "The stone confers such power to human beings that flesh and bones are soon made young again." In addition, its miraculous, food-giving properties are brought about through the power that the Grail receives from the dove on Good Friday. The stone receives "a special power to bestow every form of good-smelling food and drink on Earth, like the perfection of Paradise, I mean *everything the earth may produce*" [my italics].

Here the Easter event is understood in a subtle way as the creation of a new Paradise from which the Earth and humankind will live. This can be seen in the account of the Grail feast when one realizes that the Grail feast is a description of a hidden, unconscious process occurring in a mysterious nocturnal sphere. In the Grail feast we are able to understand the spiritual-physical process of nutrition that enables the physical-material existence of humankind on a daily basis. By means of this spiritual process of nutrition occurring in the subconscious depths of the will, with which every human being is living in the substance of the spiritual world, the human being shares in the Grail process, which is an expression of the truth of the Resurrection....

Through contemplating the Grail feast a feeling can be developed for the spiritual force that makes possible incarnation of the individual self.*

Admiring these ancient stone works is more than moving; it reminds all of us that a thousand years ago, people knew much more than they do now, and that is the true power and strength of this ancient pilgrimage route. It awakens the deep secrets "buried in stones" that need to come to life again, to teach us the real mysteries of death and life. All one needs is to *truly see,* or *pierce the veil.* That is why so many people are flocking to these ancient paths all over Europe—by the thousands, they walk. They look, they see, they search, they meet, they talk, they question, they experience: *they awake.* The death of so many pilgrims throughout the hundreds of years of the existence of this path since the ninth century, the death and sufferings of so many Cathars, Bonhommes, so-called heretics, warriors, and knights have paved the way with their blood so that each one of us can rediscover the ancient paths leading to inner freedom and eternal life. If each one who walks this path awakens just a bit they will not have died or suffered in vain.

Pierce the veil = *perce voile* = *perce val* = Parcival. Isn't that what his name means? *Perce* means "to pierce"; *val* could have been *voile,* which means "veil" in French, not *val-vallée-vallon,* which means "valley." I think it makes more sense to have the meaning being *voile,* or *val.* With the evolution in language, it is likely that, in the last thousand years, the vowel sound changed from *oua* to *oi* to *a.* Moreover, in the Middle Ages it could have been pronounced as a combination of long *ouoi* changing to a long *a,* instead of *voil,* or *val*—easily done with the *lange-d'oc.*

---

\* Von Halle, *And if He Has not Been Raised...*, pp. 33–35.

Rudolf Steiner gave us some remarkable insights into Parcival through his ability to read into the *akashic substance,* or record, owing to his powerful capacities developed over many lifetimes.

> One of the subtlest substances accessible to human striving is called "akasha." Beings and phenomena manifested in the akashic substance are the subtlest of all those accessible to human beings. What human beings acquire for themselves in esoteric knowledge not only lives in the souls, but it is impressed in the akashic substance. When we bring an idea from esoteric science to life in our soul, it is *immediately inscribed in the akashic substance.* It is significant that such inscriptions, which are significant for the general development of the world, is inscribed in the akasha only by *human beings.*\*

Here is more about Steiner's insights into *Parce-val.*

> As a result of his spiritual research, Rudolph Steiner was able to give indications of seven successive incarnations of the individuality who appeared as Mani....
>
> The earliest incarnations to which Steiner refers is that of the Disciple of Sais [Coptic = *twin*] in Egypt. Isis represents there the soul, the mother who receives the divine into herself and conceives. But Osiris, the divine father, has withdrawn, so the female element is no longer confronted by the divine fructifier, and is called "the widow." Seeking to behold unprepared the secrets of the archetypal forces of man and nature, he *unveiled* the image of Isis on the physical plane, and had to succumb to death. No mortal, no one not prepared by initiation, might at that time lift the veil of Isis. In him is symbolized the wisdom of Egypt, which had by then lost its power.
>
> He then incarnated as one of the three Magi from the East, who brought the old treasures of wisdom of the Indian, Persian, and Egyptian ages to the feet of the newborn Jesus... as Caspar the Moor from Africa, he presented the myrrh, the symbol of death and resurrection of Osiris, of the dying of the lower life and the resurrection of the higher by means of the deep forces of the will....

---

\* Steiner, *Approaching the Mystery of Golgotha,* pp. 2–3.

He was soon reincarnated *as the youth of Nain*, who was one of the three raised from death by Christ (Luke 7:11). Now literally son of a widow, he was being carried out of the city gate when Christ Jesus approached. "And a large crowd from the city were with his mother"—namely the Egyptian initiates who bury the dead. "And when the Lord saw her He had compassion on her, who represented the earthly Isis. And He said, 'Young man, I say unto you, arise.' And the dead one sat up and began to speak; and He gave him to his mother. And those around glorified God saying, 'A great prophet is arisen among us.'" This was a very special initiation in the depths of the will; it contained the mystery of the working of Christ into the future. Only a seed planted into his soul, so that he had to wait until the next incarnation for its forces to blossom in him as an initiate, and become a mighty teacher of religion who is gradually to permeate Christianity with the teaching of reincarnation and karma.

Then came the incarnation as Mani, from AD 216 to 277. This background enables us to understand why he saw it as his task to draw together the wisdom of the East and transform it through the forces of Christ, and how he gained such strong forces for the future transformation of evil. He now describes himself as "son of the widow," because he is preparing for the stage when people will lay aside all outer authority and seek for their own spirit light by gazing into their own souls....

Then, in the ninth century, just at the time when the Roman Church was denying the separate existence of the spirit, Mani incarnated as the historical Parcival, again son of a widow. Parcival prepared in advance the initiation needed for the Age of the Consciousness Soul, later expressed in the legends by Chretien, Wolfram, and others.[*]

It is important to mention that on Reichenau Island in Lake Constance (or *Bodensee*), during the Middle Ages, there was an important monastic center founded in the ninth century, whose abbots were well known at the time. It also served as a school for children of the

---

[*] Seddon, *Mani: His Life and Work*, pp. 55–56.

aristocracy, who were taught by influential thinkers to become future monarchs, abbots, and other persons of influence. One of the abbots there, Waldo of Reichenau (c. 740–814), was a close adviser to Charlemagne, who also became the abbot of St. Denis. Charlemagne's home, as we have seen, was the whole of Europe. He had numerous daughters from his many wives, some of whom married into the important houses of what is now Germany, thus establishing many abbeys and monasteries. Through Charlemagne, we know the Parcival legend because of his grandmother Flor, mother of Bertha Bigfoot.* But what I would like to mention is this:

> The island has no fewer than three surviving monastery churches: Mittelzell, the main church, Oberzell, and Nierderzell.... The well preserved, if somewhat faded, fresco cycle in the middle vessel of the church dedicated to Saint George is wonderful. It has been dated around 980. The theme of the eight-part cycle...is Christ's miracles, in particular the healings and resurrection, including *resurrection of the youth of nain*. The paintings are closely related to the style of the illuminated manuscripts of Reichenau.**

We see that in this great powerful Abbey that knowledge remained of *what lay behind the veil;* the Abbots *had pierced the veil*. They knew much more than is generally known today, when we have to rediscover all those connections through scholarship and the clairvoyance of other great human beings. It is not by chance that Frescoes are painted about the Youth of Nain, a reincarnation of Parcival.

During the past year, I spent many hours in numerous churches, chapels, and museums in Florence and in the whole of Tuscany for seven weeks. I gazed at hundreds of sacred icons, frescoes, and paintings and do not remember seeing frescoes depicting the Youth of Nain. That is why this is an important fact to me, not to be dismissed in the understanding of Parcival, the Grail, and this Podiensis path. Why

---

\*   For more on this topic, see Stein, *The Ninth Century and the Holy Grail*.
\*\*  Schutz, *Great Monasteries of Europe*, p. 324.

paint such a fresco in that particular place if it had nothing to do with Parcival? Furthermore, what were all the Cathars doing in this area? Why in this area, which is also supposedly the area of the "Grail castle." The Cathars were influenced directly by Manicheism, the teachings of Mani. Rudolf Steiner tells us that Parcival is the reincarnated Mani.

※

Filled with what I had seen, I walked back to the monastery. It was suppertime, and the host at our *gîte* strongly recommended a particular restaurant, saying, "Well, here you do not eat just anywhere," and suggested we make a reservation. I thought, do I really have to make a reservation in this little town in the middle of nowhere France? I did. When we got there it was full. That weekend was the *fête agricole,* or the county fair, and the next morning many trucks and cars would arrive from the surrounding towns with pigs, sheep, goats, cows, and farm produce.

After seeing the tympanum on the monastery, I could understand that the people of this region of France take their food seriously. With such a feast above the church, they could not serve us anything but the best. We ate soup, béarnaise, pâte, duck, mousse au chocolat, red wine, café—all in a jovial and warm atmosphere. It would not be a bad city to live in, and ski resorts were not far.

The next morning, we had breakfast with a group on a one-week walk. The Spaniard was up, but the French fellow had gotten sick during the night and had a fever, so he would stay behind. The Spaniard was taking the other path, going through Saint-Jean-Pied-de-Port ("Saint John at the foot of the mountain pass") and on through the Roncevaux path, which I had taken the previous year.* Thus we would go our separate ways.

I walked out of town looking at the small snowy peaks in the distance amid the low clouds. I took the small road, since I did not want

---

\* See Valandro, *Camino Walk.*

to climb up and down on the steep path. It was raining, so it would also be muddy. The road was quiet, with farms on both sides and meadows full of spring flowers and golden cows peacefully eating their morning breakfast. I saw forests up in the mountains and many beautiful stone homes.

I arrived in the old town of Lurbe-Saint-Christau just as it started pouring rain. It was lunchtime, so I sat in a sheltered bus stop to eat my half sandwich from the previous day. I was drenched but not cold, and I had to keep going. I could not see the mountains; it was all grey in the distance. I walked on for another four miles. The road had become a "national" route that was very busy and narrow, so I took the path that crossed the highway and over the Gave d'Aspe, a fast-moving, crystal-clear, river of melted glacier. This was the famous Vallée d'Aspe. My guidebook said that the association of *grandes randonnées* (long walks) had declassified this path. It was no longer endorsed by the association, and I wondered what that meant; I would find out soon enough.

The path was climbing a cut on the mountainside; below was the fast-moving river. It was lovely and quiet in the forest—a respite from the busy and dangerous road. It was still raining heavily, but under the canopy of trees it was not so bad. Then I noticed that the path was becoming smaller and very muddy—yellow clay mud, no rocks, and no footprints. This was not a good sign and meant that I was the only one on this path. I kept walking; there was no way I would go back. Then the path became almost impassable and so narrow that I had to walk with one foot in front of the other. It was also slippery from the rain. Thank goodness, I had my sticks to help if I slipped—and if I fell, it would be directly into the ravine and the fast icy-cold river below. There was nothing to hold on to, and with my backpack it was hard to keep my balance. I was becoming nervous about my stupidity again, but could not afford to lose my cool in this place. I told myself, "Well, you are in a mess, and the path is so narrow you can't even turn around without falling. So keep going; be as light as possible on your feet so that, if you start slipping, you can just hop on the other foot and keep going with the help of the walking sticks. Keep yourself centered with your backpack and pay attention. One moment of inattention and you will tumble into the ravine—with no one to notice."

This situation continued for three miles, growing progressively worse until the path disappeared, but I went on. I was thinking, "What the hell are you doing here? This is not acceptable—putting my life in danger is not what this is all about. This is the result of gross negligence and lack of planning on my part." Now I knew what it meant to "declassify" a whole path. It is also why no one else had gone this way. The newly printed guidebook had not mentioned anything about this. It should have warned pilgrims that the path is not passable in rainy weather, and perhaps even in sunny weather.

I gratefully entered the next town of Sarrance, a medieval town. After that walk I was totally drenched, so I wanted to stay there. It was Sunday and I had not gone shopping, so I had no food. I went into the *gîte* communal in a cloister next to an old church that used to be home to a *Vierge noire* (Black Madonna). I rang the bell at the door of the cloister and no one came for quite a while. Then an old man showed up and asked me what I was doing. I thought it would be obvious. I am muddy, soaked, and exhausted from the terrible walk; I have a backpack and walking sticks. Now I had to answer to him about my legitimacy as a pilgrim. I was disgusted. I said thank you very much, good-bye. I went back into the rain and was on my way, but he came running after me, saying that I could stay and that there might be some food in the fridge from other pilgrims. However, I thanked him and continued on.

It was in this town of Sarrance that the tales in the *Heptaméron* of Marguerite the theologian (grandmother of Henri IV) took place during a flood. How appropriate. She was familiar with the weather and France's hidden villages.

> Oisille's pilgrimage is marked throughout by her faith. Her lack of fear, her rejection of any superstitious reason for choosing Our Lady at Sarrance as her destination. And her desire to see "this

holy place" suggest a life grounded in prayer and thanksgiving that informs her every action and thought.*

Here we can mention again the importance of this highly educated woman who lived a thousand years too early, but who bravely attempted to pave the way for "a brotherhood of humanity." Carol Thysell talks about Marguerite de Navarre:

> First is... "the democratization and secularization of the mystical experience. All Christians, not just in monastics, can "enjoy immediate experience of God's presence." This experience can happen in the secular realm, in everyday experience, just as easily as in a monastic setting. For the devisants of the *Heptameron*, the mystical moments of God's presence occur, admittedly, in a monastic setting, but the author has taken great pains to distinguish this "monastic" community from any other.... Their mystical experiences, or realizations of the immediate presence of God, occur in the context of the very democratic society they have created, where neither abbot nor monk is privileged and where engagement in everyday life, rather than retreat from it, is assumed. On the eighth day, as Oisille finishes a reading in which the Holy Spirit seems to be "speaking through her mouth" and the devisants, "inflamed with this fire" go off to tell their stories, the monks are already gathered to be entertained—and instructed—by them.
>
> Second, the new mysticism emphasized a changed relationship between men and women on the spiritual path. In short, they talk with one another. While it is difficult to determine whether there were any differences between men's and women's mystical writings, women took a far more prominent role in the conversation....
>
> Furthermore, Oisille argues that "neither man nor woman is favored in the work of God" and notes that St. Paul "commends himself to those women who have labored with him in the Gospel." If the male devisants harbor objections to this leadership in theory, they consent to it in practice by acknowledging the spiritual authority of Oisille each morning.

---

\* Thysell, *The pleasure of Discernment*, p. 70.

Finally, the new mysticism of the beguines employs, "new forms of language and modes of representation of mystical consciousness." These new linguistic strategies and the genres employed were often controversial, differing as they did from the very precise scholastic treatises of theologians who wrote in Latin. Such controversy often arose over the claims of mystical experience in everyday life and the experience of the everyday. Women, and men who were not ordained, most often called upon the Holy Spirit to establish their authority, and the Church did recognize this as "the true source of all divine truth, so that women could not be totally excluded from all forms of teaching"....

Marguerite de Navarre uses her collection of tales to underscore the theological importance of the difficult social issues of her day. In so doing, she joins a theological tradition of discernment begun by a woman she admired, Marguerite de Porete, whose only subject was love.... It is in the community of equals and the tradition of vernacular theology that the process of discernment becomes pleasurable, because, "the game" that abolishes the hierarchically ordered society and its gendered virtue is more in keeping with the universal anthropology revealed in Scripture through the guidance of the Spirit.*

---

I was afraid; the place no longer felt very "holy," but one never knows what might be hidden in such little places. Wet, upset, and tired, I was in no way able to judge the atmosphere of the place. This time, I went back to the dangerous highway, and I saw a local man walking to his car, just passing me, so I asked him if I could get a ride to the next town, and he gladly took me, though I was drenched. He let me off at a very convenient place about seven miles farther on near a restaurant, and a couple of miles from a hamlet that had a *gîte* at a presbytery, the local priest's home in the town of Accous. I thanked him profusely, and he went on his way.

---

\*    Ibid., pp. 95–96.

I was beyond wet by now, dripping everywhere from my poncho. Again, the restaurant was full of Sunday drivers. As a puddle formed next to my table, I ordered food. I was getting cold now, so I sat there and chatted with the waiter and the new chef, who had previously worked in a Chicago restaurant. What was this about Chicago? This was the third person I met who had worked in Chicago. When I was full, warm, and a bit dryer, I put on my wet poncho and backpack and headed for the hamlet of Accous. By now I could see a little of the mountains; the weather was improving, and it was truly beautiful. I felt bad that I'd had to take a seven-mile ride in this glorious scenery, but I planned to come back through here with a car and rent a place. The hamlet was nestled in a little corner of the valley surrounded by mountains. Sadly, I was unable to take pictures.

In Accous I passed a little church and walked around the scenic town full of renovated summer homes. I went to the Presbytère Saint-Norbert en Aspe and rang the bell. A gentleman answered the door and said yes, he had room, asking me to please come in. *"Je ne me suis pas fait prier"* (meaning, he didn't have to twist my arm). Hugh showed me to my room on the upper floor of the ancient building. It reminded me of my grandmother's house, with an old bed and old sheets—wonderful! I had not slept on sheets in weeks. There was also a night table with a candle on it and some simple religious pictures. I changed my clothes and went downstairs.

The host offered warm tea and we talked. He had walked the Camino the previous year and wanted to serve the pilgrims, which he was doing in this priest's home. He was the caretaker of the pilgrims; the local priest was living there, as well, and he cooked for the priest and did house chores. He said that the priests were overworked now, because they had many villages and towns to take care of. He had to drive up and down the valley to see his parishioners, which kept him extremely busy. Nevertheless, we would have supper together. Then he said another French man, Marc, was also living here. He was a former seminary student who had not yet decided to become a priest. He was in his mid-forties, and the seminary student, around forty. Another, older priest also lived there; he had been in Chad, but was not part of the welcoming group. I said that I wanted to take part in Vespers at 6:30.

I went into the living room, which had a huge table and a large library of my kind of books—religious, spiritual, historical, local biographies, and much more that I didn't have time to look through. I went through quite a few and took lots of notes; then it was time for Vespers.

The old priest came and we went in. Vespers was celebrated in a little room converted into a simple chapel; it was very intimate with almost nothing in it but an altar, a few benches, and pictures of the Virgin Mary. They did not use the church because it was too cold and big to heat for just a few people. Two older women arrived, and father Philip with his resonating tenor voice read from the sacred books. It was a voice that could have belonged to an opera singer, warm and coming from the large lungs of people who live in the mountains. I had never heard such a voice, and after the trying day, I felt appeased. Everyone was praying earnestly, especially Marc, who was intense in his prayers—so intense that I felt a bit awkward being there and wanted to leave the room. Thankfully, the one sitting next to me made me feel comfortable. I really do not go to church, having stopped when I was thirteen or fourteen.

One day, while at church in France with my sisters, I remembered that I was not supposed to bite the "host," but decided I would bite it anyway and see what happens. I bit the host and nothing happened; therefore, in my mind, it was all a bunch of nonsense. That was the end of my belief in the church service, the beginning of questioning.

We sat a while longer, surrounded by the powerful words. The seminary student came back to reality, leaving behind his "cloud of rapture" that had nothing to do with the priest's words. He just seemed lost in his own self. The two older women talked to the priest and brought him a cake, and then everyone quietly left the cozy chapel.

This reminds me of another story about my sisters and me when we moved to Boston. My mother wanted us to go to church. She did not go herself because, she said, church is only for hypocrites. She meant adults; we children were not part of that. They pray on Sunday, and lie on Monday. And so, one Sunday morning, we left our house. I was sixteen, my sisters fifteen and twelve. We went to the church closest to our house in Brighton, Massachusetts. We entered the church, sat in the back, and joined the service. After a while, I noticed things were different from the regular Catholic service. We looked at each other when it was time to go to the front and receive the bread and wine. In the Catholic service we had received the only "host," so we thought it would be fun to have real bread and wine. The mood was somber, and the service was in English, which we did not speak well then. If it had been in Latin, I would have noticed something different, because I knew the service by heart through repetition. However, this was in a different country, so what the heck. Then, at the end, as we were leaving, the minister and his wife told us to please come again. I noticed that his clothes did not look like those of a Catholic priest. I knew this was not the kind of church we were used to. Then we read the sign outside, which said "Presbyterian" something or other. That was the last day of church for the three sisters. Brought up the way we were (a bit backward), we had not known about other churches, so we did not know the difference between Jewish, Protestant, Presbyterian, or Moslem beliefs.

After the intimate service at the *presbytère,* we sat down to a meal of vegetables, lentil chorizo soup (which I helped to cook), salad, the gift cake from the two older women, pudding, and tea. Father Phillip was from the area, and he looked happy and jovial, with red cheeks—definitely from the mountains, down-to-earth, and authentic. As soon as he sat to eat, there was a phone call. He had to leave because one of his parishioners, an old man, had been taken to the hospital. The priest needed to perform extreme unction, the last sacrament before one passes away. He left quickly for a half-hour drive after working all day. The rest of us ate together as if I had always lived there, in this pious and genuine atmosphere. By the end of our meal, Father Philip had returned and we talked for a while before we all retired. I had weird dreams about horsemen.

The next morning, I got up, took a warm shower, and wanted to go to their morning service, but I could not open the door to the chapel. I told father Phillip later about my attempt at the door, and he said that sometimes it locks. He said that he would give me his blessings after breakfast. I thought to myself, this is more than I deserve—a special blessing from this wonderful priest just for me.

We all shared breakfast, Hugh, Marc, Father Philip, and me. Then I stepped into the little chapel with brother Marc, and Father Philip proceeded to say some kind of service (this shows how grossly ignorant I am of church services). We recited the "Hail Mary" and "Our Father" prayers as I have never experienced them, and he gave me his blessings in his thundering, warm voice and asked me to pray for him, as well. I thought I would be glad to do so. I thought to myself that those men certainly know the power of prayers. I have always felt that I do not need anything, so why pray. I am certainly not going to pray for myself, but I can pray for others. But being with such sincere human beings who actually live each word of the prayer was a powerful and new experience. I was immensely thankful to Father Phillip and always will be.

> The Lord's Prayer resounds of course in the physical world, earthly world. But it resounds also beyond the threshold. It is a kind of mediator between these two worlds and joins them together. Of course these two worlds are always joined together, so that we can only speak of a mediating activity that joins these worlds from the perspective of our current state of human consciousness. To the seer's gaze, speaking the Lord's Prayer unites two worlds which otherwise stand distinct from one another in ordinary perception, so that one world—the spiritual—usually remains invisible. If human beings can direct their gaze to these two worlds, they gain

insight into the way they interact and the manifestations arising from them. Then we perceive that every sensory perception on this side of the threshold has a primal source, has its true existence beyond the threshold. What we see here in the physical sense world as the color of a rose is an expression of what the rose is beyond the threshold. This also holds true for the spoken word, and for the concepts and numbers linked with individual letters in Hebrew and Aramaic. Those who heard the Lord's Prayer from the mouth of Christ thus experienced the living, true being of words. This living, true being of the Word had been concealed from them previously. What they experienced through words in the sensory world approached the nature of the Word only as a kind of reflection. A reflection, it is true, is a likeness of a being, but is never that being itself. Now the truth of the Lord's Prayer beyond the threshold became a direct experience for them, and this process led them to insight into great cosmic mysteries.

The reality of words stood before them in images, colors, sounds, yet not in the way we generally perceive images, colors, and tones through sensory organs; instead they experienced the essence of a color, the essence of a sound, smell or taste, and were thus able to experience the cosmic laws underlying sensory phenomena. They saw the magnificent harmony connecting all the apparently disconnected, chance phenomena of the sensory world; they saw the most intricate and yet at the same time simple and perfect whole integrating everything with everything else; they saw that everything is embedded in a divine order, in which the human being and the spiritual hierarchies also have their place....

Anyone who speaks the Lord's Prayer today encounters something similar to those who first heard and prayed it. It is really the same living quality we encounter when we pray it....

The very special quality of this prayer, given to us directly from the mouth of Christ, is that it grows with us as we evolve. The further humanity develops its spirit consciousness, the more will the depths of these words be revealed. In early Christianity the Lord's Prayer was still fully one with the God who proclaimed it. It was simply referred to and inwardly absorbed, as "the Word of the Lord." During the Middle ages, when faith gave people support and strength, it continually accompanied them through their lives. Continually praying it strengthened the etheric (life) body in particular. Today and in the future, as we acquire the consciousness soul, the Lord's Prayer will gain ever more of an apocalyptic dimension for human beings: we will come to recognize how profound these apparently simple words actually are, and what they contain and can activate for our spiritual path of evolution.

Ever-new things about the spiritual world will be revealed to us through this prayer, in every future age. The everlasting constant, however, which never leaves us, whatever incarnation we are in—a fact that is anchored in the solace of these words—is that the moment we speak the prayer in true and honest fashion, we find ourselves as though safely mantled by the Godhead, wrapped in a spiritual space of protection against all powers of darkness.*

It was time to say good-bye, and I put a generous amount in their collection boxes. They did not have a set price but only "pay as you like." I left this idyllic *presbytère* in the Pyrenees. Today was the day of climbing straight up to the Col du Somport. The path was actually on a major highway, shared with big tractor-trailer trucks coming from or going to Spain, and some parts of the road had no room for pedestrians. In addition, there were blind curves where one could not see oncoming traffic, nor could they see someone walking. I was apprehensive of this road that I had heard should not be taken lightly. In fact, Hugh had told me that many people just take a bus through this section of the road. However, it was so beautiful that I refused to take the bus. It was bad enough that yesterday I missed walking seven miles, so I certainly would not miss the fantastic gorges and cliffs made by this thundering river as it came down from the glaciers and carved this beautiful canyon.

---

\* Von Halle, *The Lord's Prayer*, pp. 37–74.

I walked out of the quiet village and looked at the enchanting scenery on all sides. I was lucky; the sky had turned a beautiful blue with just a few clouds. I walked for a couple of miles, and then I had to begin the dreaded road. I was joined by another pilgrim, an Austrian. Like me, he was very attentive as we walked. The road was hazardous and made me nervous. A sign on the road indicated *"l'Auberge Cavalière"* (an inn with horseback riding), and the Austrian and I decided to stop there for a cup of coffee.

The host at the inn was very likeable. The inn featured horse trekking, and I told him I would come back for one of his two-week rides in the Pyrenees. As I was stepping outside, a *camionette* (small truck) pulled up. It was the kind one sees often in the French countryside, operated by shopkeepers who come to your door to deliver bread, meats, eggs, or other foods. This one was selling fresh fish, so I asked him where he was headed and about the road conditions. He told me it was very dangerous, so I asked him if he would give me a ride past the dangerous area, and he said yes, of course. I really wanted to walk, but I had to be realistic. One doesn't want to be run over.

When the driver let me off, a mile or two further on, I walked to the beautiful old hillside village of Borce. If the road had been hell, the scenery here was out of a fairy tale as I climbed into the Vallée d'Aspe. The villages were increasingly picturesque and more were tucked away in the distance. I wanted to stay there for another month and walk in every direction. The village was quiet but not abandoned. I stopped at a restaurant for a sandwich, coffee, and a conversation with the woman who operated the place. This little village has been a pilgrim stop since the second millennium or even earlier. It had a hospital, a chapel, and beautiful medieval homes throughout the village. I was ready to stay here for a while; all I would need is my library (or Father Phillip's library). I was in no hurry and enjoyed the sun on the terrace, thinking I had all day. I hadn't noticed, but I still had more than ten miles to go before reaching the top of the pass, about 5,000 feet straight up. I regretfully walked on, back on the treacherous road. It was nerve-wracking for several hours. I developed a strategy for when I was unable to see anything on a curve, with no room for me. There was a cliff that came right down to the road with a margin of three or four inches. When a big tractor-trailer would come, I ran like hell to the corner, where I could see what was coming.

The road became even more spectacular and wilder. Up above, one could see a path carved into the cliff. This was part of the *Grande Randonnée*, GR 10, which crosses the Pyrenees from east to west. I will walk it someday, way up there. I could see from below a former fortress-like structure carved into the rocky mountainside. The poet Alfred de Vigny was stationed in this area with a garrison in the 1820s.

> The day when humankind will no longer have any enthusiasm, love, adoration, or devotion, let us dig to the center of the Earth and put in 500 billion kegs of gunpowder and let the earth burst into millions of pieces, like a bomb in the middle of the Milky Way.
>
> I love humanity. I feel sorry for her. Nature is for me an embellishment, lasting impudently, on which is thrown this sublime, only passing-by marionette called the human being.*

Below, the road did not become any quieter; trucks coming from Portugal and Spain were passing here and the road was extremely narrow. I wondered what they do in the wintertime. I passed the village of Urdos and after another two or three miles on the dangerous road I finally crossed the road and said good-bye to the highway. Now I was climbing up the steep path on the east side of the road. I was glad to walk quietly, peacefully. I didn't care that it was all uphill; at least there was no rain and no trucks. I had several hours of daylight and another five or six miles of steep path.

The path was through a mountainside forest of hazelnut trees, birches, and holly. I had a view of snow on faraway peaks through dark green pine trees. I was crossing all sorts of little rivers swollen

---

\* Lagarde and Michard, *XIXe siècle: Les Grands Auteurs français du programme*, p. 152 (tr. M-L. Valandro).

from the recent rain. There were traces of wild boars, as well. The path was obvious, but other paths soon crisscrossed mine and I was again unsure of which way to go. I more or less followed the path in an upward direction hoping I was right; this was no longer a GR and no longer maintained. Very old markings were present, but nothing that helped much. The authorities probably wanted pilgrims off these paths because of the dangerous highway.

I encountered no one after the Austrian. At one point, I walked in the wrong direction and wasted a couple of miles before returning to the path. Then I saw the familiar pilgrim signs that crop up in the absence of "GR" signs. In those cases, we help ourselves and do a people do all over the world, especially in Nepal, the Himalayas, and Peru—build little stones piles or other crude markers on the road, especially where paths cross. Again, however, I had to watch carefully so as not to take the wrong path in these wild mountains. After a few hours of climbing—which seemed very long—I reached the tree line, and it all opened up so I could see more mountains in the distance—but not a clear path. Uphill I went, through meadows, and finally I thought I should go straight up toward some buildings in the distance, a short cut, but then I saw a large restaurant-inn. I had walked into Spain and to an *alberge* (no longer *"gîte"*).

Near the restaurant were beautiful signs for directions—"Santiago de Compostela"—everywhere. From now on, no getting lost. The Spaniards take their Camino very seriously, unlike the French, who don't seem to give a damn, at least not everywhere.

I entered the inn, and the woman there was pleasant. I placed my backpack in a tiny room with six beds and then met pilgrims from Spain. This is the place from which many Spaniards start their pilgrimage. They take a bus to here and then walk all the way to Santiago or just for a few weeks. Two women were walking for two weeks, then there was a couple from Brazil; the Austrian was already there, and I wondered when he had passed me. Perhaps he just kept going when I was having lunch in Borce. He was writing in his journal and made no

*Looking back at the Pyrenees from Spain*

signs of wanting to talk. I sat in the restaurant on top of the mountain and looked at the superb sunset and the high peaks surrounding us. The woman cooked supper for us—French fries and a terrible salad, and then we all retired in our eagle's nest for the night. I realized that I would not be speaking French again for quite a while—back to Spanish.

Everyone got up early, especially the new pilgrims starting on the path; it is very exciting to begin. I took my time with breakfast. Outside, a Belgian couple was taking pictures. I headed down on the path; I would have to walk down all that I had climbed. Destination, Jaca—almost the end of the road for me. The views were extraordinary, tall majestic as the Rockies—nothing like Roncevaux pass, which had little hills. This looks more like the Canadian Rockies or the Swiss Alps.

I headed down into the valley. Farther down was a beautiful ski area and resort called Candanchú. I was headed south, traversing the east side of the mountain. I could see many small cement-block houses from the war; there must have been intense fighting here—they are everywhere and tend to spoil the beautiful scenery. The large road winds its way through this great setting and disturbs its peaceful beauty. In addition, there is the very long tunnel through these mountains. The ski area brings an element of affluence and a disregard for nature. On the French side, one finds quaint little hamlets and villages that maintain the quiet life of the past. Here it is twenty-first century, with expensive hotels, weekenders from large cities here for winter sports. The life of the past is gone, but it is a beautiful place to ski.

I entered the city of Canfranc Estación, which has an enormous train station that used to be popular before the war. The train comes all the way here, but the tracks going to France have stopped service. The French government has shown no intention of renovating tracks. I walked on the train tracks a bit in France and it is thoroughly abandoned. The train ride here is spectacular; I could see it from the path—tunnels, cliffs, and incredible engineering. The Spanish, unlike the French, fully intend to maintain this huge train station that leads to the grand ski resort.

Canfranc is a tourist town with numerous shops. I stopped for a brunch (last night's inn at Somport Pass had little), so I ordered the famous egg-and-potato dish and coffee. Other pilgrims passed by, as well. Upon arriving in Canfranc, we could see a former pilgrims' hospital built on top of a rocky peak. It had been famous during the Middle Ages, but now it is in ruins. In this area, many kings have been taken hostage through the centuries, or have passed through, leading their sisters and daughters to marry the Spanish kings, including Marie de Valois's older sister Elizabeth (1545–1468), who married the king of Spain. The path itself has been written about for thousands of years. It is wild—some of the paths here are called "robbers' paths." I would have liked to walk around this city for a few days, but I continued on and crossed the beautiful old pilgrims' bridge over the River Aragón. I walked on the main road again, because the path had been damaged by a recent flood. Eventually, we were able to get back on the trail.

On one part of the path, we had to cross a very wide, though somewhat shallow river, but there was no place to cross. I walked up and down the bank and studied the river, looking for rocks to hop across the river but saw none. There was nothing to do but get my feet wet and, one hoped, not fall in and get thoroughly wet. I managed to jump on a few unstable rocks but ended up just walking in the water, saving one dry foot, the other wet. Better than both feet wet. By this point on my Camino walk, my shoes were disintegrating. The soles of my hiking boots were coming halfway off. I had used tape to keep them together for the past few weeks. I had gone thousands of miles in those shoes, but they were at the end of their life. They would have to do.

I arrived in another old medieval city of Villanúa by following a ravine of the Aragón riverbed path. It was quiet and beautiful, with pine trees and brush; the terrain was wilder, poorer, and dryer than the French side, and of course there were the beautiful mountains in the background. The Aragón River flows wildly down, gaining strength and speed and crossing a beautiful valley. This path was made for at least two horses to pass, because it was heavily used by horse riders in the past.

It was around one o'clock, so I went into a restaurant for coffee. It was full of working men having lunch. Then I saw that the whole town and vicinity seemed to be under construction with building and renovation. Spain has become wealthy in the last few decades; it is no longer the poor country of Europe. Here many well-to-do Spaniards have been buying up the countryside for second homes, condos, and hotels. I decided against going into the restaurant, which looked too busy. Many of the workers were from North Africa and former Eastern Bloc countries.

There were caves to visit, but they were closed. So I left the busy town, following a path, but realized after a while that I had taken the wrong one. Now I could see into the distance, however, so I just followed a lovely dirt road and made my own way. The pilgrims' path continued on the other side of the river, but the signs were not very good. I took a path toward the river crossing through farms, and finally it crossed the river on an old bridge. I ended up at the next town on the Camino, Castiello de Jaca. Another town in the boom stage. It was once again full of builders and carpenters renovating the whole ancient town. The result was beautiful stonework; any of these houses would suit me. Again, I asked one of the workers what was going on. It really looked like a ghost town. He said, "We can't afford to live here; it is too expensive. This place is only for people who have second homes. The villagers have gone elsewhere. Now it is deserted. The workers are here from somewhere else, too, coming to make money. People come here only in the summer, and during ski season; otherwise, it is empty."

At least the French villagers were still living in their hamlets and villages. They were not abandoned to rich city dwellers. The Spanish side of the Pyrenees is much more accessible than the French side. It reminded me of Colorado and the ski industry. Formerly, this area of Spain was extremely poor; now the Euro is waking up the region, and the wealthier middle class is waking up the sleepy towns. Perhaps in another twenty years, the younger generation will return and bring back a healthier lifestyle.

I walked on the path for a few hours toward Jaca, near the highway. The city could be seen from far away, along with some old castles on distant hills. It is a big city, and I headed for the pilgrims' *albergue*, which was very clean, modern, and much cheaper than the French *gîtes*. The whole city was in the middle of a gigantic fiesta celebration of the conquest over the invading Moors. It was opposite the mood of Pau; here the Christians were in control.

There was a bit of fanaticism in the air, which I strongly dislike. I did some shopping and found a place to download my pictures and finally had an empty memory card, which meant more pictures. I walked around the city, visited the large Cathedral, and mingled in the crowd. Many people were dressed in medieval costumes. The young crowd raised hell all night with firecrackers and so on.

The next morning I got up very early, because I did not want to be caught in their celebration. However, as I headed out of the city many horse riders in medieval costumes were on the otherwise empty city streets. To my surprise, the road going out of the city was full—it was only 7:00 in the morning and they were heading in the same direction that I was going. I said to myself, bad planning. There were many old people with picnic baskets and children, all walking into an empty field. I discovered that the major celebration would happen outside the city, where they were having a giant picnic for the day of celebration. Hundreds of cars everywhere, and people were setting up to barbecue hot dogs, drink lots of beer and wine, and celebrate the Christian conquest of the Moors 700 years ago. I left in a hurry. Police were everywhere. I did not feel comfortable at all. The message was clear to me: Get out of here!

I headed out for the final stage of my pilgrimage to the monastery of San Juan de la Peña, which was off the main path.

> At the time of the Holy Father Sixtus II (Pope, 257–258), there lived St. Lawrence, a devoted pupil to the pope.... So Sextus made him one of the seven deacons of Rome. In this capacity, it was Lawrence's duty on the one side to administer Church property, and on the other to care for the poor....
>
> During the persecutions of the Christians in the years 257 to 258 by the Emperor Valerian, Sixtus was brought to martyrdom.... Lawrence was persecuted and asked to deliver up the Church property of which he was a guardian....
>
> At this point a later legend inserts something into the story. It is said that among those Church properties was the cup that Christ had used at the Last Supper. Thus the significance of his refusal was that he was unwilling to deliver up the Grail vessel to the Romans. Instead he begged for time to reflect, and when the poor were gathered for the gifts they were accustomed to receiving, Lawrence said to the judge, pointing out the great crowd, "These are the Church's goods." The judge had no mercy. He was condemned...[and] the cup was brought to Spain to the Monastery of San Juan de la Peña. Thence, through King Martin, it was brought to Valencia, where it may still be seen to this day. But what is the meaning of this tale? For what reason did the writer of

*A festival in Castiello de Jaca to celebrate victory over the Moors*

the legend insert this Grail tradition into the story of St. Lawrence at a later time? He wished clearly to awaken us to a search as to whether a connection could not be found between St. Lawrence and the Grail stream, on the one hand, and the Monastery of San Juan de la Peña, on the other. This is still to be investigated further.*

I guess I can say that I am an investigator of some kind.

❧

After half an hour or so, the path was again deserted. I passed the Austrian, who was having his breakfast at a picnic table. We could see the mountains in the distance and the wide valley. The land was arid. It was Spain.

The path meandered through forests on both sides, going up and down hills and cutting through a large, abandoned military compound. In the future some wealthy person will find a use for that huge military

---

\* Stein, *The Ninth Century and the Holy Grail*, pp. 303–305.

estate in pretty surroundings. The river was slower here but wider. Then the path followed a river crossing where my feet got wet and I slipped stepping on stones.

After three or four hours, I saw a sign showing the way to a tiny road going to the ancient monastery. The road, surrounded by soft hills, scrubby vegetation, and wild scenery was becoming more deserted and climbed toward the distant hills. I was getting hungry; the one restaurant I had counted on had been closed, so I just walked on past nice farms and old homes. I could see why this particular place, hidden away in the calcareous hills, was chosen for a monastery.

It was getting hot, and I was probably about eight or nine miles from the main road. Two hours later, I flagged down a car driven by a young cement worker. He took me to the lovely medieval village called Santa Cruz de la Serós, just around the corner. He dropped me off at the inn in a beautiful old stone house overlooking the village. I got a room with a view of the distant mountains and the ancient chapel. I thought it was a great place to end my pilgrimage. I would be completely spoiled after the many dormitories.

It was still early in the afternoon, so I left my backpack in the room, took a water bottle, skipped lunch, and headed out for the five-mile, three-hour climb to the Monastery of San Juan de la Peña. I had seen pictures of the place, and I was very excited to get up there. The path was right outside the inn and went up a steep, rocky path to the cliffs. I was too excited to mind the climb. With no backpack, I could fly.

I had wanted to experience walking in this area and breathe its living air. I had read that this place was the site of the Grail castle—the third Grail castle; the first two were in the mountains further west, which I had crossed the previous year. Why this place and this setting? Why, of all the places in Europe, here in Spain?

The Grail saga was part of my pilgrimage, but not really part of the modern Santiago de Compostela path. I had to go out of the way to come here. These ancient paths had seen countless pilgrims, as well as the famous hero of the Grail, Parcival. He was a real human

*Headed for my destination, San Juan de la Peña*

*Nearing the hidden monastery*

being who lived around the eighth century. The first pilgrim who came to pay homage to St. James was King Alphonso II (792–842). Charlemagne (742–814) was crowned emperor in 800. That short period saw the pilgrimages begin (the outer search), the search for the Grail with Parcival (the hidden search), and the Christianization of Europe through Charlemagne.

I had wanted to understand more the life of Charlemagne, who had been through the places I had just seen, as well as Parcival, who had also supposedly walked here from northern countries, and of course the Cathars, troubadours, and the terrible tragedies that are part of the landscape I had crossed on this journey. Climbing to this monastery, the third resting place of the Grail, was a moving experience, but stone silent. The mountains, the cliffs, the arduous rocky path—nothing was speaking; it was all buried in the past. Nevertheless, these words reawaken the past:

*A cross bas relief, San Juan de la Peña*

The old mysterious abodes of the Sun oracle exerted their influence in Atlantean lands. Their wisdom was transplanted into the post-Atlantean cultures. Two streams of people came forth from Atlantis. One went through Africa, preparing the later Egyptian culture, toward Asia, toward India and the East altogether, preparing for the Christ light. The other stream of people went through Europe toward Asia and left part of the stream to settle in middle Europe.

These people were led from the mystery centers, and the task of these centers was to prepare the West for the Christ light that was to come to it later. A strong race of people with strong physical powers was to be educated: emotionally strong, courageous, the forces of the heart were to be trained; that was their striving. Invisible to the people, great spiritual leaders from the spiritual heights guided this humanity and its mystery center. One of them was the so-called Round Table of King Arthur, the other: the Druid centers, the Trotten centers, the mystery centers of the Ingäwonen.

Especially during this age of preparation there was a great spiritual individuality working from the spiritual world into Europe and its mystery centers. He was called Titurel. For his instruments Titurel used the spiritual or secular leaders of humanity, and we can understand their work only in this light. These facts are indicated in sagas and myths.

The saga of the Holy Grail says that the cup with the collected blood of Golgotha was brought by angels to Europe. Titurel received this cup. He kept it hovering above the countries of Europe, and only after centuries did Titurel descend with it from spiritual heights down to the Earth and found the mystery center of the Holy Grail on the mountain of salvation (Montsalvat). He could only do that after several people were mature enough to receive the secret of the Grail. Everyone mature enough for this initiation was called Parcival.

Charlemagne, who came from the East—he was the reincarnation of a lofty Indian adept—was an instrument of the spiritual individuality symbolized by the name Titurel. Flor and Blanchflor, called rose and lily, are called the parents of Charlemagne in a spiritual sense. They were at work presiding over this mystery.

A "Parcival" had purified his soul of all earthly wishes and self-seeking through long meditations and concentration. He was a Catharist and came as such to King Titurel. By exerting all the power that he had acquired through long exercises he managed to bring forth his higher "I." He stood over and against himself. First he had to sacrifice his intellect; then he experienced what is written down in the following esoteric script....

By exerting all the power that he had acquired through long exercises, he managed to lift up his higher "I," and he stood before himself and saw himself in a symbol. The entire physical world disappeared and in its place he saw a great sprouting dream-like form of a plant, as large as the Earth, and on top of it a white lily blossoming. The voice of Blanchflor behind him said, "That is you!" And he saw his purified soul....

The lily was glorious and perfectly formed, but it sent forth a strong aroma that had a repulsive effect on Parcival. And it

was clear to him that this aroma symbolized everything he had
set outside himself through catharsis and that it now surrounded
him like an atmosphere. From this he understood that the lower
elements that he had set aside were not destroyed, but rather were
in the atmosphere around the lily.

He learned that he must take all that back into himself in
order to transform this aroma from the lily. With this knowledge
he watched the tree wither; the symbol disappeared and it got dark.

After some time another symbol arose out of the darkness
for Parcival: a black cross entwined with red roses. The tree,
transformed into the black wood of the cross and the fragrant
roses, was created by the sacrifice of the life of the white lily. And
behind Parcival the voice of Flor, whose symbol was the strong, red
roses, spoke: "That you will become." The aroma had disappeared,
the roses had absorbed it. Parcival saw that purification was not
enough. He saw that he had to nail his lower self onto the black
cross in order for the roses to blossom.*

One just had to enter into the great silence. As I climbed ever higher, eagle like birds circled nests on the face of the rocky cliffs. What a place this was! One could not have found a more hidden place. You could see the high, snowy mountains in the distance from where I had come. The monastery was buried inside the cliffs. After crossing the high peaks of the Pyrenees into a long valley, and then again into these hills, I find this little niche in the rocks, which one cannot find unless shown where it is. It cannot be seen, even as one walks next to it.

> Parcival was sent into a place of solitude so he could meditate on
> the powerful pictures that had been conjured up before his soul.
> Day and night he let the symbols work within him. Gradually the
> pictures paled, yet the effects of the forces remained and worked
> in him like the power that germinates a seed.
>
> In the solitude of the mountains in which he stood, Parcival
> directed his gaze to the boundless sky above him, looked down
> into the boundless depths beneath him, to the right and the left

---

\* Steiner, *Esoteric Lessons, 1904–1909*, pp. 430–437.

*Monastery of San Juan de la Peña*

into the boundless distances, and an indescribable feeling of devotion and reverence for God, who was revealed in all, overcame him. He felt great unity in everything. And he directed his prayer to it. "You great enveloper, you whom I feel above, below and next to me, who are everywhere whether I look forward or backward. I would like to devote myself to you, to be dissolved in your being."

At the same time, he felt another divine power that did not overwhelm him in this way, that seemed to lead him to himself to give him a center. He felt that this point was part of the great enveloper within him, the all-encompasser, behind which he sensed unity. This second power had the tendency to take him by the hand and to guide him from that center that he felt within himself—but which he surmised was below him and which he could not consciously lead into consciousness—to the periphery. Thus he felt from one side a stream that flowed through him and strove toward complete dissolution in the Godhead, in the forces of the enveloper; but from the other side came a power that wanted to lead him to develop his own self.

*Column capital, San Juan de la Peña*

While these two forces worked on him he felt a third power that joined together the previous two and led him to the periphery of the enveloper. This third power Parcival experienced as a messenger of the great enveloper, who appeared to lead him in circles around this center. It united the two streams and brought it about that the two paths, which led apart, were led together in a circle, went together in a circle (the fatherless and motherless paths).[*]

I walked to the top of the little mountain and saw another monastery that had just been rebuilt as a hotel for wealthy tourists. I met a couple out walking and asked them where the old monastery was. They pointed back down, so I went back a mile or two and took a different path through a lovely forest and winding around the mountain.

I finally arrived at the old Monastery of San Juan de la Peña. It was so well hidden that I could not see it until it was right under my nose. It was built into the cliff. The woman in charge let me in for free as

---

[*] Ibid., pp. 437–438.

*Last supper, column capital detail, San Juan de la Peña*

a pilgrim and let me wonder around the well-maintained monastery. Inside were several little chapels, and I especially liked the pillars and their amazing carvings. They included a replica of the Grail (or what is supposed to be the Grail) carved in onyx. The real Grail is in the cathedral in Valencia. I had my camera so I took a lot of pictures of the area. I spent a lot of time looking at the carved pillars—stone story books, whose carved faces make the holy books come to life—with Charlemagne on his horse, Old and New Testament stories, Cain killing Abel, Adam and Eve, St. Joseph's dream, Herod's banquet, the two wise kings, the fish miracle, the wedding at Cana, Lazarus, the adulteress, the Last Supper, and many more. The many symbols included Christ's three years, his healings, angels and archangels—everyone was there.

The eleventh San Juan de la Peña had become a resting place for many of the nobles of Aragon and Navarre who wished to be buried there in exchange for generous donations that kept up the monastery. Several chapels from different centuries had been added.

*Bas relief, Adam and Eve*

After spending several hours there, more tourists arrived—first, Spaniards and then a couple from Tokyo. It was time to go back down to town, but it was too late to walk. I asked two older Spaniards if they would give me a ride to the little town below; it was a ten-mile ride by car. We packed into the small car, and one of the older men said, "This is supposed to be the place where the Grail was kept." They also mentioned Parcival. Then he said that this place must have something to do with the Grail. Then he added, "The wife of a Spanish king once said that there is an invisible castle here. It can be seen only by those in a state of grace." We left it at that. I had no comments. All I wanted now was silence. The place itself demanded silence.

> Every such suppressed manifestation of our unique personal existence, every such silence is a new accumulation of energy to aid us in acquiring knowledge. The more we are able to listen and not express our opinion, the faster we ascend to direct knowledge and direct vision. For those who lack insight into the organization

of the human soul, this is unbelievable. Just as certainly as electric energy is stored in an accumulator, so too soul forces can accumulate when we suppress our opinions. This gives us strength and power. Those who have opinions they need to express will be able to ascend only slowly; those who can be silent a lot, who can let things speak to them, they will ascend quickly. This is a golden rule in relation to direct knowledge: If we refrain from expressing our thoughts to things then the things will speak to us.

A very significant expression from the secret doctrine is: I have learned a great deal from those who stand above me; I have learned much from those who are equal to me; and I have learned the most from those who stand beneath me!—It is the learning from those who stand below us, learning through listening and through suppressing our opinions, that takes us into the heights. And we learn the most when we let nature speak to us and we listen to her. Then we achieve what must be achieved, namely the power to really suspend our judgments and opinions.

If we have allowed ourselves the four to five minutes needed to develop our astral body, then something else sets in. What do people do when they are confronted by a question? It may mean something big or small. What do people do there? They reflect on it, strain their minds and believe that they must be the ones to retrieve the answer from the depths of their own thinking. Those who tread the path of knowledge do not do it that way. Goethe characterized it, as he so often did, with hints as an initiate. He once said: "We are not called upon to answer the questions, but, to begin with, to pose them and to wait to see how the question answers itself."

Do not underestimate this way of answering questions. It is very powerful. We try to pose the question very clearly and do not think about the answer but about the means that are suitable to provide an answer. Let's say, for example, that I am confronted with the question of whether a person is guilty or not guilty, whether he or she acted from an innocent heart or with evil intentions. If I reflect on it I will not get a correct judgment. But I will arrive at an answer if I consider his or her life, as far as it is available to me; what have I experienced with this person? How has this person presented him- or herself to me? What did she or he say to me? What did he or she say to others?—Those are not answers but questions that I have created for myself. They are to be considered. If I do this in a very active way and suppress an answer, then I will arrive at the point where the picture I have created for myself itself gives the answer. I exclude myself, so to speak.

If you do this with all your will forces, exclude yourself, so that your self is not involved, so that your thinking is suppressed, if you overcome your desire to give an answer, but just go to sleep with these preparatory questions, then you will have the experience that you awake the next morning with an answer that is much more correct and certain than the one that might have come to you in the evening. While your physical body was resting your spirit was disembodied and retrieved the means of answering the question from higher worlds. *

⁂

I had not mentioned anything about why I was there to the two Spaniards bringing me down the mountain. I said only that I was walking on the Camino. They let me off and I walked to the inn to get ready for supper. I still had some time before supper was served; one eats very late in Spain, so I had to adapt to the new schedule even though I was starving after not eating all day. Nonetheless, they gave me a couple of fruits. No stores were open in the tiny village.

I walked through the village and of course went straight to the beautiful little church Santa Cruz de la Serós, which was also a cloister for women, dating back to the eleventh century. It was closed, so I admired it from outside, especially the beautiful, centuries-old pillars with sculptured figures on top. There is something joyful, simple, alive, and mesmerizing in the stonework. It had the same power as those in the tympanum in Oloron, Moissac, and Conques, but here there were just a few carved pillars.

---

\*    Ibid., pp. 19–20.

Then I went into the dining room, which was full of tourists. I noticed a Brazilian couple who had also hiked up here and arrived that day. An older, English woman was eating alone, so I invited myself to her table, and she warmly agreed. She was vacationing here and crossing different areas of Spain by car with her husband, but now he was a bit ill and in their room. She had been coming to Spain for twenty years and loved it, but they had not bought a house.

The Brazilian couple was more talkative; she had gotten some bad blisters on her feet and was having a hard time. Since they had just started at the Somport Pass a couple of days earlier, she was feeling the effects of the arduous hike, which everyone must endure for the first ten days or so—aches in the shoulders, legs, feet, and everything else. She had lost some enthusiasm and wanted to take a taxi from here to the main path—not a good sign when one has another 450 miles to go.

I returned to my room, looked outside my window at the mountain I had just hiked, and meditated on the past few days, which had gone by so quickly. I am walking, but it is still too fast.

Before I knew it, morning arrived with its communal breakfast. I ate with the old English man and his wife. He asked me if I had gone upstairs in the little church, and I said that I hadn't. It had been closed. He said, "You must go up there; it is incredible. There is a hidden chapel room there that one would not notice at all." I said I would not dream of missing it. We waited until it was opened.

I asked them for a ride back to Jaca, where I had to take the train in the afternoon back to Barcelona, and of course they said they would.

We all went into the little church, where a pleasant woman was at the reception desk. We climbed the stone stairs, and there was the hidden room. From the main floor, we could not see anything; it had been built not to be noticed. The woman explained that in the olden days this was a monastery for wealthy women. Often, there were wars between various factions, and the residing sisters and noble women frequently had to go upstairs to hide. They went up into a little tower, which was difficult to see. It looked as if it were part of the bell tower.

Even the stairs were hidden within the walls. I was amazed at the clever architecture. Once people had climbed into the hidden rooms, everything was closed up. We stayed there for quite a while to experience the mysterious space, looking through the narrow windows at the mountains and the village below.

Then it was time to pack up and leave for Jaca and on to Barcelona. The end of a journey always signals the beginning of another. In the beginning... the source, the spring.

> There is no end to the value of what I have seen, and how endless are the things for which I have lived, yet they are perhaps entirely without value. I must begin a new life if I no longer wish to live in the manner to which I am accustomed, if I do not want it formed and created by an influence foreign to me but want to shape and create it through my own inner life. We then do not become another to external appearances, but we are leading our lives following a different impulse. We will be guiding our lives not out of vanity, not out of ambition, not out of sensual comfort, for we will no longer be able to do that, but rather out of a sense of duty, because it must happen out of a higher insight.*

---

\* Ibid., pp. 13–14.

*Leaving Spain on my last day*

## The Grail King Speaks

Be forewarned, Oh Speaker.
Behind the quest [question] burns
Aspiration,
A yearning for the heights
So intense
That ultimate failure,
Even death itself,
Though risked,
Is no obstacle

And, as well,
You must come to know,
Indeed must embrace,
The deepest, moist sorrow
Of your heart.

Fire and water,
The marriage of yearning and sorrow,
Give birth to the quest [question].*

After sleeping on this, here is my Christian *koan:* Where does the question itself come from? Or, in other words:

> Every theory and every science begin with questions. Questions arise when we look at something twice because we were not satisfied with the first view of what we saw. That is, the existence of questions presumes two different glances, two separate views, the second of which is conscious and deliberate. These two different views necessarily originate in two different possibilities of the seeing consciousness, which can be at home on two different places.
> The first view or picture of reality is *given* to us, and it is already a picture at that moment, not a reality, as is often supposed.

---

\* Sussman, *The Speech of the Grail*, p. 21.

Reality is the last secret and can be attained only through conscious questioning. The first picture is given through the soul's superconscious and subconscious structure. It is filtered, dulled, and immobilized because of the necessary dependence of the cognizing principle in human beings on the physical organism. As a result, only a part of the totality of the world reaches conscious experience. Since our questions and answers also become part of reality, reality is not finished or fixed: it blossoms within, and through, the human being.

Our questions concern the given picture, the first view. Epistemology deals with the question of how this "given "arises. The sciences deal with the question of how to complete, correct, and understand the given picture. And the philosophy of science deals with the question of how science is possible.[*]

To strengthen your capacities and begin your quest-question-questioning journey, *practice! Graal* = Grail; *Gradalis* = degree, steps. Start climbing.[**]

❧

*So we have come to an end—which is no end, but a beginning.... A jumble, you may say; a fantastic mixture of legend and superstition and pseudo-history. But perhaps, here and there, the innocent beauty of some old tale may have stirred your heart so that you had to say, "It is true."*
—Eleanor C. Merry, *The Flaming Door*

---

[*] Kühlewind, *The Logos-Structure of the World*, p. 19.
[**] Read, for example, Lipson, *Stairway of Surprise*, and Steiner, *Start Now!*

# Bibliography

Barfield, Owen. *History in English Words*. Great Barrington, MA: Lindisfarne Books, 2002.

Bogen, Meg. *The Women Troubadours: An Introduction to the Women Poets of 12th-Century Provence and a Collection of their Poems*. New York: Norton, 1980.

Bordes, Richard. *Cathares et Vaudois: En Perigord, Quercy et Agenais*. L'Hydre, 2010.

Dark, Sydney. *St. Thomas of Canterbury*. London: Macmillan, 1927.

David-Neel, Alexandra. *Magic and Mystery in Tibet*. New York: Dover, 1971.

Dunselman, Ron. *In Place of the Self: How Drugs Work*. Stroud, UK: Hawthorn, 1996.

Fages, Brieuc and Jean Gugole. *Visiter la villa de Séviac*. Bordeaux Cedex: Editions du Sud-Ouest, 2005.

Francke, Sylvia. *The Tree of Life and the Holy Grail: Ancient and Modern Spiritual Paths and the Mystery of Rennes-le-Château*. London: Temple Lodge, 2007.

Godwin, Malcolm. *The Holy Grail: Its Origins, Secrets, and Meaning Revealed*. New York: Barnes and Noble, 1998.

Jourdan, Michel and Jacques Vigne. *Marcher, méditer*. Paris: Albin Michel, 1998.

Klocek, Dennis. *Seeking Spirit Vision*. Fair Oaks, CA: Rudolf Steiner College Press, 1998.

Kühlewind, Georg. *The Logos-Structure of the World: Language as a Model of Reality*. Hudson, NY: Lindisfarne Press, 1986.

———. *Thinking of the Heart and Other Essays*. Fair Oaks, CA: Rudolf Steiner College, 1987.

Lagarde, André, and Laurent Michard. *XIXe siècle: Les Grands Auteurs français du programme - Anthologie et Histoire littéraire*. Bordas, 1993.

Lipson, Michael. *Stairway of Surprise: Six Steps to a Creative Life*. Great Barrington, MA: SteinerBooks, 2002.

Lusseyran, Jacques. *Contre la pollution du moi: Un aveugle clairvoyant avertit...* (Against the pollution of the I: A blind seer gives warning). Paris: Triades, 1992.

Merry, Eleanor C. *The Flaming Door: The Mission of the Celtic Folk-Soul.* Edinburgh: Floris, 2008.

Merton, Thomas. *No Man Is an Island*. San Diego: Harvest, 1955.

Morizot, Pierre. *The School of Chartres*. Sacramento: Rudolf Steiner College Press, 1987.

MSM. *Les Chemins de Saint Jacques de Compostelle*. Éditions MSM, 1999.

Novalis. *Spiritual Songs*. Chestnut Ridge, NY: Mercury Press, 1986.

Raju, Alison. *The Way of St. James, France: Le Puy to The Pyrenees*. Cumbria, UK: Cicerone Guides, 2003.

Reeves, Marjorie. *Joachim of Fiore and the Prophetic Future*. Stroud, UK: Sutton, 1999.

Roschl-Lehrs, Maria. *The Second Man in Us*. East Grinstead, Sussex: Henry Goulden, 1977.

Schutz, Bernard. *Great Monasteries of Europe*. New York: Abbeville Press, 2004.

Schwenk, Theodor, and Wolfram Schwenk. *Water: The Element of Life*. Great Barrington, MA: Anthroposophic Press, 1989.

Seddon, Richard. *Mani: His Life and Work*. London: Temple Lodge, 2011.

Sernin, Jean. *La cathédrale d'Oloron-Sainte-Marie: Ou le banquet céleste*. Paris: Maison de vie éditeur, 2012.

Stein, Walter Johannes. *The Ninth Century and the Holy Grail*. London: Temple Lodge, 2009.

Somé, Malidoma Patrice. *The Healing Wisdom of Africa*. New York, Tarcher/Putnam, 1999.

Steiner, Rudolf. *Approaching the Mystery of Golgotha*. Great Barrington, MA: SteinerBooks, 2006.

———. *The Archangel Michael: His Mission and Ours.* Hudson, NY: Anthroposophic Press, 1994.

———. *Cosmic Memory: The Story of Atlantis, Lemuria, and the Division of the Sexes.* Great Barrington, MA: SteinerBooks, 1987.

———. *Earthly Knowledge and Heavenly Wisdom.* Hudson, NY: Anthroposophic Press, 1990.

———. *An Esoteric Cosmology: Evolution, Christ, and Modern Spirituality.* Great Barrington, MA: SteinerBooks, 2008.

———. *Esoteric Lessons 1904–1909: From the Esoteric School,* vol. 1. Great Barrington, MA: SteinerBooks, 2007.

———. *"Freemasonry" and Ritual Work: The Misraim Service.* Great Barrington, MA: SteinerBooks, 2007.

———. *Inner Impulses of Evolution: The Mexican Mysteries, the Knights Templar.* Hudson, NY: Anthroposophic Press, 1984.

———. *Karmic Relationships: Esoteric Studies,* vol. 2. London: Rudolf Steiner Press, 1974.

———. *The Mystery of the Trinity and the Mission of the Spirit.* Hudson, NY: Anthroposophic Press, 1991.

———. *The Occult Movement in the Nineteenth Century and Its Relation to Modern Culture.* London: Rudolf Steiner Press, 1973.

———. Rosicrucian Wisdom: An Introduction. London: Rudolf Steiner Press, 2000.

———. *Start Now! A Book of Soul and Spiritual Exercises.* Great Barrington, MA: SteinerBooks, 2002.

———. *Supersensible Knowledge.* Hudson, NY: Anthroposophic Press, 1988.

———. *Wonders of the World, Ordeals of the Soul, Revelations of the Spirit.* London: Rudolf Steiner Press, 1963.

———. *World History and the Mysteries in the Light of Anthroposophy.* London: Rudolf Steiner Press, 1997.

Sussman, Linda. *The Speech of the Grail: A Journey toward Speaking that Heals and Transforms.* Hudson, NY: Lindisfarne Books, 1995.

Tautz, Johannes. *W. J. Stein: A Biography.* London: Temple Lodge, 1990.

Thysell, Carol. *The pleasure of Discernment: Marguerite de Navarre as Theologian.* New York: Oxford University, 2000.

TopoGuides, *Sentier vers Saint-Jacques-de-Compostelle via Le Puy: Le Puy à Figéac* (6th ed.). Paris: Federation Française de la Randonnée Pedestre, 2012.

von Halle, Judith. *And If He Has Not Been Raised...: The Stations of Christ's Path to Spirit Man.* London: Temple Lodge, 2005.

———. *The Lord's Prayer: The Living Word of God.* London: Temple Lodge, 2007.

Wadler, Arnold. *One Language: Source of All Tongues.* Great Barrington, MA: Lindisfarne Books, 2006.

Wenzler, Claude. *Mémento des rois de France: Histoire, généalogie, chronologie.* Éditions Ouest-France, Rennes, 2003.